South University Library
Richmond Campus
2151 Old Brick Road
Glen Allen, Va 23060

THE ENGLISH EMPIRE IN AMERICA, 1602–1658:
BEYOND JAMESTOWN

Empires in Perspective

Series Editors: *Tony Ballantyne*
Duncan Bell
Francisco Bethencourt
Caroline Elkins
Durba Ghosh

Advisory Editor: *Masaie Matsumura*

Titles in this Series

1 Between Empire and Revolution: A Life of Sidney Bunting, 1873–1936
Allison Drew

2 A Wider Patriotism: Alfred Milner and the British Empire
J. Lee Thompson

3 Missionary Education and Empire in Late Colonial India, 1860–1920
Hayden J. A. Bellenoit

4 Transoceanic Radical, William Duane: National Identity and Empire, 1760–1835
Nigel Little

5 Natural Science and the Origins of the British Empire
Sarah Irving

6 Empire of Political Thought: Indigenous Australians and the Language of Colonial Government
Bruce Buchan

Forthcoming Titles

India in the French Imagination: Peripheral Voices, 1754–1815
Kate Marsh

British Narratives of Exploration: Case Studies on the Self and Other
Frederic Regard (ed.)

Law and Imperialism: Criminality and Constitution in Colonial India and Victorian England
Preeti Nijhar

Slaveholders in Jamaica: Colonial Society and Culture during the Era of Abolition
Christer Petley

www.pickeringchatto.com/empires

THE ENGLISH EMPIRE IN AMERICA, 1602–1658:
BEYOND JAMESTOWN

BY

L. H. Roper

LONDON
PICKERING & CHATTO
2009

Published by Pickering & Chatto (Publishers) Limited
21 Bloomsbury Way, London WC1A 2TH

2252 Ridge Road, Brookfield, Vermont 05036-9704, USA

www.pickeringchatto.com

All rights reserved.
No part of this publication may be reproduced,
stored in a retrieval system, or transmitted in any form or by any means,
electronic, mechanical, photocopying, recording, or otherwise
without prior permission of the publisher.

© Pickering & Chatto (Publishers) Ltd 2009
© L. H. Roper 2009

BRITISH LIBRARY CATALOGUING IN PUBLICATION DATA
Roper, L. H. (Louis H.)
The English empire in America, 1602–1658: beyond Jamestown. – (Empires in perspective)
1. Virginia Company of London 2. Virginia – History – Colonial period, ca. 1600–1775 3. Virginia – Politics and government – To 1775
I. Title
975.5'02

ISBN: 9781851969920
e: 9781851965946

This publication is printed on acid-free paper that conforms to the American National Standard for the Permanence of Paper for Printed Library Materials.

Typeset by Pickering & Chatto (Publishers) Limited
Printed in the United Kingdom by MPG Books Ltd.

CONTENTS

Acknowledgements ix

Introduction 1
1 Deep Background 21
2 Genesis 35
3 Birth Pangs 51
4 Fatal and Near-Fatal Attractions 73
5 An Empire of 'Smoak' 93
6 Some Measure of Success 121

Notes 141
Works Cited 181
Index 203

ACKNOWLEDGEMENTS

The chance to thank publicly those who so kindly gave their time and expertise constitutes one of the greatest boons to the research and writing of history. For *The English Empire in America*, the list of contributors has grown to a considerable length.

First, staff at a number of institutions assisted with enquiries and provided materials with invariable expertise and good cheer: the Department of Special Collections and Western Manuscripts, Bodleian Library, University of Oxford; the British Library; the Centre for Kentish Studies, Maidstone; the Huntington Library, San Marino, California; and the National Archives, Kew, Richmond.

I would like to extend my gratitude to the offices of the Provost/Vice President of Academic Affairs and the Dean of the College of Liberal Arts and Sciences which provided a term of sabbatical leave, as well as essential travel funding to conduct research at the above institutions and to present my preliminary findings at conferences. I would also like to thank the Beinecke Rare Book and Manuscript Library at Yale University for the award of the Alexander O. Vietor Memorial Fellowship in Early American History and Cartography, which subsidized the cost of working in New Haven for a wonderful month in March 2004.

I would like to extend special applause for the crucial continuing efforts of staff at the Interlibrary Loan Office of the Sojourner Truth Library, State University of New York–New Paltz. Their unceasing dedication and resourcefulness in obtaining materials for me, as well as their good cheer, especially in the face of frequent assaults on their profession, enables the pursuit of scholarships at institutions such as mine.

A number of fellow labourers in the vineyard have kindly lent their knowledge, helped the working out of issues, read and commented upon drafts of various parts of this project, and/or rendered various kindnesses. For those efforts, I would like to thank Sarah Barber, Thomas Festa, Katherine French, Evan Haefeli, Lauric Henneton, Joyce Hoad, Jaap Jacobs, Maija Jansson, Heather Morrison, Thomas Olsen, Michael Questier, François-Joseph Ruggiu, David Smith and, last but by my no means least, Bertrand Van Ruymbeke.

Several venues kindly extended invitations to present chunks of the material included herein, once these became suitable for public consumption, and I am grateful to the Program Committee for the 2006 North American Conference on British Studies; my colleague, Jeff Miller, director of the Honors Program at SUNY–New Paltz; Evan Haefeli, coordinator of the 2006–7 Columbia University Seminar on Early American History and Culture; and P. Guillaume, F.-Ch. Mougel, C. Laux, F.-J. Ruggiu and P. Singaravelou, *comité scientifique* for the colloquium 'Servir outre-mer: Les élites européennes dans les colonies du début du XVIe siècle au milieu du XXe siècle', held at the Université de Bordeaux 3–Michel de Montaigne.

I would like to acknowledge specially Bernard Bailyn and his indefatigable (although just recently retired) associate, Pat Denault. In 1996, Professor Bailyn granted me the great boon of an invitation to participate in the inaugural International Seminar on the History of the Atlantic World at Harvard University. I can say unequivocally that involvement in this Seminar has had the greatest significance for my professional life and I was very pleased to be able to present a key component of this project at the 10th Anniversary Conference of the Atlantic Seminar in August, 2005. Moreover, I find it most remarkable and immensely gratifying that this renowned scholar has chosen to spend his 'retirement' cultivating the careers of young scholars with similar interests, even those with somewhat different views.

A version of that Harvard paper, which forms the basis for Chapter 4, subsequently appeared in a number of *Itinerario*, the international journal on the history of European expansion and global interaction, as did an article on the failed colony of New Albion, which has been incorporated into Chapter 5. In addition, an essay on Anna of Denmark, queen-consort of James I/VI, and her circle, which forms the core of Chapter 3, appeared in C. Levin, J. Eldridge Carney and D. Barrett-Graves (eds), *High and Mighty Queens of Early Modern England* (New York: Palgrave Macmillan, 2003). I would like to note my appreciation to the editors of those publications for permitting me to publish some of that material here.

I would also like to acknowledge the editorial and marketing staff at Pickering & Chatto for their help and patience in getting this project into print.

My deepest gratitude, as always, goes to Rosemarie Frisone. My spouse's continuing acceptance of life with a stereotypical academic whose head is always in a book or in the clouds or lost in the seventeenth century allows me perhaps too much liberty to pursue my passion for investigating this increasingly remote but always fascinating period.

Finally, I would like to thank my students and my own teachers for all of their assistance, guidance, observations and learning, and I dedicate this volume to them.

INTRODUCTION

On 20 December 1606, three ships, containing settlers for 'Virginia' with their baggage and sailing under the auspices of the Virginia Company, chartered in London for this purpose, shipped anchor in the Thames. After weathering 'many crosses in the downes from tempests', they crossed the Atlantic Ocean, arriving in Chesapeake Bay in the middle of the following April where, after some consideration, they established themselves at a site on an island in the James River.[1]

As every proverbial American schoolchild knows, the Jamestown pioneers endured years of misery, suffering bouts of dysentery, as well as harassment from the neighbouring 'Indians', while they squabbled incessantly amongst themselves. They also failed to find either mines from which to extract precious metals or a quick 'Northwest Passage' to the lucrative East Asian trade, preoccupations which prevented them from growing the crops necessary to sustain themselves. Only the reform programme implemented by the heroic Captain John Smith – at least, according to Smith's own account – saved the colony. Even so, a further 'starving time' rendered its situation precarious after Smith's departure: the survivors of the desperate first years had packed up to return to England when a relief ship and a new governor, Thomas West, Lord de la Ware, arrived in 1611. In the meantime, the Virginia Company manned the public relations pumps against the flood of derogatory reports generated at home by disgruntled colonists and other naysayers as they sought to keep their endeavour afloat.

Subsequently, matters became easier: the famous marriage between John Rolfe, a leading Virginian, and the Powhatan 'princess', Pocahontas, stabilized relations with her father and Rolfe's equally famous introduction of tobacco cultivation provided the English with the all-important 'staple crop' which generated a 'boom' as hundreds of people made their way to Virginia. In addition, some time before 1619, the first Africans arrived at Jamestown thereby facilitating the introduction of the transatlantic system of slavery to the Chesapeake region.

The influx of white migrants, however, created headaches in the form of further antagonism from their indigenous neighbours, who attacked the colony in 1622 killing a quarter of the inhabitants, and overcrowding, which made it difficult to feed the 'sot-weed'-crazed colonists. These difficulties added fuel to bickering within the management of the Virginia Company, prompting the royal takeover of the colony in 1624. Yet, despite these difficulties and continued concerns about the possible effects of Virginia's overdependence on tobacco, the end of the 'company period' saw the English presence along Chesapeake Bay permanently established.[2]

So reads the seemingly well-known narrative of the early history of Virginia. As one of the first examples of English overseas colonization, there can be no question that it provides a profound example for our understanding of the development of the British Empire as well as of Anglo-American colonies. The chronological primacy of the first permanent English settlement in North America moved the study of Jamestown to privileged historiographical ground for students of United States history during the nineteenth century and it has remained there ever since. This privilege arises naturally from the important, perhaps fundamental, cultural links – language, most importantly – and the 'special relationship' which continues to exist between Great Britain (for which read 'England', customarily) and the United States. These links, in turn, have generated analyses of the connections as manifestations of 'modernization'. This term has incorporated a variety of intertwined phenomena and perspectives, including, most notably, colonization, empire and 'state formation'. Invariably, though, authorial conceptions of the character of 'liberty', including the place of the United States in the history of that concept, both domestically and generally, have occupied a place very close to centre stage in these reflections.

In the first instance, from the period preceding the American Civil War until the 1960s, Virginia constituted the chronological ace in the sectional struggle with adherents of New England over the 'origins' of American society and the cultural attributes which Great Britain bequeathed to the thirteen colonies which won their independence from it in 1783. This self-consciously Whiggish view attempted to place early American history within a wider context of the progress of Anglo-American liberty and, so, trumpeted such 'achievements' as the creation of the Virginia House of Burgesses, the first representative assembly in the 'New World'. It also lauded, particularly, the yeoman-adventurer persona of Captain Smith as the prototype of the American character against the rival claims made by 'Yankees' on behalf of the 'Pilgrim Fathers' and 'Puritans' as the progenitors of the United States.[3]

This debate over the 'origins' – and, thus, the essence – of American society received a famous fillip in 1893, when the young Frederick Jackson Turner famously lamented the demise of the catalyst role of the 'frontier' (as defined by the United States Bureau of the Census) in the development of American society. While Turner never wrote on early Virginia, his preference for 'the West' and his corresponding view of purportedly self-sufficient yeomanry operating as the vanguard of a civilization advancing across the continent provided the characterization of a distinct, even unique, American nation which has resonated most profoundly. Moreover, it set out the frame for subsequent considerations of United States history in terms of the degree of the distinctiveness of that history and of the society which spawned it.[4]

The post-World War II generation of American historians, many of whom entered the profession during the period of the Civil Rights Movement and the Vietnam War, moved away from these celebratory views. Instead, these scholars placed a greater emphasis on 'history from the bottom up' (known at the time as the 'new social history') and the contributions of women, people of African descent and others previously ignored by historiography. According to the investigations of the element of this group which formed a 'Chesapeake school', colonial society in the region surrounding Chesapeake Bay underwent a series of phases en route to 'modernity'. In the first decades of English settlement, according to this scholarship, the relatively egalitarian character of the early population coupled with a keen desire for advancement and the exigencies of frontier life, exacerbated by the reality of routine premature death, created a rough-and-tumble socio-political environment in which only the fittest prospered, tobacco became the be-all and end-all, and a bizarre form of the metropolitan social structure developed. By 1660, however, the population had settled to the degree that a recognizable elite had emerged and enslavement of Africans had become part of the 'success' equation. After the convulsions of Bacon's Rebellion (1676) and, in Maryland, the 'Glorious Revolution' (1688–9), the membership of the colonial elites became further entrenched and, in accord with their counterparts in other colonies, copied, as best as they could, the behaviour and characteristics of the metropolitan aristocracy; they became increasingly 'anglicized'.[5]

More recently, practitioners of 'Atlantic history', apparently in line with the emergence of post-modernist perspectives in other disciplines and with the break-up of the Soviet Union after 1989, have proclaimed their intentions to move away from a reliance on the nation-state as a basis of historical inquiry. This perspective has proved eminently adaptable to the study of the early modern English Empire as an increasing number of treatments have endeavoured to situate the English settlement of North America within the wider context of an 'Atlantic World'. In general terms, the pupils in this new school stress the importance of the commercial and social links – generated by the unprecedented movement of people and commodities during the early modern period, especially among the various English colonies and between those colonies and other European-American settlements, as well as Africa and Europe – as a key element in the development of 'modernity'.

From this perspective (like that of contemporaries), the establishment of Jamestown holds no great import in and of itself. Indeed, the arrival of the English in the Chesapeake, so far from providing the platform for the creation of the United States, constitutes 'an almost trivial event', a small tributary of 'a migratory stream that was altering the four continents bordering the ocean'. A proper appreciation of its significance, instead, arises from considering it within a wider 'Atlantic' context of activity in Africa and South America, as well as North America and Europe. Led by a vanguard of 'cosmopolitans' or 'boundary-crossers' – merchants, interpreters and others travellers to exotic parts – the expansion of early modern European interests had formed a manifestly new world in which peoples from four continents interacted. 'By the middle of the seventeenth century', according to a recent analysis, this movement of people

> had put in motion effects that would produce much of the modern world as we know it today – a Western Hemisphere in which most people speak European languages; an African diaspora that has spread across the Americas and, to a lesser extent, Europe; a drastically reduced Native American population that has survived through cultural adjustment; and a global market that circulates goods around the world.[6]

Yet, while this body of work avowedly eschews a national perspective, it maintains, ironically, the age-old presumption that the formation of colonial worlds resulted in inherent and fundamental socio-political novelties. In a related sense, to what degree does the present-day quest to find the origins of a global, diverse, modern world (and the place of English-speaking people in it) in the sixteenth and seventeenth centuries differ from the old Turnerian search for the origins and catalyst of American society? The nature of both enquiries has privileged the modern outcome and even, despite the cautions presented by the horrors of transatlantic slavery and the decimation of American Indian populations noted by the most recent generations of historians, a sense of progress.[7]

This enduring whiff of Whiggishness has meant an enduring obscurity of the nature of colonization and empire during what we call today the early modern period. In the first instance, in the English case, it shrouds the important links that were maintained between the 'Old World' and its Anglo-American offspring, especially their cultural and political aspects. This tendency arises from the tendency of 'Atlanticists' – shared, again ironically, with their predecessors – to regard the phenomena they study, especially prior to 1760, as one-way traffic westward, whether in terms of the 'Atlantic basin' as a whole ('circum-Atlantic history', as David Armitage has styled it), comparatively ('trans-Atlantic history') or in terms of situating 'particular places within their more general Atlantic context' ('cis-Atlantic history'). Thus, while they have pointedly eschewed the old-fashioned national perspective, this new perspective has found it difficult to shed the enduring desire to comprehend the role of the English settlement of the future United States as an important part of a fundamentally distinctive modernizing process.[8]

Thus, according to an 'Atlantic' account of Jamestown released in conjunction with the 400th anniversary of its founding, 'the first permanent English settlement in the territory that would become the United States' constituted 'the tiny seed from which would grow a powerful nation where all the world's people would mingle'. This seed came to flourish through 'trial and error – and error often predominated' employed by the settlers, a number of whom 'had had experience of other Atlantic and Mediterranean regions before they came together on the James River', over a decade or so after 1607. In doing so, the emerging society overthrew the 'hierarchical arrangements' devised by the Virginia Company, which had also conceived 'notoriously unrealizable goals' for its colony. The 'improvisation, undertaken by ordinary people' with the people and the land they found, created 'the outlines of genuinely American society, with all its virtues and defects' and made 'elites nervous' as they 'set about the task of building families and family farms' – a characterization with which the Progressive historian Turner would have readily concurred.[9]

The shadow of another eminent Victorian also still hovers over the counterpart of colonial British America, the early history of the Anglo-British Empire. Five years before Turner's appearance at the World's Columbian Exposition in Chicago in 1893, Sir J. R. Seeley declared that the British Empire was founded in a 'fit of absent-mindedness'.[10] Even today, historians of the early modern English state offer their considerations (in which the expansion of its 'empire' during the seventeenth century, of course, played a part) in terms of Seeley's characterization of an essentially accidental empire. They do so even as they have struggled to come to terms with a revamped understanding of the social and political world over which the Tudor and Stuart monarchs ruled. At the same time, the Whiggish/Marxist 'high road' to the English Civil Wars, culminating in the triumph of 'liberty' or of the bourgeoisie (depending on one's point of view), which was first laid coincidentally with Turner's construction in the United States, has undergone substantial revision and post-revision. These investigations have yielded a re-evaluation of the meaning of 'liberty' to contemporaries, a more nuanced understanding of the powers and limits of early modern English government, and a greater appreciation of the importance of politics and religion to this history.[11]

The most cogent of these analyses have sought to reconcile the apparent indifference towards overseas empire on the part of the early Stuarts with the reality that English overseas interests rapidly expanded during their reigns, while the Anglo-British state, like its peers, became increasingly modernized. According to Michael Braddick, the growth of English long-distance trade and colonization accompanied a halting but inexorable seventeenth-century 'state formation' – the increasing manifestation and centralization of state functions accompanied by the acquisition and control of those functions for political advancement. In the case of Anglo-American colonies, elites 'had vested interests which could be protected by crown authority, and mutualities of interest with the metropolitan authority'. Thus, the manner of development for these places both 'shored up the interests of developing local elites' and 'bore considerable similarities to the activities of the patriarchal state in England. None the less, these developments took place within the shell of a developing fiscal-military empire, the interests of which overrode the interests of particular colonies'. This scenario, in turn, gave rise to 'a potential tension between the interests that bound local elites to the crown and the autonomous interests of the state'.[12]

Chartered companies, especially of the joint-stock variety, proved particularly popular mechanisms for engineering overseas trade and colonization between 1550 and 1640. Their structure helped minimize the huge risks involved and they provided a banner under which English interests could rally against foreign rivals, while the issuance of a royal charter granted these entities quasi-governmental functions, such as recruiting settlers and building fortifications. Their nature also removed the financial burdens necessarily incurred in these activities from the shoulders of the Crown while providing spearheads for involvement in areas from Russia to the Moluccas to the Gold Coast to Hudson's Bay to Virginia. In the latter case, however, divisions within the company, compounded by its indebtedness and continuing 'reports of hardship and disorder', punctuated by the 1622 Indian attack on the colony, led to a royal takeover: 'This confirmed the emerging consensus, that these settlements represented an extension of the English polity'; this consensus, partly, 'was the product of sentiment in the colonies themselves'.[13]

In order to ascertain the character of this imperial meeting of the minds in the North American case, Braddick has relied on the scholarship of the Chesapeake noted above. He notes that, as colonial societies matured, they turned to 'Old World' governmental and social examples, 'not [as] a survival of the presumptions of the original settlers but a product of later mimesis, as complex societies sought models for their political and social order'. The colonists also 'drew upon diverse local experiences and responded to conditions with which they were not necessarily familiar', such as slavery and demographic diversity, but primarily relied upon the importation of English law and governmental institutions as well as a presumption of the superiority of patriarchal authority. In the Chesapeake, where 'the imbalance in the sex ratio, high mortality rates and dispersed settlement made patriarchal authority more difficult to attain than in' New England, 'individualism and competition' resulted. While a self-conscious provincial elite emerged in Virginia and Maryland 'by the early eighteenth century', the imperial state, after 1640, 'accelerated' its direct involvement in the colonies.[14]

At the same time, the appearance of a recognizable English imperial ideology (at least *ex post facto*) – based upon the expansion of Protestantism (despite the vagueness of the term to contemporaries) and free maritime trade – became evident through the work of writers such as John Dee, the younger Richard Hakluyt and Captain John Smith. These efforts, according to Armitage, provided the intellectual impetus for pursuing economic and political advancement in faraway places during the Tudor-Stuart period, although they began to bear their fullest fruit after 1730.[15]

The book you are about to read constitutes a different sort of attempt to bridge the histories of early modern England and 'colonial British America' and so improve access to our understanding of both subjects. It does adopt an 'Atlantic' view of what happened in the early English Chesapeake since a proper comprehension of the significance of this subject can only come from a transatlantic context and perspective. It does not, however, pursue an investigation related to the emergence of an 'Atlantic World'; not only because contemporaries remained wholly unaware of this concept, but because most early modern Europeans did adhere to their own sense of nationhood and abhorred those, such as the Jesuits, who they found blurring political and cultural boundaries. Nor does it seek to place American colonization within the context of the history of 'modernity'. Instead, this book adopts an unfashionable 'national' perspective in order both to provide clearer insights of what transpired in what passed for the English Empire during the first half of the seventeenth century and to enable the use of the English case for comparison with others. In doing so, it situates the expansion of English interests overseas within the context of medieval and early modern English social and political history, as sketched in Chapter 1 below.

Of course, some of the English people who spent considerable time with other societies, notably John Smith and John Pory, actively participated in the Virginia Company; naturally, their colleagues – persons with deep mercantile and political experience – drew upon their knowledge. Equally obviously, Jamestown's indigenous neighbours had profound effects on the early history of Virginia. And, of course, as others have observed, English people living in a 'New World' necessarily had to adapt to rather different social and environmental realities from the situations they had left.[16] Most famously, they lacked an aristocracy as those few members of the armigerous order who ventured to Jamestown, such as George Percy, eighth son of the eighth Earl of Northumberland, returned to England. Moreover, this group received the scorn of Captain Smith both for their alleged failure to govern the colony properly and for their refusal to contribute to the production of food. The absence of this customary leadership created a vacuum into which the aspiring Jacobeans could and did step – often over each other – in assuming prominence in this colonial backwater.[17]

At the same time, however, for all of the novel environmental circumstances that early English migrants encountered in the Chesapeake, they ultimately retained – and successfully applied to their new surroundings – an 'Old World' sensibility of how society and politics were supposed to operate, as Braddick, for one, has noted. Indeed, 'modernization', if it did come, came hard: the socio-political understanding of colonists shared the same belief in a hierarchy based upon landed income as the best means of ordering society, a system of reciprocity which required the cultivation of patronage links through deference to 'superiors' and condescension towards 'inferiors', and a keen sense of locality, especially in terms of local administration and in negotiation with the central government with their counterparts in England.[18]

This sensibility also included a long history of fierce factional jockeying for political, religious and economic advancement. Thus, as Braddick and others have also observed, while distinguishing socio-cultural traits certainly developed out of necessity and contingency in Virginia, to regard the colony as the platform from which sprang something fundamentally new and improved – not to mention exceptional – means to look, anachronistically, for something that did not exist in the first part of the seventeenth century. Again perhaps paradoxically, the mechanism for socio-political change (if not 'modernization') came to a manifest degree from within the shared political culture through the pursuit of advantage on both sides of, as well as across, the Atlantic Ocean. *The English Empire in America* contends, however, that this shared political culture not only came to exist at a later point in Anglo-American colonial history; it came into existence very early in the history of the Jamestown settlement. Correspondingly, 'anglicization' never needed to take place as those who assumed control of the colony and its offshoots always maintained a metropolitan orientation.

Thus, this volume, first, casts aside the inherently teleological preconceptions that have, by extension, remained embedded in discussions of 'origins', especially, in the debate over Anglo-American 'exceptionalism'. Instead, it widens the chronological context from which Anglo-American settlement arose. In Chapter 2, it concentrates on those in the metropolis who became interested in colonization, who amassed the necessary political and economic capital to support overseas settlement, who provided the ready socio-political model for their colonists, and who had to overcome the doubts which were raised about their endeavours. 'Peopling' entailed far more than pioneering and interacting with indigenous neighbours: without the continuing willingness of investors to undertake the significant risks and costs of colonization and pay the settlement freight, Hakluyt, Smith and the rest of the 'Jamestown project' would constitute little more than historical footnotes. Not coincidentally, what we can glean – largely from the promotional pamphlets which the Virginia Company generated – about the motives for migration suggests that both colonizers and would-be colonists identified the 'wilderness' and American 'opportunities' largely in terms of landed estates, which remained the benchmark for socio-political status on both sides of the Atlantic.

In a related vein, this book offers a reassessment of the management of the Virginia Company, which has generally attracted opprobrium practically since its first fleet landed. On the face of things, the undoubted misery of succeeding waves of settlers, the inability to sort out relations with the Indians, the colony's subsequent addiction to tobacco, and the ultimate dissolution of the corporate entity itself make a lengthy list of serious charges to answer. Underpinning them lies the belief that the merchants, such as Sir Thomas Smythe who led it until 1618, the gentry, such as Sir Edwin Sandys who oversaw the affairs of the company from that point until its dissolution, and their aristocratic patrons, such Henry Wriothesley, third Earl of Southampton, did not make adequate provision for the American situation, did not devote adequate time and resources to the colony, and insisted on imposing impractical social and governmental schemes upon their settlers. Even the reforms undertaken after 1618, which included the establishment of the celebrated House of Burgesses, as well as private plantations, turned sour as the throngs of migrants the company sent arrived without adequate provisions and the colony lacked supplies to maintain them, resulting in more death and finger-pointing among the shareholders.[19] Indeed 1624, when the court of King's Bench dissolved the corporate charter, remains a benchmark of Virginia history.[20]

The English Empire in America thus takes the view that the absence of an aristocracy in the early Chesapeake, the dissolution of the Virginia Company and the attempt to link English overseas colonization with modernity constitute red herrings to our understanding of these imperial and colonial histories. In the first instance, as Chapter 1 discusses, English society had experienced such 'modernizing' phenomena as widespread migration and a devotion of substantial resources to commercial agriculture as far back as the thirteenth century, especially in, but by no means limited to, the Home Counties. Accompanied by continuing demographic recovery from the nadir of the Black Death of the late 1340s and the great land-grab generated by the dissolution of the monasteries in the 1530s, these activities continued through the period of what proved to be the genesis of the English Empire in America.[21] This reality, however, did not signal the 'origins of English individualism', the identification of which has, in turn, provided the foundation for an influential treatment of the formation of Anglo-American colonial societies.[22] Rather, it manifested the history, which sometimes incorporated profound changes, of the enduring attempt in England to reconcile social order and individual behaviour.

Those who led the management of Virginia on both sides of the ocean and who constituted the real engineers of this enterprise, providing the investment and maintaining the interest in the venture in the teeth of frequent hostility, ridicule and disinterest, were products of this environment. As outlined in Chapter 4 below, in accordance with principles of good management and the character of early modern English politics and society, the company's leaders remained willing to defer to their men in charge on the scene. Unfortunately, these realities, aggravated by the distance between London and Jamestown, entailed issues which proved insoluble. In particular, generations of colonial leadership took to cultivating patronage connections and socio-economic interests of their own, just as their 'superiors' at home did. It proved beyond the capacity of the company to compel their officers to devote their attentions to the corporate good. As a consequence, a recognizable Virginia elite emerged by 1614, as suggested by the typically paradoxical career of John Rolfe.

The name of this planter, as noted above, has long been enshrined in Jamestown lore as the spouse of Pocahontas and as the midwife of tobacco cultivation. But for all of this notoriety, we know very little about Rolfe's life, especially before his life in Virginia.[23] Yet, he did, of course migrate to America and, more importantly, he established the early template for Anglo-American colonial success: the acquisition of a landed estate fuelled by an exportable commodity and the formation of connections in the metropolis. He also took an active role in promoting the colony.[24]

The case of Rolfe also illustrates how contemporaries resolved the fundamental ambiguities inherent in the expansion of early modern English overseas interests. Colonizers – and colonists, for that matter – had to square their comprehension of proper social order in terms of phenomena which meshed uneasily with the prevailing view. Both the metropolitan reality and the colonial ideal rested on the belief in hierarchy derived from the ownership of landed estates. Yet, the migration required to build colonies was twinned, by definition, with individual initiative and opportunity, not to mention commercial activity, which seems to rest uneasily, in retrospect, with the socio-political pillars of civility and gentility erected in the sixteenth century.[25] Of course the distance between metropolis and colony, of which colonizers were aware and sought to manage, together with the 'wilderness' character of America, aggravated the situation. In all of England's colonies, when it suited colonial leaders to cooperate with colonizing officials such as the Virginia Company they did; when it did not, they did not; officials in London could do little to affect this scenario.[26]

Then, although the company's management certainly made mistakes, some very serious, over the years, and did lose its charter, a significant number of the people involved in that management remained in charge of proceedings after 'royalization' – on both sides of the Atlantic. As noted in Chapter 4, once the military situation became ensured after making peace with the Powhatans in 1614, this leadership and its successors worked together to realign Virginia into a settlement colony devoted to the production of commodities for export. Not only did this appeal to 'mercantile' thinking, of the sort espoused by Hakluyt and others; it appealed to migrants seeking the status – as well as the wealth

– generated by the income from landed estates in accordance with the prevailing norm. Correspondingly, then, the absence of contemporary intent, accompanied by the largely successful adaptation of the metropolitan socio-political system to the new, casts doubt on the degree to which we can consider Anglo-American colonization in terms of modernization. At the same time, given that England had experienced both a lengthy period of overseas empire and substantial long-haul migration prior to 1550 (and 1350), it remains unclear to what degree the British Empire constitutes a 'modernizing' phenomenon.[27]

Chapter 1 of this book, then, sets out the structure of that world – as much as can be done, in light of the continuing convulsions it endured – especially in terms of its government and society in order to provide the context from which early English overseas activity arose. Chapter 5 then analyses the attempts of the governments of James I and Charles I to imagine and effect what might be termed an 'imperial' policy, especially after tobacco became established as a lucrative export commodity in the Chesapeake, which the government tried to conduct in accord with private interests. The existence of these efforts, despite their tentativeness and ultimate failure, demonstrates that these monarchs and their officers, pace Seeley, did have a sense – perhaps tentative, but nevertheless, palpable – of an overseas empire and visions of how to coordinate that empire. The problem, both for contemporaries and for historiography, was that these views, along with the policies which guided them, often emerged incoherently and, so, sometimes conflicted. The 'fiscal-military shell', identified by Braddick, seems to have developed particularly slowly on the imperial side of things.

The record – and, therefore, predictably, the scholarship – remains preoccupied with the miserable little groups of settlers at Jamestown and its counterparts. Significantly – perhaps either because they feared neglect or because they sought to justify themselves – early colonial promoters, such as Sir Walter Ralegh and Captain John Smith – spent considerable time and energy creating tracts, 'histories', diaries and other documents that created a durable lens through which the light of history has continued to shine. But does this lens prevent the light from hitting more important regions of reality for our understanding of early English colonization?

In the case of Virginia, the figure of Smith has long dominated. The Captain composed three versions of his *History of Virginia* during his lifetime, which, *inter alia*, famously bemoaned the laziness of Jamestown's gentlemen and the perfidy of the Indians. It also privileged Smith as the saviour of the settlement and the champion of Anglo-American expansion whose sound suggestions failed to register with the stubborn gentlemen-amateur incompetents who had control of the Jamestown project following his enforced departure from the colony in 1609. As the most in-depth first-person account we have of Jamestown, Smith's *History* provides unparalleled access to the colony's early tribulations.

And because generations of subsequent readers have identified its author – by his own account a forthright, pragmatic, 'can-do' leader quick to point out the shortcomings of his aristocratic 'superiors' – as an early American, it has also cemented the Captain's status as a household name even today as a progenitor of American identity although those involved in Virginia scarcely noted him.

Yet, Captain John Smith, his career and *History* comprise only one, relatively unimportant, aspect of the actual history of early English colonization. For leading English colonizers, Smith and his ilk were, literally, foot soldiers in a greater game, of which empire constituted only a part: the colonizing itch developed from the frustration felt by some, both personally and philosophically, with the character of England some time around 1575. Some of these people were concerned about the refusal of Elizabeth I to marry (thereby ensuring the Tudor dynasty as well as security for the realm) and about her government's seeming tendency to drift, especially with respect to combating the pretensions of Catholic power in France, the Netherlands and Germany; this group, in its initial incarnation, coalesced around Robert Dudley, Earl of Leicester, and Sir Philip Sidney. Its members shared the humanist belief, tied to 'medieval' notions of chivalry, that true aristocrats should take direct action – act as true leaders of their society – to solve problems whenever they saw occasion to do so; their tools included literature, patronage and drama (both theatrical and personal). Thus, Sidney, Mary Wroth and others composed a battery of social critiques of the sort found nowhere else in Europe. Members of this circle cajoled Elizabeth and her ministers, notably William Cecil, Lord Burghley, to adopt a more forceful policy on behalf of the Huguenots against the Catholic League in the Wars of Religion in France, on behalf of the Dutch rebels against Spain, and against the pretensions of Mary, Queen of Scots, to the English throne. They also supported greater English colonization in Ireland and overseas.[28]

After Sidney's death during a skirmish with the Spanish at Zutphen (which, predictably, transformed him into a martyr for international Protestantism), the group carried over its allegiance to Leicester's stepson, Robert Devereux, second Earl of Essex. Essex maintained both a spy network on the Continent to monitor and counter the activities of 'papists' and a patronage network designed to promote the Essex agenda at home against Burghley, perceived as overly cautious with respect to the Catholic threat.[29]

But here the equation of English imperial pursuits with anti-Catholic, or even anti-Spanish, agendas becomes too simplistic: the Essex faction did not maintain a common intellectual 'front' outside of the perceived need for reform and to protect English national interests (although they did not use the term) against foreign plotters. Most particularly, its leader – paradoxically, given his foreign policy predilections – favoured religious toleration by the standards of his day and so attracted those English Catholics, such as the colonizer Sir George Peckham, who accepted a Protestant monarch, to his side. Also, as a self-styled protector of the interests of the old aristocracy, Essex opposed the pretensions of perceived parvenus such as Burghley, his son, Sir Robert Cecil and Ralegh.

Although the latter supported, as Essex did, international Protestantism and colonization, his alienation from the earl's patronage and his corresponding inability to create his own network (compounded by his secret marriage to the queen's handmaiden Bess Throckmorton which enraged Elizabeth, who banished Ralegh from court) shunted his own career to an imperial cul-de-sac. Despite all of the later publicity heaped on him as the founder of Roanoke, his employment of Hakluyt as a colonial theorist, his efforts to settle Guiana and his tragic end, purportedly at the hands of the 'scheming' Count Gondomar, Ralegh failed either to generate significant state support for his colonizing activities or to establish any sort of enduring colonial model for future settlement. Instead, his legacy consists of the knowledge he and his associates gathered about America and its inhabitants and the enduring sensibility that the Spanish ambassador 'duped' the 'tyrannical' James I into carrying out the death sentence that had hung over this romantic hero following his implication in the 'Bye plot'. Ralegh's execution in 1618 came to symbolize both the struggle of 'Elizabethan adventurers' to advance the liberties purportedly manifested by Anglo-Saxon Protestantism and the fate of that struggle at the hands of perfidious Spain and a feckless king.[30]

While Ralegh languished in the Tower for fifteen years and then went to the block after one last Guiana fling, his great rival, Essex, despite his own execution following his failed rebellion in 1601, retained rather more significance. In the first instance, the survivors of the Essex revolt and the close relatives of others, notably Henry Wriothesley, third Earl of Southampton, and Sir John Danvers, younger brother of the executed Sir Charles Danvers, carried on the Essex legacy.

Moreover, a number of members of the Essex network served as espionage agents both before and after 1601. As such, they inhabited a particularly shadowy and dangerous world, in which constantly shifting allegiances and fortunes at various levels meant advantage at one turn and ruin at the next. Serving as diplomats and soldiers in Italy, the Netherlands, in Germany, even in Hungary, and as double-agents in the English seminaries in Rouen and Louvain, they often played the tricky game of switching sides (and back again), most scandalously at the 'betrayal' of Deventer to besieging Spanish forces in 1587: some survived, received pardons and even prospered, others, such as the playwright Christopher Marlowe, who became unreliable or deemed a threat were condemned to death, while other veterans, such as Edward Maria Wingfield, Captain Smith, Peter Wynn and Sir Samuel Argall, pitched up at Jamestown after the Spanish war ended in 1604. In this era of constant plot and counter-plot, the stakes and targets, including the hapless Scottish queen who finally fell in the same year as the Deventer betrayal, remained high.[31]

Chapter 2 and, in part, Chapter 3 set out what we might regard as a 'prehistory' of the settlement of Virginia. As they discuss, the requirements of early seventeenth-century colonization necessarily included a substantial military component. This meant, in 1606, recourse to employing men who had served in the wars in the Low Countries and/or in Ireland. The problem, then, for the Virginia Company was not so much the inexperience of its officers with the American environment or even their arrogant presumption in dealing with indigenous people. Rather, the military operations in which these men had made their careers had generated atmospheres of treachery, switching sides and plots, including the infamous handover of Deventer to besieging Habsburg forces by Sir William Stanley and the madcap attempt by Essex to seize control of the government in 1601. We find men involved in both of these events also involved in Virginia.

Their situation, however, improved somewhat when Elizabeth died in March 1603 and was succeeded by James VI of Scotland. Essex (like Robert Cecil) had been in secret correspondence with the Scottish monarch and had generated a favourable impression. Thus, when James came to the English throne he released Southampton and the other Essexians from the Tower and remitted their fines – although they remained on the margins of power. Arguably, the leadership of the faction passed, at least temporarily, to Lucy Russell, Countess of Bedford (whose husband seconded Essex in his ill-advised tilt at supreme power), in the absence of viable male direction in the aftermath of the 1601 fiasco. Thus, politics became wedded to the theatre as Bedford and her associates included the leading literary figures of the day – William Shakespeare, George Chapman, Ben Jonson, John Marston, Samuel Daniel, John Donne and William Drayton – amongst their clients. A number of these pens became employed in support of views espoused by the remnant of the Essex faction, most notably in the play *Eastward Hoe!* (1605), a collaboration between Chapman, Jonson and Marston, which lampooned Scottish graspers, wastrel apprentices and also colonizers.

In the meantime, as Chapter 3 discusses, a combination, which included another old Essexian and Dutch veteran, Sir Thomas Gates, Hakluyt (whose former patron, Ralegh, had become implicated in a plot against the new king and went to the Tower at the end of 1603) and the leading London merchant Sir Thomas Smythe, had begun investing in efforts to find likely locations for a 'Northwest Passage', a North American version of the Mexican and Incan empires, and locations for trade with Indians. Building on the efforts of Ralegh and others, they sent a fleet under Bartholomew Gosnold to inspect the New England coast in 1602, founded one of two Virginia Companies in 1606 and undertook the settlement of the Chesapeake the following year.

The coming to England of the Stuarts presented an alternative power base to those who chafed for the chance to improve England by employing their talents for government: James's queen-consort, Anna of Denmark, left Edinburgh with intentions of making her presence known politically. Can it have been a coincidence that a number of old Essexians, including, most prominently, the Countess of Bedford, rushed north to meet their new queen on her progress?[32]

Anna had claimed an independent political existence in Scotland, on occasion thwarting the will of her husband, for all of his claims to authority bestowed by 'divine right'. Clearly, James moved, in conjunction with Cecil, who remained in place as chief minister, to circumscribe his wife's political movements in his new kingdom. Cecil and the leaders of the Howard family, including, especially, Henry, Earl of Northampton (the recipient of a Spanish pension), as well as Thomas, Earl of Suffolk (Northampton's brother), and Charles, Lord Howard of Effingham, the lord admiral, had allied themselves against those they regarded as dangerously anti-Spanish. All of these men, for various reasons, planned an end to the long war that had brought on attendant miseries at the end of Elizabeth's reign, a view that completely agreed with those of the new monarch, the self-styled *Rex Pacificus*. Thus, while Southampton and his fellows emerged from disgrace and threat of attainder, Ralegh went to the Tower on treason charges. At the same time, the arrival of James's friends from Scotland complicated the royal patronage mix; they assumed many of the new, plum 'bedchamber' offices.[33]

The presence of these foreign favourites added insult to the injury inflicted by the continued limited access to the centre of authority for the legatees of Essex and their corresponding policy fears – the peace treaty with Spain signed in 1604, proposals for a formal union between England and Scotland, and the seemingly inordinate bestowal of royal wealth on Scottish favourites. A number of their clients, including, perhaps most significantly, the parliamentarian Sir Edwin Sandys, joined Queen Anna's council. Since until very recently, Anna has received short, if any, shrift from scholars and this organization has received scant notice as a potential locus of opposition to policies favoured by James. Yet, coincidentally or otherwise, her council included the most prominent of the spokesmen against those policies speaking even to the point that the king complained that they encroached upon his prerogative.[34]

By this time, the tentative connections that had existed between colonization and the Essexians during Elizabeth's time had gone into abeyance. Instead, with the Spanish war winding down – ironically given the attention paid to the anti-Spanish rhetoric of colonizing theorists such as Hakluyt – the merchants, interested in commerce in the Mediterranean, in Africa and in the East Indies and with no interest whatsoever in linking their overseas activities to a crusade against the Habsburgs, began to move to include North America in a new, related zone of commerce: interest in finding a 'Northwest Passage' to East Asia remained keen, the fishing off of the North Atlantic coast remained exceedingly promising, and trade with the indigenous inhabitants might, in itself, prove profitable. In 1602, a group of Londoners, led by Smythe, who as the lord mayor of London had famously turned Essex away from his door the previous year, sponsored the exploratory voyage of George Weymouth in order to identify likely locations for bases for trade.

Weymouth identified Chesapeake Bay, which was supposed to have been the location of the Roanoke colony in 1585, as promising on all fronts: money-making constituted the only spur to investigations of remote places here. From the point of view of the Essex relicts, however, this sort of activity demonstrated the fundamental problems with English society under its new monarch. Instead of vigorously pursuing and defending the nation's interests abroad, especially against the Spanish 'menace', the government lavished power, office and wealth on dubious companions of the monarch and granted perquisite privileges to those unwilling to defend the interests of the realm. This, in turn, created a serious financial shortfall that obliged James's ministers to seek various dubious means, from collecting impositions without parliamentary approval to selling baronetcies, in order to maintain solvency. Not only did these expediencies put kingly government in a poor light; they caused all sorts of social disruption as people of 'inferior' backgrounds – 'ordinary' or otherwise – sought to take advantage and move into the aristocracy by dint solely of their ability to pay. This, of course, debased the old aristocracy and the noble values that the late Earl of Essex, for one, had regarded as crucial to the national interest – and they made their displeasure known as well as they could from the political sidelines.

Yet, as Chapter 4 notes, this situation became transformed after 1616 when the queen, in conjunction with Southampton and other allies, seized the chance provided by the erratic behaviour of James's incumbent favourite, Robert Carr, Earl of Somerset. They ingratiated a replacement, George Villiers, whom they used to orchestrate the eclipse of Carr's Howard in-laws and manoeuvred themselves, temporarily as it proved, into power. At the same time, Southampton and his clients took over the management of the Virginia Company, with Sandys taking the leading part and his own clients, brothers John and Nicholas Ferrar, assuming the day-to-day management. Famously, the 'new broom' swept away Smythe's philosophy that the company's interests should remain paramount; the Southampton-Sandys-Ferrar regime astutely realized that the local interests on the ground should have primacy. This attitude sat better both with contemporary socio-political views and the realities of imperial administration and, thus, they created a 'little parliament' for the colony.[35]

In conjunction with these developments, the leading Virginia planter, John Rolfe, famously married the 'Indian princess', Pocahontas (daughter of Wahunsonacock, the sachem of the neighbouring Powhatan people), and successfully introduced tobacco cultivation at Jamestown. The former act ended the series of wars between English and Indians that had begun in 1609. Rolfe brought his bride to England where she was introduced to the court at, as it happens, the masque at which Villiers met the king. The tour of the 'American' couple generated renewed attention in Virginia and, coupled with the news of tobacco, prompted a successful recapitalization of the Virginia Company. Given the historical links of this group, we can postulate that something more than profit became included in their thinking about colonization. At the same time, public jibes against colonization and social climbing, tellingly, ceased.

With new corporate resources in hand, together with peace with the Indians, and a staple crop offering a substantial incentive for crossing the Atlantic, the Southampton-Sandys-Ferrar organization recruited an unprecedented number of migrants for Virginia. Unfortunately, they became victims of their own success: the Crown, always keen to find new revenue streams, quickly became interested in devising a means of controlling the tobacco trade; the encroachments made by the new settlers rekindled tensions with the Powhatans, who attacked the colony in 1622 killing over a quarter of the inhabitants; and another faction involved in the Virginia Company, led by Robert Rich, second Earl of Warwick, alleged malfeasance by Sandys in their attempt to wrest control of the enterprise. The ensuing struggle, discussed in Chapter 5, only came to an end when the Crown intervened in 1624, filing a writ of *quo warranto* which abrogated the company's charter and placed Virginia under royal government, although this was envisioned as a temporary move, at least initially. The Southampton group exacted a measure of revenge by leading the successful fight in the parliament of 1624 to impeach the lord treasurer, Lionel Cranfield, Earl of Middlesex, who had led the government's fight to establish a contract for the collection of the customs revenue.

As noted above, the royal takeover – invariably regarded as the beginning of a new epoch of Virginia history following the 'mismanagement' of the company era – did not constitute a break with what had transpired previously, as Chapter 5 also relates. In the first instance, although Nicholas Ferrar retired to the religious retreat they founded at Little Gidding, Huntingdonshire, and Sandys became a victim of poor health, many of the key figures remained on the scene and assumed even greater prominence.

These included Edward Sackville, fourth Earl of Dorset, who had joined the Virginia Company board as early as 1620 and who led the commission of enquiry appointed by James I following the 'massacre'. Such familiar names as the London merchants Sir John Wolstenholme and Sir John Zouch and the colonial planters William Claiborne (a client of Sandys who arrived in the colony in 1621), Samuel Mathews and Sir Francis Wyatt (a once and future governor) affiliated themselves with Dorset. Subsequently, the earl headed the government committee charged with colonial matters in the 1630s. By virtue of their respective positions, these understudied individuals – sometimes in combination, sometimes not – came to control the socio-political character of the colony. Most particularly, they succeeded in 'thrusting out' the governor, Sir John Harvey, in 1635.

The case of Harvey, who had also participated in the post-'massacre' investigation, provides another acute example both of how politics worked in the early English Empire. It also demonstrates how the 1632 granting of the Maryland patent to George Calvert, Lord Baltimore, became the focus of transatlantic political activity. Baltimore's proprietorship incorporated territory that the Crown had granted to the Virginia Company. By this time, operating under the presumption that Virginia still had claim to the company land, notwithstanding the *quo warranto*, Claiborne and Mathews, as part of their transatlantic (including an African component) venture with the London merchants William Clobery and Maurice Thompson, had established a lucrative trading post at Kent Island in Chesapeake Bay. Unfortunately for the Virginians, Whitehall ignored their enterprise and included the island in 'Maryland' and the next twenty-five years saw a running battle between Baltimore's successors and Claiborne and Mathews. Harvey, who mistakenly believed his royal commission would trump any opposition, became a victim of this strife when he offered assistance to the Marylanders: an outraged Claiborne used his metropolitan contacts to outflank and embarrass the governor.[36]

These contacts, notably Dorset, Wolstenholme and Zouch, supported Claiborne because they shared a desire to promote Virginia, especially by extending its boundaries – a dream with which Maryland, on its face, interfered. Since the subjects of Charles I, like all early modern 'projectors', did not differentiate between 'private' and 'public' interest, their personal interests in the colony naturally dovetailed with this particular 'imperial' view. At the same time, however, serious disagreement existed over the prospect of a resurrection for the Virginia Company. As late as 1640, George Sandys, brother of the now-deceased Sir Edwin, petitioned the Long Parliament for a restoration of the company and its rights. Alarmed that this plan threatened their land titles (and, possibly, their autonomy), the planters responded with counter-petitions to both parliament and to Charles I at York at what proved to be the onset of the civil wars.

Thus, a paradoxical concept of 'imperialism' came to the forefront in Virginia by the mid-1630s: on the one hand, various colonists, backed by important figures in the metropolis, and proprietors from England, pursued expansionist schemes (not always in accord) both to the north and south of Virginia. In doing so, they encountered posts established by the Dutch and Swedes in the Delaware, which, in English eyes, violated their North American claims and so required removal. The Dutch presence at New Amsterdam, however, constituted less of a thorn – at least for Virginians – since it provided a base for the smugglers who helped keep up the price of tobacco. On the other hand, these ventures made no pretence of advancing the interests of the English state. Some of them, like Baltimore's and Sir Robert Heath's contemporaneous grant to 'Carolana', did arise from a charter granted by the Crown; but Sir Edmund Plowden's patent to 'New Albion' (near present-day Philadelphia, Pennsylvania) came from the government of Ireland, while the efforts of a group from New Haven which attempted to settle in the same area had no greater official sanction.

The history of New Albion, moreover, provides a further demonstration of the shifting sands of early English 'imperialism'. To a greater degree than its counterparts, the English government prior to 1649 conducted its foreign and, by extension, imperial policy on a decentralized basis. Monarchs could and did involve themselves, as in the case of the dissolution of the Virginia Company, the granting of Maryland to Lord Baltimore or the grant of the tobacco receivership to the diplomat Sir William Boswell and the Huguenot gentleman Pierre de Licques. While Dorset and his transatlantic cohort worked out the sociopolitical character of Virginia, Plowden pursued colonization as a means of demonstrating Roman Catholic loyalty to the English state. Although the Privy Council at Whitehall never endorsed his patent, he received some support, notably a patent under the seals of the kingdom of Ireland, within the political nation from those, such as Sir Thomas Wentworth, the lord deputy in Dublin, who favoured an anti-Dutch foreign policy and saw New Albion as a means both of combating the mercantile activities of the Dutch Republic and of putting added pressure on New Netherland. After overcoming Claiborne's initial reservations, Sir Edmund finally moved to take up his patent, but found the Swedish colony on the Delaware too strong to dislodge.

This largely periphery-driven pursuit of 'empire' continued naturally as the imperial centre collapsed with the outbreak of civil war in August 1642, as set out in Chapter 6. Plowden and the New Haven colony made efforts along the Delaware River and some Independents from Bermuda tried colonizing Eleuthera in the Bahamas in 1647. At the same time, Claiborne, Mathews and their allies, especially one Captain Richard Ingle, used the hostilities to resume their personal offensive on Maryland: a miniature civil war and a barrage of pamphlets from both Virginians and supporters of the Calverts broke out. After the Battle of Dunbar (1651) eliminated the royalist threat in Britain, the central government began to catch up, passing the first Navigation Acts in 1651 in an effort to curb Dutch smugglers. Virginia governor Sir William Berkeley, in conjunction with John Ferrar and others in England, continued the promotion of Virginia's southerly expansion.

The expulsion of the Rump Parliament in 1653 ended the English dalliance with republicanism in favour of the protectorate of Oliver Cromwell. For the first time, an English government – thanks, ironically, to the demise of the monarchy – possessed both the means and the will to carry out an imperial policy fighting wars against both the United Provinces (1652–4) and Spain (1655), the latter marking the first time England had sent a force to attack an overseas target (Santo Domingo). The disappointing results it achieved, however, revealed that, having developed a clearer and more ambitious sense of its reach, the government's grasp remained relatively stunted.

At the same time, the Protector's regime, despite the continued lobbying of Claiborne and Mathews, upheld the legality of the Maryland patent and ended Virginia's northerly pretensions in 1658, although an aged Claiborne made one final appeal for 'justice' to Charles II, practically from his deathbed, following Bacon's Rebellion eighteen years later.[37] The Calvert triumph in this desperate struggle removed a festering sore in Anglo-American settlement and laid out a clearer line demarcating imperial authority. As with the Cromwellian 'Great Western Design' against the Spanish West Indies, this result illustrated the practical limits on 'imperial authority' even after the mid-point of the seventeenth century. While Whitehall did make the final adjudication, it did so to resolve a provincial battle and at local behest; the Marylanders made the better case and, unlike Harvey two decades previously, had better connections than their Virginia enemies did. Correspondingly, despite creeping 'state formation', the English state continued to delegate, in practice and ambiguously, primary responsibility for colonial affairs to colonists, in accordance with understood practice within the metropolis itself.

At the same time, through colonial success stories, such as Rolfe, Claiborne and Berkeley, the royal appointee who became a dominant figure on the colonial scene between 1642 and 1676, a metropolitan-style elite both became quickly entrenched in the Chesapeake and integrated into an imperial version of the preferred socio-political pyramid. These men understood the importance of currying metropolitan links to establishing and maintaining their positions. This cultivation, however, never came at the expense of local connections, interests and identity. Thus, through the combination of their socio-political cosmology and the character of their state (compounded by the disruptions of the civil wars), the English, on both sides of the Atlantic, manufactured an imperial sensibility in the seventeenth century which had a particularly local emphasis and, correspondingly, maintained a relatively underdeveloped imperial apparatus.[38]

1 DEEP BACKGROUND

2. That all other englishe Trades are growen beggerly or daungerous, especially in all the kinge of Spaine his Domynions, where our men are driven to flinge their Bibles and prayer Bokes into the sea, and to forsweare and renownce their relligion and conscience and consequently theyr obedience to her Majestie.
3. That this westerne voyadge will yelde unto us all the commodities of Europe, Affrica, and Asia, as far as wee were wonte to travell, and supply the wantes of all our decayed trades.
4. That this enterprise will be for the manifolde imploymente of numbers of idle men, and for bredinge of many sufficient, and for utterance of the great quantitie of the commodities of our Realme.[1]

In 1584, the clergyman Richard Hakluyt famously compiled a 'particuler discourse' setting out 'the greate necessitie and manifolde comodyties' which he presented to Queen Elizabeth I. Alarmed at the advantages the Spanish had gained at the expense of England and Protestantism by their head-start in America, Hakluyt and his patron, Sir Walter Ralegh, presented American colonization as a remedy for a variety of ills and so worthy of royal sponsorship: 'Western discoveries' would do everything from increasing trade and customs revenue to drawing Ireland 'to more Civilitie' to easing unemployment to curbing the ambitions of Felipe II. The queen received this brief, however, with rather less enthusiasm than its author had hoped; as we know, state support for imperial ventures remained intermittent until the middle of the seventeenth century. The prescience of Hakluyt's characterization of colonies as entities by which exotic, but useful, commodities could be obtained at lower cost and with much less hazard than through exchange with other countries, along with his conception of the English Empire as 'a great bridle to the Indies of the kinge of Spaine', has brought the tireless promoter considerable long-term significance despite the lack of impression his arguments made in the immediate term.[2]

It would seem self-evident that the history of Anglo-American colonization arose from the history of early modern England itself. We have a fairly clear idea of the world in which Hakluyt lived, as well as the despairing views the most persistent and prolific of English colonizing advocates had of it. Yet, despite this knowledge, and all of the ink spilled on English 'state formation' and the social development of various English colonies, no systematic treatment of the place of the expansion of overseas interests within the context of Tudor-Stuart England exists. Even the emergence of an 'Atlantic' perspective, while it has widened the lens trained on the founding of Virginia and its counterparts, has generally preferred to track Mediterranean and African links with what early modern English merchants, explorers, officials and colonists were doing, rather than delving too deeply into what was going on in England, or non-Ottoman Europe in general at the time. The Habsburg service of Captain John Smith, the 1578 'battle of the three kings' at Alcazarquivir in Morocco and the character of the slave trade in Angola certainly had effects on the character of the 'Atlantic World'. But surely, when considering the character of English overseas activity, we first require a better understanding of the history of the socio-political world which gave birth to colonial variations of it?[3]

The period in which English settlement in America was conceived and in which it developed – the one hundred years between the accession of Elizabeth I in 1558 and the death of Oliver Cromwell, Lord Protector, in 1658 – continues to rank as one of the most enduringly fascinating in human, let alone English, history, if the volume of films which continues to stream from cinema projectors, not to mention scholarly works from university presses, offers any guide. Hakluyt himself, born in 1552, the last year of the reign of Edward VI (1547–53), and, thus, thirty-two years old when he composed his 'Discourse' and fifty-four years of age when the Virginia fleet sailed in December 1606, would have celebrated a dazzling array of English achievements, including in 1588 the seemingly miraculous defeat of the Spanish Armada and, eight years before that, the triumphant return of Sir Francis Drake from his circumnavigation of the globe, which the colonial theorist included, of course, in his massive compilation of *Principal Navigations, Voyages, Traffiques and Discoveries of the English Nation*, published in 1589 and again in 1600.

Contemporaries of Hakluyt with cultural inclinations might have attended productions of such new plays as Shakespeare's *Macbeth* and *Antony and Cleopatra* or Ben Jonson's *Volpone*. The cleric himself would certainly have been aware of the work begun two years prior to the departure of the Jamestown colonists, under royal patronage, to create a new English-language version of the Bible. As an integral participant in the effort to expand English overseas interests, he had a direct role in the dissemination of the descriptions of the indigenous people of 'Virginia' of Thomas Hariot, made available through the efforts of the Flemish engraver Theodore de Bry, and the description of Guiana composed by his patron, Ralegh (languishing in the Tower of London in 1606). In another ten years, the findings of the physician-scientist William Harvey on the workings of the human body would begin to circulate.

Yet, rather less triumphantly and much more significantly, Hakluyt lived in particularly fraught and deeply uncertain times, as he well knew. Customarily, students of history, especially of the 'colonial American' stripe, tend to emphasize the 'modern' in their examinations of the 'early modern' period, as they are invariably and naturally interested in the nature and history of 'modernity' and how things came to be the way they are in North America: the development of constitutional government, 'liberty', individualism, commerce, the bureaucratic state, even theatre. Overseas trade and, especially, migration have fit into this schema all too nicely.[4] Correspondingly, the earlier history of England, certainly prior to 1570, receives very little consideration, even though, as we shall see below, 'modern' phenomena manifested themselves routinely in the 'medieval' period while, on the other hand, 'medieval' socio-political sensibilities remained stubbornly apparent during the early modern period, even in circumstances related to colonization.

Much of the demarcation drawn then and now between medieval and modern – and the general perception that this demarcation sets out a transforming progress in the history of England and elsewhere – arose due to the Reformation. The overthrow of 'enslaving' papal authority, the dissolution (and often destruction) of the 'corrupt' monasteries, the casting out of 'superstitions' – such as, most pointedly, transubstantiation – from divine service (which correspondingly replaced the popish Mass), the publication and dissemination of the Bible in English (rather than Latin), and the correspondingly deeper and more direct involvement of the congregation in their religious experience all counted as progress on the spiritual front. On the secular front, the history of the English people celebrated, by definition, liberation from the 'tyranny' exercised by medieval monarchs and barons as well as the chaos of the 'Wars of the Roses', and from the 'feudalism' which held an illiterate and ignorant peasantry in thraldom and which checked the aspirations of 'ordinary people' to better themselves. In sum, such a scenario had no place – and holds no place – in a progressive and ever-progressing world, especially in the 'New World order' which ultimately came to include the United States.[5]

Inevitably, then, historians of the expansion of English overseas interests, and of Anglo-American colonization in particular, have paid scant heed to the comprehensive revision of our understanding of pre-Reformation English history which has occurred over the last twenty or so years. For the stereotypical view of a hidebound, insular medieval England finally gave way to a realization that social mobility, the movement of people and commercial activity – all hallmarks of 'modernity' – also constituted readily apparent characteristics of English society prior to the Reformation. A demographic explosion, during which the country's population increased by two to three times during the twelfth and thirteenth centuries, triggered, in turn, an increase in cultivated lands, a corresponding increase in rents and prices, 'a growing dependence on non-agricultural employment and a sizeable increase in both the number and size of markets and towns'. In addition to the creation of over 2,000 'weekly village markets and 500 boroughs', the population of London, by the turn of the fourteenth century, had climbed to between 70,000 and 100,000 inhabitants. At the same time, the amount of circulating specie in England increased tenfold from the eleventh century to £1,100,000. Accompanying these changes came 'political centralisation, the relative growth of freedom, changes in socio-property relations, and growing occupational diversity, all [of which] encouraged the emergence of factor markets in land, labour and capital'.[6]

These phenomena, in turn, contributed to an increasingly commercial agricultural system, which 'peaked in aggregate terms in the early fourteenth century'. Even with the onset of severe population decline and economic disruption brought on by the Black Death (1348–50), 'it is certain that the commercial infrastructure did not disappear or become moribund' as 'sharper competition between markets had produced a more lean and rational marketing system'. The elimination of approximately a third of the English population at a stroke placed a substantial damper on these developments but also contributed to the collapse of serfdom in much of the country between 1350 and 1500 which, in turn, accelerated the shift of agricultural production for the market.[7]

Correspondingly, this 'marketing system' meant a continuation of earlier patterns of urbanization – not just in London, whose pre-eminence continued to increase exponentially – and migration of the Middle Ages. While the founding of colonies in a later period obviously permitted the expansion of the geographical scope of English migration to beyond the seas, it has become quite apparent that English people have always been on the move and that towns of various sizes have always attracted migrants. Seaports from Exeter to Newcastle to Bristol and inland towns from York to Coventry to Salisbury, linked by a network of water and land routes, possessed the natural symptoms of urban life, including shops and markets, taverns and municipal governments devised by royal charter quite early on. Towns also cooperated and competed with another for commerce and resources.[8]

These municipal endeavours reflected the continued striving of individuals to advance themselves during the Middle Ages (and before). Degree of success in trade, of course, always provides the readiest means for social mobility along with the readiest means of social decline, although the inherently unsettled nature of commerce always placed it beneath the relative security of landed wealth in contemporary idealizations of social character. Prior to the mid-sixteenth century, English merchants primarily involved themselves in domestic agricultural production and in the export of woollen textiles to Continental markets, especially Antwerp. The acquisition of land and the 'rationalization' of agricultural production, notably through enclosure, provided another significant avenue of mobility, especially for aspiring yeomen, while the seizure and redistribution of monastic lands following the Dissolution enabled supporters of the Crown to augment their estates substantially. As commentators, such as Sir Thomas More in 1516, observed and as the recurring protestations which periodically convulsed the countryside manifested, a substantial number of people had reservations about the effects of agricultural 'improvement': it appeared both to facilitate inordinate gain for some individuals at the expense of others and to further the erosion of the reciprocity between degrees of rank which underpinned an essential sense of community and, in the worst case scenario, threatened the dissolution social order and established religion. For John Winthrop, leading light of the Massachusetts Bay Company writing some thirty-five years after Hakluyt and over a century after More, colonization came to provide a means for stemming this threat and creating a godly model of Christian charity.[9]

The continuing increase in population after 1500, however, accompanied by increased migration, only aggravated the fears of social collapse. According to the leading estimate, England contained 2,773,851 people in 1541, 4,253,325 in 1606 (the year in which the Virginia Company received its charter) and 5,140,743 in 1660, despite the recurrence of plague, smallpox and other epidemic diseases. Indeed, Hakluyt himself weathered plague outbreaks in 1563, 1578, 1592–3 and 1603. His descendants had to cope with the return of the disease in 1625, 1636 and 1665. The cleric had already surpassed the average life expectancy of thirty-eight years for the period at the time the Virginia 'first fleet' sailed. The population of London continued to outpace that of the country at large, thanks to in-migration, despite horrifying mortality: the capital recorded 220,716 baptisms and 239,221 burials between 1600 and 1624 (the country as a whole recorded 3,504,446 baptisms and 2,744,538 burials during this period), although its population grew from between 61,000 and 75,000 in the mid-sixteenth century to over 200,000 by the beginning of the seventeenth.[10]

These demographics, compounded by the consecutively disastrous harvests of 1596 and 1597, generated dire socio-economic effects: scholars of the period regard the 'nasty nineties' – just a decade before the founding of Jamestown – as the worst for most ranks of English people until the aftermath of World War II. This situation arose, notwithstanding, for instance, the adoption of the Poor Law of 1597, due to the combination of high prices and low wages generated by the fundamental reality of more people: as many as 'two-fifths of the total population of four million fell below the margin of subsistence'. Dearth and the costs of waging indeterminate war in Spain, the Low Countries and, above all, Ireland combined to render the position of many 'ordinary' English people increasingly desperate, for 'while the population of the nation between 1541 and 1656 nearly doubled, the price of essential commodities over the span more than tripled'. The collapse of England's long-standing trade with the Low Countries after 1550, punctuated by the siege and sack of Antwerp (1576–82) during the Dutch Revolt, added further fuel to these problems especially in the south-east part of the country.[11]

In reality, the kingdom's population had returned to pre-Black Death numbers by the mid-sixteenth century, but the gap of two centuries rendered the earlier demographic experience outside of the reckoning of later commentators and it was the perception of those commentators that unprecedented numbers of unattached people roamed England threatening their 'betters' with begging, crime and even rebellion over their circumstance.[12] The Reverend William Harrison, for instance, claimed in 1587 that it was 'an easy matter to prove that England was never less furnished with people than at this present' by checking the decline in the number of tenancies. Moreover, he observed, a palpable number of the realm's 'cities and towns [had become] either utterly decayed or more than quarter or half diminished'. These observations, however, did not quell either the purported threat posed by the seemingly indiscriminate movement of masterless men (and women) or the inability of government to address that threat. Hakluyt had these issues firmly in mind when he promoted Western planting.[13]

The pursuit of status and wealth – which, it should be noted, has never been restricted to a particular element in English society – meant, by definition, competition and required the subordination and control of 'inferiors'. It also, then, entailed a further erosion, aggravated by the Reformation and the Dissolution as well as by population increase, of the ideal of reciprocity between social orders. In 1500, the impoverished could and did seek relief from monasteries and other religious establishments as well as from fellow Christians duty-bound to render assistance in hope of receiving salvation. After 1560, despite the intentions of the proponents of the Church of England that the reformed establishment would step into the shoes of the old faith, no entity assumed entirely the charitable functions of the old church. Moreover, for the increasing number of English people who professed adherence to the beliefs of John Calvin, the salvation equation no longer required a 'good works' factor. The absence of this requirement further reduced the need to give to the less fortunate, especially those who adhered to a different doctrinal persuasion.

Indeed, the extent and character of the Reformation itself remained a notoriously and frustratingly open question, notwithstanding the fervent exhortations of the enemies of the papal Antichrist and the ceaseless attempts by governments to herd their subjects into a reformed orthodoxy. Instead of a seamless transfer from papal to kingly governance of religion and the creation of a theology to which all loyal English people would subscribe, the ultimate establishment of Protestantism only further refracted the spectrum of religious belief. Within this refraction, people could find themselves compelled to conform as the government shifted its religious tack; and they could convert from one creed to another, both for reasons of conscience and, alarmingly to contemporaries, for reasons of convenience. This reality further bred suspicion of others and a corresponding concern about the future of society if such beliefs and their followers were allowed to fester.[14]

Seventy years after the first attempt of Henry VIII, Thomas Cromwell and Thomas Cranmer to devise an English church and just over a year before the three ships sailed off for Virginia, the continuing existence of committed 'papists' – and the threat that group posed – had its clearest demonstration in the 'miraculous deliverance' of the nation from the Catholic plot intended to blow up those, including the new king, James I, attending the opening of parliament in November 1605.

The 'Guy Fawkes' conspiracy also manifested the mutually deep fear and loathing that had developed between many 'papists' and Protestants. This sentiment, in turn, rendered consistently problematic the various attempts which had been made from various tacks, including the 'King James Bible', to establish a wholly satisfactory religious settlement under the government of the Crown. Hakluyt subscribed wholeheartedly to the theology and government of the Jacobean Church of England. Others, however, craved a 'further reformation': they might have conformed outwardly, yet maintained a private conscience oriented towards popery or Presbyterianism or they might have held separatist tendencies, holding, in accordance with the Gospel of St Matthew (22:21), that state control over the church necessarily polluted the latter with worldliness; they might also have held radical, 'antinomian' views about the relationship between humanity and heaven. The diocese of London, as the largest within the established church, was traditionally difficult to manage for ecclesiastical authority and had persevered, correspondingly, both as a haven for religious heterodoxy and as a source of acute anxiety for the orthodox since the fourteenth-century days of the 'Lollards'.[15]

These spiritual concerns had secular relations. In theory, power and the corresponding order it generated flowed from the top in the form of the 'Great Chain of Being'. English monarchs, by virtue of their coronation oath, comprised the link between their subjects and their God. Beneath those monarchs on the social pyramid lay the hereditary aristocracy, the gentry and independent yeomanry: the 'producers'. Beneath those layers (with merchants and artisans sandwiched in between) came the vast majority of the population (or 'drains'): copyholders, tenants, servants, wage labourers and the indigent. The ownership of landed estates constituted the barometer of social status and co-requisite responsibility to provide the government of one's locality and even of the nation. The deference, in the form of doffed caps, rents and general obedience, owed to 'betters' was supposed to be matched by the condescension, in the form of casks of ale and roasted bullocks at Christmas and the adjudication of customary rights, showed to 'inferiors'.[16]

Of course, this static ideal could barely withstand the endemic jockeying for social and economic position which marked England under its Tudor (1485–1603) and Stuart (1603–49, 1660–1714) monarchs. But while individuals certainly bought and sold land in order to make money, the ownership of real property constituted more than just an avenue to acquiring wealth. Those pursuing opportunities tended to define advancement as more than wealth: the twin ideals of the possession of landed estates both as the barometer of socio-political status and as the corresponding basis of social order remained controlling in the minds of early modern people on the make, as we know from the multitude of contemporary examples, such as Lionel Cranfield, prominent Jacobean London merchant and Earl of Middlesex, who acquired lands from Gloucestershire to Yorkshire to Essex. Thus, the promotional literature disseminated to attract migrants to overseas colonies advertised prospective means for generating landed income: the Maryland proprietor, Lord Baltimore, for instance, promised one hundred acres to every man who transported himself to the colony, another one hundred if he brought his wife and fifty acres for every child under the age of sixteen.[17]

Estates in land, aside from the income they generated, also signified the commitment of the landowner to the community. At least in theory, the lord, by virtue of his holdings, had the responsibility of condescending to maintain order in the locality both by creating and overseeing manorial courts and by occupying local offices, such as sheriff, parliamentary representative and justice of the peace, which connected the shires to the central government. The greatest landholders, who tended both to be ennobled and to hold the 'greatest' offices (such as lord-lieutenant), served as patrons for networks of clients, as demonstrated, for instance, by Robert Devereux, second Earl of Essex, and George Villiers, first Duke of Buckingham.[18]

While patrons could derive their position from inheritance, invariably they, at the least, improved their estates and their political situations by successfully currying favour with those already entrenched in power and, especially, monarchs. The cases of Essex and Buckingham also manifest the reality that, despite the official desire to further stability and order (provided by heritability), those who assumed pre-eminent socio-political status in the kingdom often overcame social, political and economic disadvantage: Essex received a bankrupt legacy from his father and required the support of his stepfather, Robert Dudley, Earl of Leicester, for his initial advancement while Buckingham rose from genteel obscurity through his good looks and the ability to link up with powerful connections, as we shall see below. The aspirations and attendant activities of such people served as the hallmark of socio-political behaviour in early modern England. Thus, their example provided the model for those who sought to become the 'weightier sort' in English America.

Politically active aristocracy and gentry pursued their ambitions within the frame of a body politic which extended down from the monarch and the Privy Council through various strata of officialdom to hog reeves, constables, jury-men, churchwardens and overseers of the poor. These offices, customarily held by yeomen or other representatives of the 'middling sort', did a substantial amount of the governmental work of the time while, paradoxically, serving both as examples of the enduring importance, even centrality, of locality in the political orientation of English people and as instruments of increasing direct involvement by the governmental centre in those localities – as reflected, for instance, by the common law with its emphasis on the role of the jury: people chosen from the locality with, supposedly, the clearest understanding of its circumstances, customs and history. Perhaps the most important governmental result of the early modern period was the successful negotiation between this enduring sense of locality, and the private interests with which it was intertwined, and the increasing demands of the central authority. This outcome, however, was by no means foreordained even in areas of the greatest national concern: the period up to 1642 saw numerous examples of the indifferent success the monarchy had in compelling the obedience of its subjects or even in compelling the cooperation of local officials: the reality of distance between Whitehall and the shires, as well as a 'combination of bureaucratic inefficiency and [the] sheer pressure of business', 'often resulted in the inconsistent enforcement of policy'.[19]

The case of Wiltshire, the bailiwick of the shadowy Virginia Company leader Sir John Danvers and his family, sheds particular light on the importance of office to status at both local and metropolitan levels and how, correspondingly, relations between localities and the centre operated in the late sixteenth century and the first decades of the seventeenth century. It thus reveals the inevitable and crucial parts played by faction and patronage in the make-up and history of local governments. The degree of one's social position was reflected in the offices one acquired. While these derived from patronage connections and estates in land, rivals for positions could and did call on their own resources and could and did resort to questioning (sometimes without foundation) the character of rivals.

Infamously, in the 1590s, the Danvers family became embroiled with Sir Walter Long. Clients of the latter allegedly robbed the senior Sir John Danvers and his elder sons, Charles (later executed with the Earl of Essex) and Henry (Earl of Danby under Charles I). Sitting as justice of the peace, the elder Danvers sentenced the thieves to imprisonment, but Long encouraged some of the Danvers tenants to pursue alleged common rights to lands purportedly enclosed by their lord and supported their petition to the Privy Council against Lady

Danvers for chopping down their trees and inflating their legal costs. These cases went to the court of Star Chamber. The involvement of that august body did nothing to calm hostilities, however, which culminated in the murder of a Danvers servant followed by the death of Sir Walter Long's brother at the hands of Henry Danvers. Henry and Charles Danvers then fled to the Low Countries while their father died of 'dolour and grief'.[20]

Kent, the early home of prominent Virginians William Claiborne and Sir Francis Wyatt, as well as a location with strong connections for Sir Edwin Sandys, leading light of the Virginia Company, and Edward Sackville, fourth Earl of Dorset, who had a long-standing interest in Virginia, provides another clear example of how Tudor-Stuart government and society worked – and did not work. The county was (and is) a place adjacent to, and economically intertwined with, London, with an active land market, where gavelkind (partible inheritance among heirs male) rather than primogeniture (the quintessential feudal practice of sole inheritance by the eldest son) was practised, where, according to lore, villeinage had never existed, where enclosure ended relatively early, and where a relatively free peasantry worked their holdings (some as freehold, some as tenancies). By 1606, thanks to the provision market, especially for cereals, provided by the capital, and the healthy soil (with the exception of Romney Marsh), it also enjoyed relative wealth. Although dotted with various liberties, such as the Cinque Ports, and towns whose inhabitants did not come under county government, most of Kent's population did come under the shire's institutions, such as the hundred.

As with Wiltshire (and every other shire), the gentry of Kent provided the connection between the central government and order in the locality. But, perhaps helped by the short distance from Whitehall as well as its importance to national defence, which may have brought increased attention from the central government, no rebellions occurred in the county between that led by Sir Thomas Wyatt (grandfather of the Virginian Sir Francis Wyatt) in 1554 and the outbreak of the civil wars in 1642. During those eighty years, the gentry, through intermarriage and the cultivation of their estates and connections, consolidated their position. By the latter date, however, the increasing demands of the government, fuelled by its continuing financial problems, accompanied by novel claims of authority and differences over religious policy contributed to the same fracturing of that 'county community' which occurred elsewhere.[21]

The career of Henry Wriothesley (1575–1624), third Earl of Southampton, patron of Sir John Danvers and Sir Edwin Sandys, and chief of one of the dominant factions within the Virginia Company, provides yet another illustration of how this socio-political world worked. At the beginning of his political life in 1597, Southampton joined the faction of the second Earl of Essex and dedicated himself to what Essex stood for: anti-Spanish crusade; a following bound by kinship; a 'politique' religious stance; and, above all, noble leadership, both military and political. The younger man joined Essex in the 1597 attack on Spain and then accompanied him first as second-in-command on his ill-fated expedition to Ireland two years later and then on his 1601 rebellion. Convicted of treason, Southampton escaped his patron's fate at the block through his successful cultivation of Sir Robert Cecil and James VI of Scotland. When James succeeded to the English throne in 1603, he restored Southampton's lands and titles and awarded him Essex's right to receive customs revenue from the importation of sweet wines. He did not, however, go so far as to award him the high office Southampton believed he deserved as a representation of the high aristocracy; the creation of a wholly Scottish English bedchamber added insult to injury and seemingly threatened the position of Cecil.

These issues came to a head in 1604 when James tried to push the union of England and Scotland through the English parliament. Fearful of Scottish influence on both the public good of England and their personal situations, Cecil and Southampton, along with Southampton's clients in the House of Commons, including the future Virginia backers Sir Edwin Sandys and Sir Maurice Berkeley, raised sufficient objection to run the proposal into the sand. Southampton and his associates had joined the Council of Anna of Denmark, queen-consort of James, in the meantime.

This 'patriotic' group, which took pains to defend the 'liberties of the subject' through the parliaments of the reign through 1614, continued to confound the hopes and expectations of the king using the relatively open forum offered by parliament to defeat the prospect of union again and to scupper the 'Great Contract' designed to bring order to the Exchequer in 1610. In addition to the Scots, they counted the Howard family, especially Henry Howard, Earl of Northampton, as public and private enemies. Until 1614 (Cecil had died in 1612), the two factions battled with each other over office, policy, and access to the monarch and power, until the murder of Sir Thomas Overbury in the Tower by the royal favourite Robert Carr and Frances Howard, the cuckolding wife of the third Earl of Essex who had, at Northampton's instigation, married Carr, put the Howards into the shade. Southampton's group, as we shall see further in Chapter 4, moved into the ascendancy.[22]

Aware of the limitations of government power, contemporaries drew a far narrower distinction between 'public' and 'private' affairs than modern polities do. While people in Tudor-Stuart England certainly experienced and denounced official corruption, the combination of relatively small governments with the corresponding need for delegation in the exercise of power meant that 'private' interests often undertook policy, especially colonization, to a far greater degree in the sixteenth and seventeenth centuries. Thus, in 1663, Sir William Berkeley, long-time governor of Virginia, wrote to the Earl of Clarendon of his expectation within two years that his family would, with an annual investment of £500 for wages, 'bring home a ship laden with Flax, Hemp, and Potashes for a Tryall of their Goodness' from which 'I shall return with no wants' while helping wean the colony from its over-dependence on tobacco (about which more below).[23]

Indeed, the reigns of James I and Charles I might even be styled an 'Age of Projectors and Projects' as a veritable parade of personalities appeared with suggestions for improving the governmental coffers, whose dire situation (aggravated by James I's inability to curb his spending) became increasingly apparent. These ideas had the twin virtue of bringing prospective benefit to the projector as well. Most of these projects became moribund as the government became distracted or overwhelmed by other matters. Others, such as Alderman Cockayne's idea to compete directly with the Low Countries by exporting dressed cloths directly rather than sending undressed cloths to the Netherlands, failed dramatically: the Netherlanders simply ordered a boycott of all English cloths thereby providing the final nail for the coffin of the Anglo-Dutch cloth trade with attendant further distress for East Anglian ports.[24]

The increasing infusion of projectors with their projects – and of entrepreneurs in search of the main chance generally at this time – reflected an understanding that new opportunities, especially overseas in places like the Levant, the Baltic Sea and the East Indies (as well as America), presented themselves for exploitation through trade in exotic commodities, privateering, colonization or fishing for those with the nerve to negotiate the risks involved, underpinned perhaps by the reality that old economic ways would no longer serve. Unquestionably, those members of the older generation of merchants, such as Sir Thomas Smythe, governor of the Virginia and East India Companies, who used their pre-existing connections and capital to great advantage, as well as a new generation of traders and privateers, including Maurice Thompson, his associate William Claiborne and Samuel Vassall, who had to resort more directly to cunning and ruthlessness, gained the advantage of new, especially uncertain times.[25]

This prevalence of factional back-biting (and, in the case of Essex, for instance, worse violence), deep suspicion of religious differences, commercial competition and general uncertainty and even fear about the future gives rise to a further important point concerning the character of the evidence generated by the pursuit of empire by the English after 1580 or so. The fierce disputes amongst those involved in colonization, including, for instance, over the activities of the officers and directors of the Virginia Company, generated a substantial literature from various quarters, much of it employed for polemical purposes. Perhaps those who composed these documents, and those who oversaw their production for publication, believed themselves to be sincere, virtuous pursuers of the public good, keen to denounce evil and corruption wherever they saw them, especially if, as noted in this chapter, they subscribed to the customary belief that private good equalled public good. Perhaps also, however, these historical actors exercised disingenuousness. Certainly modern historians have been, surprisingly, willing to accept their versions of events and the personalities involved with relatively little question. Given, however, the very thin line between public and private which contemporaries drew, along with the social, political and economic stakes involved in these battles, it would seem that caution should be the watchword when judging the credibility of the evidence.[26]

The often overheated nature of this record, however, does demonstrate clearly that those who became involved in overseas settlement and trade during the first half of the seventeenth century did so with an awareness that England had fallen behind most, if not all, of its Western European rivals – even the new Dutch Republic. They also knew, on the one hand, that exciting chances existed for those with the resources to grasp them; on the other, quick oblivion seemed to beckon for those who missed their step, suffered setbacks or stayed still. Those who succeeded in harnessing this mixture of ambition and fear provided a compelling starting engine, in retrospect, to propelling the country's rise to new global prominence by the time of Oliver Cromwell's death in 1658. They also succeeded, often in tandem, in establishing colonial societies headed by other men with the same success and corresponding attitudes towards society. Such a drive for success meant, on both sides of the Atlantic, failure for others, both in the outcomes of particular political and economic battles and in terms of the laying out of the social fabric of these 'new' places, notably American Indians and people of African descent.

2 GENESIS

> It is come to pass, right worshipful, with the business and plantation of Virginia, as it is commonly seen in the attempt and progress of all other most difficult things, which is, to be accompanied with manifold difficulties, crosses, and disasters, being such as are appointed by the highest Providence, as an exercise of patience, and other virtues, and to make more wise thereby the managers thereof, by which occasion not only the ignorant and simple minded are much discouraged, but the malicious and looser sort (being accompanied with the licentious vaine of stage poets), have whet their tongues with scornful taunts against the action thereof, insomuch as there is no common speech nor public name of anything this day (except it be the name of God), which is more vilely depraved, traduced, and derided by such unhallowed lips, than the name of Virginia.[1]

Twenty years after the production of the 'Discourse of Western Planting', the English had precious little to show for their colonizing endeavours; their presence in the western hemisphere remained epiphenomenal. By the beginning of the seventeenth century, the arguments of Hakluyt and his promoting counterparts may well have been all too familiar – and, perhaps, stale – in the eyes of readers even as the promoter published a second edition of his *Principal Navigations of the English Nation* in 1600. After all, as they fretted over the succession to a queen who had lived too long, the English had little but memories to show for the endeavours of their adventurers: the celebrated 'sea-dogs' Drake and Hawkins had died miserable deaths, while the Earl of Essex, the leading advocate of opposing Spain on all fronts, had gone to the block after his madcap rebellion and his leading supporters had either suffered the same fate or languished in the Tower. The efforts of Sir Walter Ralegh, his brother-in-law Sir Humphrey Gilbert and others to establish a beachhead in the Americas had come to naught. Indeed, the litany of Ralegh's failures – in 1585–8 to establish the Roanoke colony and then in 1595 to find cities of gold in Guiana – underscored the high degree of risk involved in pursuing overseas exploration and colonization.

Even so, the English maintained some interest in America, and a steady trickle of expeditions made their way across the Atlantic. This interest increased, ironically, after Ralegh's incarceration on charges of plotting treason against the new king, James I, and the end of the long Spanish war through the Treaty of

London in 1604. Ironically, also, despite James's pacific nature and his abiding desire to effect a general European peace, his government, not that of his celebrated predecessor, provided the requisite state impetus, albeit a hesitant one, to the permanent establishment of American colonies.

Much of this activity continued, inevitably, to be directed at the Amazon basin and at the Caribbean, the areas which provided the best access to the honey pot of Spanish treasure coveted by those who pursued privateering and settlement. Despite the problems of greater distance from England and, especially, the active hostility of the Spanish and Portuguese, the attractions of a tropical climate for the production of commodities such as sugar, the reputed access to the riches of Peru through Amazonia and the enduring belief in El Dorado, along with the continuing profits generated by plunder and the clandestine tobacco trade in Venezuela, made this region on paper the likeliest location for permanent English settlement.

A battery of English (and Irish) colonists made their way to the Amazon between 1608 and 1633 and settlers did establish themselves on St Christopher in 1624, Barbados in 1627, Providence Island in 1630 (but only until 1641), Montserrat in 1632 and Antigua in 1633. The timing of these expeditions, as well as their prospects for their success, however, remained dependent, as Roanoke had been, on the nature of relations between England and Spain. As noted above, one of the first acts of the government of the new monarch, James I, was the negotiation of an end to the war with Spain. The resulting treaty permitted for the first time, at least by omission, an English presence in American territory not occupied by subjects of the Spanish king. This omission enabled James and his ministers to employ colonization as a diplomatic tool.

The new king had pursued empire in the Western Isles as James VI of Scotland and would do so again in Ireland in his new 'British' guise. But those endeavours involved territory which James regarded as already part of his imperium, not claimed or occupied by other Christian monarchs. America, where the Spanish had exercised claims for over a century, presented a different question. Furthermore, in terms of his foreign policy, James I envisioned himself as a European peacemaker between Spain and the leading Protestant nations, such as the Dutch Republic, both temperamentally and economically. Despite the charges levied by some of his subjects, however, '*Rex Pacificus*', a very experienced monarch by the time he arrived in London in 1603, did not hold himself hostage to the machinations of Felipe III and the very able Spanish minister to England, Diego Sarmiento de Acuña, Count Gondomar, although his pursuit of peace, which included firm prosecution and execution of pirates, confounded the anti-Spanish views of Amazon projectors. In the first instance, the outbreak of peace enabled the sanctioning of colonizing activity. On occasions when relations between England and Spain soured over, for instance, the Spanish seizure of English traders, the government, especially in the person of Sir Robert Cecil, the lord treasurer and chief of James's ministers, who held a less sanguine view of Spain than his sovereign, signalled its support for American settlement by providing charters to colonizing entities such as the Virginia Company. Not coincidentally, then, English colonists appeared in Chesapeake Bay in 1607, the Amazon in 1608 and the Caribbean in the 1620s. On the other hand, an improvement in Anglo-Spanish relations, always a greater diplomatic goal of James I, could make colonization problematic, as Roger North and the Amazon Company learned to their cost in 1620. Ultimately, the Spanish and Portuguese proved too powerful for the English, especially with relatively limited governmental support, to effect a permanent establishment in South America in the seventeenth century.[2]

The lack of a Spanish presence north of Florida, however, gave the English free access as far as James was concerned. While obviously less convenient to the silver of Peru and less conducive for tropical products, North America did offer its own prospects: access to a 'Northwest Passage' to the lucrative Indies trade; the prospect of hitherto undiscovered Indian 'empires' ripe for conquest in accordance with the Aztec and Inca examples; control of the Newfoundland fishery and the lucrative fur trade; a temperate climate suitable for the production of naval stores and other merchantable commodities. Moreover, it had geographical advantages as it was closer to England and further from the Spaniards than Amazonia. In 1602, a group of interested parties, including Hakluyt, sent an expedition led by Bartholomew Gosnold to scout out likely locations for a North American colony. Gosnold's investigation confirmed the belief that Chesapeake Bay provided the best balance of proximity and distance from Spanish America.[3]

Unfortunately for the supporters of Gosnold's voyage and similar ventures, their probing of the North American coastline generated some remarkable reactions even before the Virginia Company came into being. Some time ago, David Armitage reconfigured the relationship between the canon of English literature and the development of the British Empire: once, 'Empire spurred the growth of literature, as the planting of colonies went hand-in-hand with the building of a canon; now, it seems, William Blake had it right when he concluded that "Empire Follows art & Not Vice Versa as Englishmen suppose"'.[4]

Yet, as the indignant complaint made by Robert Johnson on behalf of the Virginia Company in 1612 and cited at the beginning of this chapter indicates, a deeply adversarial relationship also existed between 'English literature' and the 'British Empire' at what proved to be the dawn of the latter phenomenon. Indeed, a number of works were published and performed in early Jacobean London that not only ridiculed colonization and colonizers, but depicted overseas colonization as contrary – even as a threat – to prevalent social ideals, wherein order was achieved when the occupants of the various social ranks duly performed their respective responsibilities towards each other. The message conveyed by these plays, which linked overseas activity with alchemy, usury and even treachery, compelled defenders of colonization, such as the Virginia Company mouthpiece Johnson, to proclaim the propriety of their endeavours while they railed against the 'players' – dubious personalities themselves, according to the prevailing norm – who attacked their 'noble enterprise'.[5]

Eastward Hoe!, written by George Chapman, Ben Jonson and John Marston in 1605, and *The Tempest*, written by Shakespeare in 1611, constitute the most significant – at least in terms of their endurance – instances of this dramatic assault. Both plays, furthermore, reflect the reality that the dispute between players and colonizers comprised just one element in the greater battle for political power in early Jacobean England. It may well have been more than a coincidence that the attacks from the stage ceased after 1615 when, temporarily, as it turned out, the anti-Spanish faction led by William Herbert, third Earl of Pembroke, and Henry Wriothesley, third Earl of Southampton, ousted their rivals, led by the Howard family, from the leading position at the court of James I.

The accession of the Scottish king to the English throne in 1603 had generated disappointment for this group. Although James, as noted in Chapter 1, pardoned Southampton and other surviving participants in the doomed 1601 rebellion led by the Earl of Essex, the new monarch had not restored the old Essexians to what they regarded as their proper place in his councils. As the legatees of Essex – aristocratic champions of a vigorous anti-Spanish foreign policy – the Pembroke-Southampton group believed that they had an inherently superior right to involvement in government at all levels, especially over their enemies, the pro-Spanish Howard family and the bureaucratic Sir Robert Cecil. Indeed, the new monarch had retained the Howards and Cecil to lead his government. His court also made a mockery of Essexian ideals by reaching a peaceful accommodation with Spain, while it presided over a further dilution of the aristocracy: James brought with him a clutch of Scottish favourites to whom he quickly granted a bevy of English offices, while English parvenus found new opportunities to advance in the far more liberal Jacobean atmosphere, most notoriously by purchasing baronetcies. Some of these parvenus employed overseas trade, privateering, and colonization to 'better' themselves, most notably Ralegh, even though they shared a hatred of Spain with Southampton and his supporters.[6]

But while Hakluyt and Ralegh and his associates may have shared an anti-Spanish attitude, along with a desire to act on that attitude, with the old Essexians, for the Pembrokes and Southamptons they were part of the deeper problem – as typified by Ralegh himself, the scion of minor Devon gentry who rose to captain Elizabeth's guard (but no further). The founder of the 'lost' Roanoke colony had a number of scuffles with Essex in the 1590s resulting in a famous falling out.[7] In the meantime, faced with a continuing obstacle to advancement at court, underscored by what they regarded as seriously misguided foreign policy and a society whose preoccupation with 'projects' threatened to unravel itself, a number of Howard enemies, notably Pembroke, sponsored a campaign, assisted by their literary clients, of lampooning the character of James I's England in which, over a period of five years after the Treaty of London ended the Spanish war in 1604, many issues – including colonization – provided targets for the sharpest pens of the day.[8]

Chapman, Jonson and Marston combined their talents to fire one of the first and most comprehensive of these salvoes when they composed *Eastward Hoe!* This play's spoof on colonization and those involved in it is, in itself, readily apparent, although scholars have continually downplayed – even overlooked – the reality that 'players' readily incorporated jests at the expense of this sort of social climber. Moreover, the corpus of theatrical literature indicates that early seventeenth-century English dramatists, actors and audiences shared a sceptical attitude towards plans for American settlement and the advertised prospects of land, climate and benevolent government in Virginia.[9]

Thus, *Eastward Hoe!* stresses the virtues of hard work, substance and a good name, while it lampoons those characters engaged in all sorts of dubious schemes to elevate their standing, including 'grasping' Scots – a reference that landed the authors in the Fleet Prison in fear for their ears.[10] Master Touchstone, an honest, respectable London goldsmith, has two apprentices: the lazy, irresponsible Quicksilver and the loyal and hardworking Golding, both younger sons of gentlemen, those particularly recognized as most in need of advancement and, thus, the primary audience for colonial promoters. Touchstone likewise has two daughters: the fashion-conscious would-be lady Gertrude and the sensible and virtuous Mildred.

Gertrude cannot abide life as a goldsmith's daughter and accepts the suit of another character on the make – Sir Petronel Flash, baronet. In reality, Sir Petronel has invested all of his resources in a Virginia voyage: he has his eye on Gertrude's estate from her grandmother, which he obtains by false pretences after their wedding, in order to prevent the attachment of his ships for debt by the usurious money-lender, Security.

Nor can Quicksilver abide his situation as a goldsmith's apprentice. His disdain for his trade earns him the corresponding disdain of his master: freed from his indenture, he requires money to maintain himself in the gentlemanly lifestyle to which he aspires. Thus, he ensnares 'gentlemen', such as Flash, in Security's clutches. In the meantime, 'honest' Golding and Mildred have become betrothed, at the behest of Touchstone.[11]

Sir Petronel had taken on Captain Seagull on as a partner. After separating Gertrude from her inheritance, the pair meets with their associates Spendall and Scapethrift at the Blue Anchor public house to discuss their plans. There, the colonizers adopt the language of promotional tracts as well as Sir Thomas More's *Utopia* (1516), although the nature and circumstance of the ludicrous assemblage renders their speech ironic. Seagull leers, 'Come boys, Virginia longs till we share the rest of her maidenhead'. To which Spendall queries 'Why, is she inhabited with any English?' Yes, according to the captain, the descendants 'of those that were left there in '79 [an erroneous reference to Roanoke]' who have intermarried with the Indians to 'bring forth as beautiful faces as any we have in England'.[12]

These relationships, he claims, have yielded other 'treasure' as well, echoing the attitudes towards gold and personal wealth held by More's Utopians:

> Golde is more plentifull there then Copper is with us: and for as much redde Copper as I can bring, Ile have thrice the waight in Golde. Why man all their dripping Pans, and their Chamber pottes are pure Gold; and all the Chaines, with which they chaine up their streetes, are massie Golde; all the Prisoners they take, are fetterd in Gould: and for Rubies and Diamonds, they goe forth on holydayes and gather 'hem by the Sea-shore, to hang on their childrens Coates, and stick in their Cappes, as commonly as our children weare Saffron guilt Brooches, and groates with hoales in 'hem.
>
> *Scapethrift.* And is it a pleasant Countrie withal?
>
> *Seagull.* As ever the Sunne shinde on: temperate and full of all sorts of excellent viands; wilde Boare is as common there, as our tamest Bacon is here: Venison, as Mutton. And then you shall live freely there, without Sergeants, or Courtiers, or Lawyers, or Intelligencers, onely a few industrious Scots perhaps, who indeed are disperst over the face of the whole earth. But as for them, there are no greater friends to Englishmen and England, when they are out an't, in the world, then they are. And for my part, I would a hundred thousand of 'hem were there, for wee shoulde finde ten times more comfort of there, then wee doe here. Then for your meanes to advancement, there, it is simple, and not preposterously mixt: You may be an Alderman there, and never be a Slave; you may come to preferment enough, and never be a Pandar; to riches and fortune enough, and have never the more villanie, nor the less wit.[13]

Seagull, 'the thirty pound knight' Sir Petronel and the rest of their company drink freely to their success before taking ship for Virginia.[14] Meanwhile, the baronet arranges for Quicksilver to spirit Security's wife, Winifred, away from her jealous husband to a rendezvous at the tavern and a new life in America. Unhappily, the group, disregarding the warnings of their landlord, runs afoul of a prodigious tempest that shipwrecks them on the Isle of Dogs and washes away their cuckolding, defrauding, shifting, grasping scheme. In short order, they are arrested by the constables and brought before the Aldermen's Court. There, they encounter honest Golding who has, in the meantime, stuck to his craft, married the good daughter, Mildred, and quickly become both a freeman of the City and an alderman's deputy, despite his abhorrence of ambition. The new deputy and his father-in-law confront the miserable miscreants, Touchstone seizing the chance to heap scorn on the hapless Quicksilver.[15] To cap their humiliation, the apprentice-turned-adventurer and his associates are committed to the Counter.

In that place, the fraudsters abjectly repent of their frippery and felony; after their pleas for pardon fall on Touchstone's deaf ears, they appeal to divine mercy. In the end, the honest but excitable goldsmith softens to the importunities of Golding, who contrives, under the cover of his own imprisonment, to bring his father-in-law in person to witness the penitence of Flash, Quicksilver and Security. The prisoners are duly bailed: Sir Petronel and Gertrude reunite (and she dutifully apologises to her father for having assumed the airs of a lady and expressed such contempt for him and his profession), while Quicksilver resumes his apprenticeship. Thus, the unseemly breaches in the social fabric are repaired, as Touchstone observes to his satisfaction at the conclusion of the play.[16]

Eastward Hoe!'s portrayal went beyond making colonization the butt of a joke. We can well imagine theatre-goers ridiculing the inept behaviour of the would-be aristocrats – younger sons like Quicksilver, would-be lords like Sir Petronel who bought their 'rank' from the cash-strapped monarch, and social-climbing snobs like the baronet's wife and goldsmith's daughter, Gertrude – as they pursued situations and stations for which they were not suited, and wound up courting disaster before thrift, prudence, and honesty restored the proper order of things. London audiences (also the primary target of the promotion literature) witnessed here, then, a portrayal of American venturing as inherently comic; a harebrained vehicle for aspirations to illegitimate station and wealth held by flash baronets, drunken sea captains (and their crews), usurers, wastrel apprentices, and other ludicrous posers. 'Real' gentlemen, honest artisans, and earnest merchants sneered at such activity and those involved in it.[17]

The appearance and publication of this play meant that colonization supporters had to respond quickly. Indeed, in the first instance, its characters touched all-too-closely on reality for comfort: many in the City audience would have known that Christopher Newport, the captain of the 'first fleet' that headed for the Chesapeake in December 1606, had married Elizabeth Glanville the daughter of Francis (can it have been entirely a coincidence that this is Quicksilver's first name?) Glanville, one of his goldsmith partners in privateering; Newport's partner in Virginia venturing, Gosnold, a scion of a Suffolk armigerous family, actually married a woman named Mary Golding.[18]

To combat those reports which cast aspersions on their endeavour (and which threatened to render it stillborn), a battery of tracts appeared under the aegis of the Virginia Company after 1607 purporting to describe Jamestown and the desirability of life there. These pamphlets also had to address accounts, quickly conveyed back to England, of the dismal reality of the colony, which will receive further discussion in Chapter 3. Rancorous disputes between factions in its government and among the directors of the company in London, unwillingness on the part of many colonists to plant subsistence crops, and enervating outbreaks of disease nearly put paid to the settlement. As late as 1611, the survivors of these travails had gathered at the quay to return to England when relief ships arrived, in the end salvaging the enterprise.[19]

Taking to the promotional pumps, then, the author of *Nova Britannia* (1609), for instance, proclaimed that he had overcome his initial reservations about migrating and that his removal to Virginia had yielded happy results: the English had 'spread the kingdom of God' to the indigenous people. At the same time, they had seen off the pretensions of popery in this 'earthly paradise', a country 'commendable and hopeful every way; the air and climate most sweet and wholesome, much warmer than England and very agreeable to our nature'. The pamphleteer further asserted that while the colony's neighbours were a 'wild and savage people ... they are generally very loving and gentle, and do entertain and relieve our people with great kindness. They are easily brought to good, and would fain embrace a better condition'. While encouraging these 'infidels' to accept Christianity, Jamestown could, as Hakluyt had argued, employ 'artificers' in their trades and produce commodities not available in the metropolis, thereby augmenting the customs revenue and relieving dependence on foreign states. Finally – and most importantly to Englishmen sensitive about their liberties – the colonial government included a royal charter 'with many ample privileges'.[20]

The following year, William Barret offered *A True Declaration of the Estate of the Colonie in Virginia*. This author also intended his 'confutation of such scandalous reports as have tended to the disgrace of so worthy an enterprise' – based upon his understanding of the history of British involvement in America, including the purported visit of Madoc, twelfth-century Prince of Wales, to present-day Alabama and 'the secrets from the judiciall councell of Virginia' – to promote the worthiness of spreading Christianity and combating Rome while he hastened to dispel rumours of the 'unwholesomeness of the climate' and turbulence of the voyage. Granted, difficulties had cropped up for the colonists, including the harassment of that 'greedy vulture', the powerful neighbouring sachem, Wahunsonacock, aggravated by 'scandalous reports' of cannibalism amongst the colonists spread by 'a viperous generation'.

But, according to Barret, the horizon had brightened considerably by 1610: now that Sir Thomas Gates and Lord de la Ware had arrived, placing the colony's government on a solid footing, and with 'the French preparing to plant the Vines, [and] the English labouring in the woods and groundes, every man knoweth his charge, and dischargeth the same with alacrity': Jamestown had moved to the verge of success, notwithstanding the doubters. Can status-conscious readers have missed the significance of the proclamation here that peace and prosperity had finally come to Jamestown in the form of recognizable aristocrats rather than of the younger sons of gentry or other opportunity-seekers?[21]

In the end, a meaningful measurement of the effect of all of this literature on the inhabitants of early Jacobean London must remain elusive, but placing the pro-colonization response into context provides the added historiographical advantage of enabling us to reconsider 'the origins of the British Empire' from a metropolitan perspective, as opposed to reading present-day issues into the past.[22] To do so requires more than rehashing the story of the Virginia Company, Captain John Smith and Pocahontas, or, as has become fashionable lately, to 'recover' the cultural attitudes held by early modern English folk towards the 'other', especially in a 'post-colonial' sense – in particular since the colony was not firmly established until, at best, 1612 and, quite possibly, as late as 1623.[23] It requires that we first understand the expansion of English interests overseas as contemporaries in the first decade of the seventeenth century – before a 'British Empire' came into being – understood that phenomenon: they were inextricably harnessed to the career and goals of the anti-Spanish, anti-Howard faction led by Southampton and Pembroke, as we shall see in Chapter 4.

For present purposes, we should note that the Pembroke-Southampton group scored a significant triumph in 1616 when their protégé Villiers secured his position as royal favourite. The dramatic fall of his predecessor, Robert Carr, Earl of Somerset, along with Carr's Howard in-laws, and a corresponding shift in governmental policy against Spain accompanied the rise of Villiers and his backers. During the same period, the Virginia Company underwent its third reorganization in a decade that, finally, put the company on a firm financial footing. The survival of the company – and, thus, of its colony – occurred largely thanks to a renewed surge of interest from those who had earlier backed a lampooning of the venture: in its heavily promoted capital campaign of 1618, Pembroke himself topped the list of subscribers with his £400 investment while Southampton contributed £350. These old Essexians, having gained some of the levers of governmental power, now moved to the forefront of the colonization effort.

The combination of royal affection now showered upon Virginia's advocates and the publicity generated by the tour made by Pocahontas and Rolfe helped overcome the general lack of interest in America that had threatened – even before the venture started – to strangle Jamestown in its infancy. Somewhat confusingly, much of the adverse impression generated about Virginia had also arisen from the hothouse of Jacobean politics, and Pembroke and Southampton, leading patrons of literature and theatre, as well as of overseas settlement, found themselves in the middle of it.

The history of English theatre further helps to track the emergence of the Pembroke-Southampton group as key supporters of the Virginia Company to the key period of 1611–16. But doubts remained in dramatic circles. Probably the most celebrated early modern work that deals with issues related to English involvement in exotic lands is *The Tempest*, first performed in 1611 in the midst of the Virginia Company's efforts to recover from its settlement's disastrous start (which will be discussed in Chapter 3). Recent scholarship has successfully attacked the canard that Shakespeare plotted out the English colonization of a 'New World' here. Rather, possession of foreign territory and interaction with other cultures constitute two strains of a wider reflection, drawn from a variety of references, on the dangers presented by adventuring overseas to the already fragile society of orders.[24]

Yet, ironically drawing on the account of the shipwreck of the Gates fleet on 'still-vexed Bermudas' made by William Strachey, secretary of the Virginia Company and one of the shipwrecks, in 1610, the playwright, Southampton's client, clearly styled colonization, from the very beginning of the play's action, in a manner at odds with that of its promoters and his patron.[25] The eponymous storm, conjured as an illusion by Prospero, testifies to the inherent uncertainty of the sea as it renders both social hierarchy and the Neapolitan flagship asunder. When Alonso, King of Naples, and his nobles appear on deck to investigate, the boatswain dismisses them as worse than useless with oaths.[26]

Having landed on Prospero's island, situated between Tunis and Naples, as planned by the exiled and usurped Duke of Milan, the shipwrecks, amazed at having survived the tempest, find themselves in a weird place.[27] The nobleman Adrian observes not only that 'this island seem a desert' and 'uninhabitable, and almost inaccessible', but also 'it must needs be of subtle, tender and delicate temperance'.[28] This last remark occasions an exchange on the virtues of the place that reads as a spoof of the descriptions offered in *Nova Britannia* and other promotional pamphlets as the characters are drawn into reflections on the qualities of the island.

> *Antonio.* Temperance was a delicate wench.
> *Sebastian.* Ay, and subtle, as he was most learnedly delivered.
> *Adrian.* The air breathes upon us here most sweetly.
> *Sebastian.* As if it had lungs, and rotten ones.
> *Antonio.* Or, as 'twere perfumed by a fen.
> *Gonzalo.* Here is every thing advantageous to life.
> *Antonio.* True, save means to live.
> *Sebastian.* Of that there's none, or little
> *Gonzalo.* How lush and lusty the grass looks! How green!
> *Antonio.* The ground indeed is tawny.
> *Sebastian.* With an eye of green in't.
> *Antonio.* He misses not much.
> *Sebastian.* No; he doth but mistake the truth totally.
> *Gonzalo.* But the rarity of it is, which is indeed almost beyond credit –
> *Sebastian.* As many vouched rarities are.[29]

Shortly afterwards in the same scene, Gonzalo, the 'wise councillor' to Alonso, perhaps still 'mistaking the truth', muses that 'Had I plantation of this isle', he would turn Hakluyt on his head, to the merriment of his companions. Spoofing language from the running debate (and hand-wringing) over the character of English society dating from *Utopia*, he observes:

> I'th' commonwealth I would by contraries
> Execute all things, for no kind of traffic
> Would I admit; no name of magistrate;
> Letters should not be known; riches, poverty
> And use of service, none; contract, succession,
> Bourn, bound of land, tilth, vineyard – none;
> No use of metal, corn, or wine or oil;
> No occupation, all men idle, all;
> And women, too, but innocent and pure;
> No sovereignty –
>
> *Sebastian.* Yet he would be king on't.
> *Antonio.* The latter end of his commonwealth forgets the beginning.
> *Gonzalo.* All things in common nature should produce
> Without sweat or endeavour; treason, felony,
> Sword, pike, knife, gun, or need of any engine
> Would I not have; but nature should bring forth
> Of its own kind all foison, all abundance,
> To feed my innocent people.[30]

Having rendered the climate, government and society of a hypothetical colony dubious, *The Tempest* also casts considerable doubt on another professed motive for Virginia settlement, the prospect for 'improving' the indigenous folk by extending to them the 'benefits' of Christianity and English 'civility': Caliban, a 'born devil, on whose nature Nurture can never stick' has proven immune to Prospero's 'pains'. When Prospero arrived on the island, he placed Caliban in his household as a servant and taught him his language. The 'savage', though, repaid this 'kindness' by 'learning to curse' and by trying 'to violate' Miranda, the duke's daughter, for which act he was enslaved.[31] Yet, while many scholars have contributed to the literature on Caliban, especially in terms of his 'native' qualities and the treatment he receives from Prospero, this literature tends not to compare his situation with the only actual indigenous inhabitant of the island, Ariel, who, of course, is also Prospero's servant.[32]

The respective careers of this pair echo, oddly, those of the *Eastward Hoe!* apprentices: one loyal and industrious, who receives due condescension from his master; the other, dismissive of his place and aspiring unnaturally, has his ambitions dashed and must remain in the status quo. Ariel, for reasons that remain undisclosed, suffered imprisonment in a tree at the hands of Caliban's mother and original migrant to the island, the witch Sycorax, who died before Prospero's arrival. The exiled duke frees the 'airy spirit' who, like Caliban, is forced to join his household. Yet, while Ariel, cognizant of (and frequently reminded of) the great favour Prospero has done in liberating him, continues to render faithful service throughout the play resulting in his freedom, Caliban refuses to accept servitude to the magus-duke. His attempt to have 'peopled else this isle with Calibans' by forcing himself upon Miranda having failed, he resorts to railing against his master and dithering in his assigned tasks for which dalliance he receives pinches and other pains.[33]

The arrival of the shipwrecks provides Caliban with a means of escaping his bondage, although, curiously, unlike Ariel, he does not work towards freedom. Rather, he kneels and swears his obedience, in a parody of the due allegiance owed by subjects to a proper sovereign, to his new 'king', the drunken butler Stephano. He then hatches a plot with his new master and the jester Trinculo to murder Prospero and govern the island themselves – with Caliban destined, apparently, to remain a servant – an attempt duly thwarted through the agency of the loyal Ariel.[34] Like Quicksilver, though, Caliban comes to recognize the error of his ways in the end: when Ariel brings the plotters before Prospero and the Neapolitan court, the 'monster' fears he 'shall be pinched to death'. Instead, Prospero, despite the plan to rob and murder him, 'acknowledges' him and, like Touchstone, pardons 'this thing of darkness'. Caliban, in turn, acknowledges the error of his ways: 'I'll be wise hereafter / And seek for grace. What a thrice-double ass / Was I to take this drunkard for a god, / And worship this dull fool.'[35]

This attempt by 'the rabble' against Prospero mirrors the scheme planned by Prospero's brother, Antonio, and Alonso's brother, Sebastian, against the Neapolitan king. Having found usurpation to their taste once, this pair view their arrival on the island, and the apparent death of Alonso's son and heir, Ferdinand, in the storm, as a chance to murder Alonso (along with 'wise' Gonzalo) and seize the throne. They get so far as drawing their swords before Ariel, acting on Prospero's foresight, intervenes with more magical music.[36]

As in *Eastward Hoe!*, the plot here remains fundamentally concerned with a reconciliation, in this case effected by Prospero, of the proper order after unnatural behaviour had unsettled it. Taking the chance presented to him, the magus uses his arts both to recover the throne from which he had been deposed and to preserve his dynasty (as well as to unite Milan and Naples legitimately) by facilitating the betrothal of Miranda to Ferdinand. Then, having resorted to the dubious expedient of magic to achieve these goals, Prospero famously jettisons his powers; left with his 'most faint' strength, he also provides the platform for restoration by forgiving Antonio, Alonso and Sebastian (he calls them 'three men of sin') rather than reveal the treason of the last pair.[37] He also accepts the submission of Caliban and frees Ariel as he had promised. The Europeans then depart the island.

The Tempest, like *Eastward Hoe!*, not only derided overseas colonization and those involved in it. By employing the language of humanism, the 'players' cleverly added an impressive dose of form to the substantive scorn they heaped on colonizers, who themselves relied extensively on humanist thinking and rhetoric in their own literature. Having been wrong-footed by the portrayals of Sir Petronel Flash and Captain Seagull as early as 1605, the promoters of the Virginia Company – in order 'to redeeme our selues and so Noble an action from the imputations and aspertions, with which ignorant rumor, virulent enuy, or impious subtilty, daily callumnieth our industries, and the successe of it' – repeatedly cast themselves in humanist terms, as selfless, civic-minded labourers the 'excellencie and goddnesse' of whose 'principal ends' of 'the plantation of a Church of English Christians there, and consequently the conversion of the heathen from diuel to God' did 'appeareth evidently'.[38]

Ultimately, of course, the English did establish themselves in the Chesapeake despite the theatrical allusions about the character of Virginia and those who supported it. In the first instance, they did so because, unlike earlier irregular ventures to more southerly parts, the Virginia Company received, between 1606 and 1612, a series of three charters from the government which, in addition to granting it American lands, gave it certain powers, including the authority to recruit migrants, to form a government (under the authority of a council in England), to build fortifications and to dig mines. Even though Ralegh and Gilbert had received similar grants from Elizabeth I, their ventures lacked both a wider platform of investment and a clearer connection with the central government: Cecil's name takes pride of place in the third Virginia Company charter, along with that of Thomas Howard, Earl of Suffolk, and those of Southampton and Pembroke. Thus, through a combination of chronology and the character of its enterprise, Virginia may claim priority both as an English imperial venture and as a benchmark for English colonial development.[39]

Having acquired its first charter within six months of the first performance of *Eastward Hoe!*, the Virginia Company began sending out colonists at the end of 1606. The 'first fleet' – and its successors – carried the sorts of people anticipated as colonists by the play – gentry, younger sons of aristocrats and apprentices (although, in a remarkable lack of prescience generally duplicated in such ventures, only a handful of women). And, while the survivors of the famine and dysentery which beset Jamestown in its first years had planned to abandon the colony by the year *The Tempest* received its first performances, the settlement ultimately managed to maintain its place on the map thanks to the accidental success of the tobacco staple, the good offices of Virginia's 'Calibans' (between the 1616 wedding of Pocahontas and John Rolfe that ended the 'Powhatan Wars' and the 1622 attack on the colony launched by Pocahontas's uncle, Opechancanough), and, later, the introduction of bound labour from Africa – a formula applied with even more vigour in the West Indies after the founding of the English settlements on St Christopher and Barbados.

Yet, indentured servants like the fictional Ariel and Caliban, who constituted the highest percentage of English migrants, have left little evidence that they gave much deliberation to transatlantic migration, which seems to have been part of the ongoing migration of 'middling' to poor English folk from countryside to city to other parts which, as noted in Chapter 1, dated back to the Middle Ages; slaves and convicts, of course, had next to no choice at best. Since four out of five migrants to Virginia in the first decade of the colony's existence died soon after their arrival, it would seem that few, if any, of those who did have a degree of choice took ship to pursue 'happiness' or 'opportunity'.[40]

As also noted in Chapter 1, modern American scholars looking back at the English colonization of North America tend to regard their subject as a 'modern' one; that is, both the settlement phenomenon itself – through its promotion along with the movement of people – as well as the process whereby, through 'a European confrontation with a wilderness environment', migrants became 'Americans', reflected, consciously or otherwise, a need to change the character of 'Old World' reality. Western Europeans flocked, according to Bernard Bailyn, to an 'open country, full of promise' in colonial British North America. There, they inhabited a 'loose, ill-organized, world on the margins of European civilization', with a new society 'far less intricate, structured, and continuously interactive than the one they left behind, but one that allowed them autonomy ... a more open world' befitting their 'expensive energies, a world where difficulties could be bypassed ... and where the imagination was released'.[41]

Unfortunately for this sweeping characterization of Euroamerican migration, as the plots of *Eastward Hoe!* and *The Tempest* suggest – and as the anxieties betrayed by the hot retorts of promoters further reveal – not everyone in early seventeenth-century England seems to have shared an enthusiasm for – or turned their imaginations to – the 'promise' of life in North America. And certainly notions of individualism and happiness – qualities in short supply in early modern England in any event – had little to do, except negatively, with conceptions of English colonization at that time, outside of the purple prose of pamphleteers. Considering the popular characterization of colonization and its supporters, as well as the reality – dysentery, 'Indians' and other hardships – faced by the settlers on the ground, even in those plantations that did take root, the establishment of what came to be the British Empire in America, in retrospect, seems far more incredible than inevitable. Perhaps more fundamentally, the entire prospect of removal to a 'brave new world' – the opportunity to join what proved (after the fact) to have been the march of 'modernity' – seems to have provoked hilarity and even contempt, rather than sympathy, from a significant number of Jacobean audiences. Could it have been the shift in Jacobean politics and the corresponding shift in the attitude of Southampton and his allies towards Virginia that not only brought new funds to the Virginia Company but also silenced the 'scornful taunts' about colonization, which had emanated from the pens of Jacobean playwrights prior to 1612?

3 BIRTH PANGS

The particular carriages of this first Governmet, are too long & would bee too displeasing to yor Lopps ears.[1]

There have bene of late divulged manie ympressions, judiciallie and trulie penned; partlie to take awaie the ignomiynie, skandales and maledictions wherewith this Action hath been branded: and partlie to satisfie all (especially the best) with the manner of the late proceedings, and the prosperitie likely ensue.[2]

Undaunted by the jibes of 'players' and whatever scorn for colonization their productions might have generated amongst their audiences, the London merchant Sir John Zouch, who maintained long involvement in Virginia, bankrolled a second voyage in 1605 to reconnoitre the North American coast for likely locations for a colony.[3] Following the recommendation of that expedition's leader of Chesapeake Bay as a site, and armed with as much support as any Jacobean colonizer might have hoped for from their government and their other knowledge of America, Hakluyt, Sir Thomas Gates, Edward Maria Wingfield and the other Virginia patentees assembled a company of 105 settlers and dispatched them to the proposed site a week prior to Christmas 1606 (although they did not clear the Downs until 5 January 1607). The colonists duly arrived at their destination in April via the West Indies, having experienced just one instance of doubt, in reasonably good order as 'God the guider of all good actions, forcing them by an extream storme to hul all night, did drive them by his providence to their desired port, beyond all their expectations'.[4]

While Hakluyt may have articulated a reasonably clear vision of the virtues of having English colonies in America, he offered no suggestions either how such an empire might be obtained (aside from bringing Christianity to the Indians) or how it might be governed. The blunt reality of these endeavours, albeit one that has largely, and oddly, escaped the accounts of historians, is that the proper establishment of new overseas colonies meant a military adventure. First of all, they required the successful control, as aliens in the demographic minority, of the substantially larger indigenous population. Any sanguine presumption by the Virginia colonists that they might establish this control without resistance from the incumbents would have been dispelled by the attack 'by 5 Salvages' on the first English party to venture ashore in the Chesapeake. Correspondingly, 'Western Planting' required substantial attention to defence.[5]

Second, the Virginia colony included, in accord with the Spanish example, the discovery and conquest of wealthy Indian empires in its brief, along with the identification and location of a 'Northwest Passage' to the East Indies; to pursue these activities naturally required an armed force. Then, of course, the new venture required defending from the Spaniards – who did not share James I's view that the English could now legally settle any American territory not inhabited by Europeans – as well as from French pretensions to North America that had developed coincidentally to the English ones.[6]

Unsurprisingly, then, the colony had a predominantly military character for the first eight or nine years of its existence. Its first council included, in addition to the ship captains Bartholomew Gosnold and Christopher Newport, four other 'captains' – John Smith, John Ratcliffe, John Martin and George Kendall – and, named as president, another veteran officer, Wingfield. The rest of its complement of settlers included several carpenters, a smith and a surgeon, as well as several builders and a dozen 'labourers' for building the requisite fort. It also included a list of 'gentlemen', including, in addition to the colony's minister, a sergeant and at least two other officers (Gabriel Archer and George Percy). The first orders of business, following the landing on James Island (itself a defensive position) and the appointment of the government, were the construction of the fort and investigation of the prospects of the surrounding countryside.[7]

Significantly, these expeditions, even as they travelled further afield in succeeding years, failed to uncover a northerly counterpart to the Mexican and Incan empires, the conquest of which had famously provided the Spanish with the wealth of the Indies and had, correspondingly, generated such alarm for Hakluyt and other English colonization advocates. Moreover, the English never assembled the strength of the native allies commanded by Cortes and Pizarro, while their new neighbour, the Powhatan sachem who ruled the area surrounding Chesapeake Bay, Wahunsonacock, declined to follow the example of the Mexican emperor, Moctezuma, and the Inca, Atahualpa, in allowing the newcomers to seize his person. Nor did Wahunsonacock, unlike Moctezuma, respond to the unexpected arrival of armed, bearded, pale, smelly strangers in large ocean-going vessels with hand-wringing and prevarication: while a party of English conducted the very first foray into the surrounding country, the Indians attacked their comrades in the fort and 'had it not chanced a crosse barre shot from the ships stroke down a bough from a tree amongst them caused them to retire, our men had all been slaine'.[8]

Relations between the two neighbours scarcely improved over the next seven years. So far from welcoming English-style religion and 'civility' (and failing to provide either mines of gold and silver or helpful guidance towards the 'South Sea'), the Powhatans maintained an alternating policy of harassing the unwanted newcomers and neutralizing them with diplomacy while they dealt blows to their indigenous – older and, possibly, more powerful – enemies such as the Susquehannocks to their north. Their activities certainly hampered English efforts to cement their position – not the least since reports of Indian hostility were naturally believed to deter migration – let alone extend their influence into the interior (significantly, Samuel Argall effected the furthest English incursion of this period – the destruction of French settlements in present-day Nova Scotia in 1613 – by water). If the English arrival at Jamestown constituted an 'invasion', we cannot regard it as having the dramatic success enjoyed by the Spaniards in Mexico and Peru.[9]

What proved to be the first of three Anglo-Powhatan Wars (customarily dated at 1609–14, but, as noted here, which seems actually to have started with the arrival of the English in the Chesapeake) only ended with the kidnapping and ransoming of Wahunsonacock's favourite daughter, Pocahontas. This episode, also carried out by Argall, with the assistance of the friendly 'King of Pastancy', compelled the Powhatan sachem to come to terms, including a return of prisoners and the provision of 'some quantitie of corne, for the Colonies reliefe', which manifested a tacit acceptance of the English colony, in order to secure her return.[10]

This opportunistic, shall we say, seizure of the Powhatan 'princess' also provides a further demonstration both of the centrality of warfare to the history of early Jamestown and of the ruthless streak the English all too often demonstrated in their military dealings with those societies they regarded as inferior during the early modern period. This is not to say that ruthlessness did not occur in other interactions: for all of the talk of English law and liberty, governmental agents could resort to kidnapping and even murder with palpable frequency. The general ferocity of relations – wholesale destruction of towns, 'massacres', murder and plots to murder between the English and Powhatans (which recurred subsequently, as we shall see) – tracks the ferocity that had developed somewhat earlier in the Elizabethan involvement in Ireland. Yet, although violence permeated much of the interaction between the English and 'inferiors', the colonists could and did regularly reach accommodation of interest – even alliance (as the Pocahontas incident also demonstrates) – with those indigenous Americans and Irish who regarded it as in their own interest to do so, although they maintained a clear tendency to suspect 'treachery' amongst their neighbours (throughout the territory which the English came to occupy) and to strike pre-emptively based upon those suspicions.[11]

Virginia, of course, did not constitute the first experience of empire, and corresponding attempts to dominate native people, for the English. From 1066 until 1453, England controlled territory in France, notably the Aquitaine, until its final defeat in the Hundred Years War. Ireland, however, provided a far more important precedent for seventeenth-century English imperial practice.[12] First, the French precedent had passed beyond living memory (the vestige of this 'first English empire', Calais, which had actually been represented in parliament, having finally fallen to the French in 1558) by 1603. In addition, various interests in England had, especially since the Middle Ages, regarded Ireland as both an opportunity to acquire lands and, after the Reformation, as a security risk. From the later twelfth century, the Pale incorporating Dublin and its immediate environs had constituted an English colony, with its own parliament, albeit controlled after 1495 from Westminster, and with the English monarch styled as, first, lord and, after 1541, king (with a deputy exercising royal authority *in situ*).

After the accession of Elizabeth I at the end of 1558, English involvement in Ireland became increasing intensive. Fearful that the Spanish would manipulate the substantial Roman Catholic population of the neighbouring island to further an invasion of England, Elizabeth's ministers sought to bring 'civility' and 'liberty' in the form of English government and religion to the 'wild Irish' who would, according to this thinking, welcome these reforms and throw off the authority of their priests and clan chiefs. This view provided the pretext for the state sponsorship of colonization in Ireland. Unfortunately for those who held this view, however, Irish peasants tended to side with their leaders, thereby confirming their 'depravity', leading to endemic and increasingly nasty warfare from 1572 to 1603. English colonies were established in Leinster and Munster and a degree of English authority further north and south of Dublin. As we know, a number of those involved in Anglo-American colonization, including Sir Humphrey Gilbert, Sir Walter Ralegh and Sir Ralph Lane, first governor at Roanoke, played important roles in this particularly brutal phase of Anglo-Irish history. These careers make it possible to argue that the perceptions held by colonizers of the colonized in Ireland and the behaviour which those perceptions generated – such as Gilbert's practice of lining the path to his tent with the skulls of those he and his forces had killed – were carried to America.[13]

In addition to the particular brutality of imperial warfare of the day, the character of English martial society between 1570 and 1642 had a further effect on the early history of Virginia. For early modern English military life involved more than taking to the battlefield, manning the ramparts and developing contempt for enemies: it incorporated, as behaviour in other aspects of society did, the machination of faction and the pursuit of patronage, changing sides (otherwise known as treason) and back, and the attendant smoke of suspicion – sometimes breaking out into the fire of attack – around others. Of course, the Tudor-Stuart English military world necessarily overlapped, as well as reflected, the wider socio-political world. As in the wider world, confessional fractures in society –aggravated by orthodox fears of 'popery' – had significant influence, especially since religion deeply coloured the wars in the Low Countries and in Ireland which the English fought.

The close chronological proximity of the Irish and Virginian adventures, along with English involvement in the Dutch Revolt, meant that a number of men took part in the last phase of the Elizabethan Irish wars which ended in 1603, fought in the Low Countries prior to the Twelve Years Truce of 1609–21 and appeared in the ultimately successful imperial push which began at the end of 1606. The outbreak of peace in Ireland and the winding down of the Continental conflict put these veterans out to pasture; they required employment and Virginia required the services of experienced officers. Inevitably, a number of these men were clients of Robert Devereux, second Earl of Essex, leading military figure of the late Elizabethan period, and fervent enemy of Ralegh; they served under the command of Essex in the Netherlands, in the attack he led against Cádiz in 1596, and in the army the earl sent to Ireland in 1599. The Essex men whose names also appear in the annals of the early English Empire in America include the original Virginia patentee, Gates, the first president at Jamestown, Sir Thomas Chaloner, first president of the Council of Virginia, Wingfield, the Welsh captain Peter Wynn, and Henry Wriothesley, third Earl of Southampton, who assumed the leadership of the colony after 1616 (for which see Chapter 4). Others with close connections to Anglo-America and the Essex circle included Sir John Danvers, sixteen years old in 1601 and brother of the Essex conspirator Sir Charles Danvers, who worked closely with Southampton and remained deeply involved in Virginia until his death in 1656, and George Percy, the eighth son of the eighth Earl of Northumberland, who had two brothers who were Essexians, and who served on the Jamestown council (twice as interim president) between 1607 and 1612. A number of the followers of Essex, attracted by the earl's toleration of their religion, which barred them from orthodox participation in society and politics, were Roman Catholics. Some of these Catholics, such as Wynn, became involved in the Gunpowder Plot four years after Essex self-destructed in the streets of London.[14]

The failed attempt to blow up king, royal family, Privy Council, and parliament naturally brought fear and loathing of papists to a head. But, these feelings – and the real and imaginary plots which fuelled them – had been bubbling all too healthily since the 1560s. English involvement in the long war in the Netherlands, in which nothing less than the stakes of Dutch independence and curbing of Habsburg pretensions to universal monarchy appeared at stake, was itself a product of the religious-political need to preserve 'true religion' and the English state against the machinations of the pope and the king of Spain.[15]

With its constantly shifting frontiers and fortunes, its high political and religious stakes and the proximity of popery in the form of the Spanish forces, the

Dutch Revolt provided seemingly endless opportunity for spying, the switching of sides and plotting. This was a shadowy world inhabited by double agents, whose 'spymasters' sought, sometimes in vain, to keep them under control, as well as the armies of the combatants.[16] The most spectacular manifestation of the thinness of the intellectual and political lines that 'traitors' and 'patriots' constructed to separate themselves appeared in the handover by Sir William Stanley of the Dutch town of Deventer to a besieging Spanish army in 1587. Stanley and his Irish Catholic troops received employment from Madrid for their 'services' and Sir William composed an elaborate justification of his actions (and, in 1608 advocated the destruction of Jamestown to Felipe III). Needless to say, the English government declined to accept this rationale and the Stanley family and their associates, relatives of the Earl of Derby, quickly fell under a cloud. Yet, some of these associates had political and biological links to the Earl of Essex, as the Stanley and Devereux families shared patronage in northern Wales and in the west of England, while others, who had served with Stanley but who had come to reconsider the consequences of their desertion, such as the Irish and Dutch veteran and future Jamestown councillor Wynn, returned to English service, as the careful research of Paul Hammer has demonstrated.[17]

Despite the furore of the recent quadricentennial of the founding of Jamestown, we shall never know, with entirely satisfactory certainty, what happened in the very first years of the settlement. In large part, we have inherited this historiographical situation thanks to the destruction by fire of most of the early records of the Virginia Company which were housed at the house of Sir Thomas Smythe, who became its leading light after 1609. Moreover, the stakes – both in terms of career and reputation along with the national interest – involved as well as the traumas which the colonists experienced led those who have composed the documents we do possess to resort all too readily to rancour, finger-pointing and self-justification practically from the moment the 'first fleet' set anchor in the James River.[18]

We do know that the first settlers breathed a fairly toxic political atmosphere which bred discord and suspicion. Here, their military and political backgrounds may have played as important a part as they did in the laying out of the fort and in carrying out raids against the Powhatans. As soon as the 'first fleet' left the Canary Islands on its voyage across the Atlantic, Captain John Smith, another veteran of the Low Countries wars, had been imprisoned for thirteen weeks, 'upon the scandalous suggestions of some of the chiefe (envying his repute)' that he plotted a mutiny against the colony.[19]

The hopes and expectations held by the Virginia Company for the management of their colony on the ground fell on this stone. On paper, the inclusion of Wingfield, one of their own number, and the other officers named to the first council would have looked promising enough: substantial military experience, including Irish colonization, and a degree of 'quality', both quantitatively and in terms of background, that should have encouraged the deference of the colonists.

In reality the Jamestown broth nearly spoiled from the involvement of too many cooks. Smith, as noted above, had earned suspicion and imprisonment on the voyage. Once cleared, however, he, along with Martin and Ratcliffe, overthrew and imprisoned the suspected papist Wingfield (Ratcliffe assuming the presidency), whom they charged with incompetence and for 'ingrossing to his privat' all sorts of foodstuffs while the settlers starved. Over the next twenty-plus years, Smith underscored his characterization of Wingfield in the series of increasingly (and, it must be said, increasingly self-congratulatory) lengthy 'histories' of Virginia he published. By September of 1607, Smith wrote the following year, Wingfield had 'ordred the affaires in such sort that he was generally hated of all, in which respect with one consent he was deposed from his presidencie' in favour of Ratcliffe. Smith reported that, after the deaths of 50 colonists (out of an original 105) over the first summer, the survivors 'seeing the Presidents projects to escape these miseries by flight (who all this time had neither felt want nor sicknes) so moved our dead spirits, as we deposed him)' while Smith himself, to whom Ratcliffe and Martin had 'committed the managing of all things abroad', managed, 'by his owne example, good words, and faire promises', to set the colonists to building houses ('neglecting any for himself') while he set out to find food. Wingfield, predictably, although in manuscript, vigorously denied both the charges brought against him and the jurisdiction of the new council to try him.[20]

The career of Captain George Kendall shines one shaft of light through the obscurity which surrounds the first years of Jamestown and illuminates a corner where we can make out some of the suspicions and fears of early modern English people. After the colonists arrived, according to the famous account of Captain Smith, Kendall directed the building of the fort. By the beginning of September, Captain Newport had departed for England, Captain Gosnold had died suddenly (by all accounts a devastating blow), and the company had been 'destroyed with cruell diseases as Swellings, Flixes, Burning Fevers, and by warres, and some departed suddenly, but for the most part they died of a mere famine'. At the same time, Kendall began 'to sowe discord' in the colony's government, for which he was imprisoned. Then, Gabriel Archer, according to the accounts of Wingfield and Percy, along with councillors Smith, John Ratcliffe and John Martin, overthrew and imprisoned president Wingfield, released Kendall, designated Ratcliffe as president, and named Archer to the new office of recorder of Virginia. Needless to say, Wingfield remonstrated sarcastically to his captors over 'their lawe so speedie and cheape' and the allegations made against him prior to the arrest and execution of Kendall. He then told 'the best sorte of the gentry' that he would 'goe into England to acquaint our Councell there, with our weaknes; I said further their lawes, and government was such as I had no joye to live under them any longer' or, if Ratcliffe or Archer went to England, he would stay with them or 'furnish them with £100 towards the fetching home of the Colonnye, if the action was given over'. His legal difficulties (as well as those of John Smith, who had fallen into trouble for the deaths of two men at the hands of the Indians on another trading voyage to the interior) only ended with the return of Captain Newport. In preparing his defence, Wingfield especially denied 'that I Combyned with the Spanniards to the distruccion of the Collony'.[21]

In September, as Wingfield was answering the case against him, a most curious turn of events took place. President Ratcliffe had struck the colony's blacksmith, James Read (a routine sort of occurrence that Wingfield claimed 'would drive many well affected myndes from this honorable action of Virginia'), who struck back. This effrontery earned the smith condemnation to the gibbet, 'but before he was turned of the Lather he desired to speake with the President in private, to whome he accused Master Kendall of a mutiny, and so escaped himself'. Kendall, though, was not so fortunate and was executed by firing squad despite his claim that the president had no authority since his real name was Sicklemore; 'then Master Martyn pronounced Judgment'.[22]

Something extraordinary (and unknown) must have occurred for Ratcliffe to have accepted the evidence of an artisan, especially one on trial for striking his own person, against an officer (and, possibly, a gentleman). Although the narratives bequeathed to us by the first settlers disclose nothing further, Philip Barbour has suggested that Kendall was a Spanish spy and that the Jamestown government executed him to prevent his escape to Spain with an in-depth report on the colony. In support of this argument, he found tantalizing references to a George Kendall as a denizen of the world of espionage sketched above, who had connections to Sir William Stanley and English Catholics on the Continent and who acted, in turn, as a spy on their activities for Sir Robert Cecil around 1600.[23]

This is certainly a plausible reason for this incident. But if Kendall had really been a spy, why did the Jamestown leadership bury the discovery of his treason rather than trumpet the blatant example of Spanish perfidy in their midst at a time when the king remained unconvinced of Habsburg pretensions to global supremacy? And what are we to make of the reality that the usually loquacious Captain John Smith had curiously very little to say on the subject of Kendall, and that at odds with the narrative of his enemy, Edward Maria Wingfield? Both Smith's account of 1612 and his much enlarged *Generall Historie of Virginia, New-England, and the Summer Isles* of 1624 only note that Kendall (and Wingfield) lived 'in disgrace' in September 1607. Meanwhile, Smith, having set the colony to work, undertook 'to search the Country for trade'. During his absence, the disgraced pair 'strengthened themselves with the sailers, and other confederates to regaine their former credit and authority, or at least such meanes abord the Pinnace, (being fitted to saile as Smith had appointed for trade) to alter her course and to goe for England'. Smith happened to return; learning of this scheme, 'much trouble he had to prevent it, till with store of sakre and musket shot he forced them stay or sinke in the river, which action cost the life of captaine Kendall': no mention of a blacksmith, a trial, a firing squad, or even Ratcliffe/Sicklemore (other than 'the compnies dislike of their Presidents weaknes'), let alone Spain, here.[24]

Perhaps these witnesses developed an honest discrepancy between these respective characterizations, although the wild degree of difference between their accounts would make this seem unlikely. On the other hand, for whatever reason, Smith and/or Wingfield exercised disingenuousness. Did Wingfield, a charter member of the Virginia Company, who had, by Smith's own account, lent early support to the colonizing venture, become so enraged at the treatment accorded him by his fellow councillors as to abandon the colony with Kendall (possibly to Spain to commit treason)? Did, he, on the other hand, wish to minimize the importance of Smith to the colony by identifying a plot against Ratcliffe rather than the captain as the means by which Kendall sought to destroy the venture? Whose version of events is more credible? Was Wingfield so bent on his own comfort that he hoarded food while his comrades died of hunger or was he a judicious administrator of the settlement's stores while 'many hungry eies did behold to their great longing' the overloaded spits of his enemies?[25]

The answers to these questions, unless and until we obtain a larger record, must remain unknown; consequently, pursuit of answers to them must run afoul of the historiographical law of diminishing returns. Indeed, the quixotic quest for the 'historical truth' of early Virginia, including the assessment and reassessment of the credibility of the various witnesses, has its own tiresome history, closely intertwined with the red herring of 'American origins' and the establishment of the first permanent English settlement in North America.[26] But despite the partisan and, therefore, overheated body of literature which the first Virginians created (quite deliberately), the fears and ambitions which contributed to it, we also know that Jamestown suffered acutely, practically as soon as it was established, from the ravages of disease as well as the close and hostile attention of the Powhatans. By the end of its first summer (some three months after the arrival of the English in the Chesapeake), the colony's leading light, Gosnold, had died and it contained just 'six able men' to defend it.[27]

Matters scarcely improved on the ground over the ensuing months, which undoubtedly aggravated the degree of finger-pointing and self-justification on all sides. The discovery, for instance, that two messengers sent to negotiate with the 'king of Nancemonde' for ownership of an island 'were 'sacrifysed and thatt their Braynes weare Cutt and skraped outt of their heades with Mussell shelles' led to a reprisal for 'their trechery' whereby the English 'Beate the Salvages outt of the Island burned their howses ransaked their Temples, Tooke downe the Corpes of their deade kings from their Tombes, and Caryed away their pearles Copper and braceletts wherewith they doe decore their kings funeralles'.[28]

By this time, Captain Newport had returned to the colony with almost one hundred men, including two goldsmiths, two refiners, a jeweller and a coppersmith, along with a supply of 'all things could be imagined necessary'. Yet, the joy with which Smith and the other colonists greeted Newport's arrival soon turned sour: the free involvement of the ship's company in trading with the Indians meant 'that could not be held for a pound of Copper, which before was sould us for an ounce', while Newport (whom Smith had, in his absence, portrayed as his 'father' in his negotiations with Powhatan) gave 'the unsatiable desire of the Salvage' too much credence. Newport and his crew, moreover, stayed in the colony for fourteen weeks ('when shee might as wel have beene gone in 14. Dayes') eating up the food and leaving the settlers with a poor diet of meal and water, 'whereby with the extremitie of the bitter cold frost and those defects, more than halfe of us dyed'. But 'the worst was our guilded refiners with their golden promises made all men their slaves in hope of recompences; there was no talke, no hope, no worke, but dig gold'. Smith, 'admitted not to the sight of their trials nor golden consultations', had little truck 'with their durty skill, breathing out these and many other passions, never any thing did more torment him, then to see all necessary busines neglected, to fraught such a drunken ship with so much guilded durt'. At last Newport departed again for England, taking Wingfield and Archer with him 'to seeke some better place of imployment', according to Smith, 'we not having any use of Parliaments, Plaies, Petitions, Admiralls, Recorders, Interpreters, Chronologers, Courts of Plea, nor Justices of peace'.[29]

The departure of Wingfield and Archer (the latter returning soon enough), however, improved neither the condition of the colony nor the character of its historical record. Ratcliffe's performance as the colony's leader apparently fell far short of expectations. When Smith returned from another expedition on 7 September 1608, he found 'many dead, some sicke, [and] the late President [Ratcliffe] prisoner for mutiny'. While, 'by the honest diligence of Master [Matthew] Scrivener', an arrival with Newport named to the council, the colony had performed its harvest, much of their provision had fallen victim to rain. In short, 'was that summer (when little wanted) consumed and spent, and nothing done (such was the government of Captaine Ratliffe)'. Three days after his return to Jamestown, Smith assumed the presidency: accordingly, 'the building of Ratliffes Pallace stayed as a thing needlesse; the Church was repaired; the Store-house recovered', and the fort, boats and watch rehabilitated.[30]

Even as president, however, Smith's efforts at maintaining the colony, according to his own account, suffered from the ambitions and failures of others.

Although 'we had the Salvages in that decorum (their harvest being newly gathered) that we feared not to get victuals for 500' people (the colony numbered 130 inhabitants at the time), the company and Newport, who had returned with a second supply, pursued the 'coronation of Powhatan [Wahusonacock]', which dangerously increased the self-importance of that 'subtile Savage'. They also sent 'Poles and Dutch-men, to make Pitch, Tar, Glasse, Milles, and Sope ashes [which] when the Country is replenished with people, and necessaries, would have done well, but to send them and seaventie more without victualls to worke, was not so well advised nor considered of, as it should have beene'. These 'projects' caused the colonists 'to loose that time, spend that victualls we had, tyre and starve our men', and 'guilded mens hopes with great promises'. The rest of the council, including two newcomers (both military men), Wynn and Richard Waldo, approving of these plans, overruled Smith's objections 'and ruled it as they listed'.[31]

Thus, partisanship continued, although Smith sent home Ratcliffe/Sicklemore, 'a poore counterfeited Imposture'.[32] Meanwhile, the 'Dutch-men' had gone to live with Wahunsonacock ('who kindly entertained them'), where they plotted to ambush the captain, but by his bravery in defeating the 'King of Paspahegh' in single combat he learned of the treachery. Then, Smith, despite the 'negligence' of Captain Wynn first in allowing a 'Dutchman' who had been taken prisoner to escape and then allowing 'the Savages' to escape when Smith sent him on a punitive expedition, recovered the situation by seizing two Indians ('the two most exact villaines in all the Country'), burning a town and taking their boats and fishing tackle. The combination of this force and the occurrence of various 'pretty Accidents' convinced the Powhatans to pursue peace and to cease 'stealing'.[33]

Despite this success, as well as the equally important progress made in survival (Smith claimed only seven colonists out of 200 died, aside from drowning, under his leadership), the 'Dutch-men' continued to plot and Smith received word that the company in London (the membership of which, Smith noted, had never been to Virginia, except for Newport) was unhappy with his 'heard dealing with the Salvages, and not returning the shippes fraughted'. Moreover, another supply, part of the fleet sent under the command of Sir Thomas Gates (famously shipwrecked on Bermuda, about which more below), arrived at Jamestown. 'Happie', according to Smith, 'had we beene had they never arrived, and we for ever abandoned, and as we were left to our fortunes: for on earth for the number was never more confusion, or misery, then their factions occasioned'. Indeed, their 'infinite dangers, plots, and practices' encouraged him to think of returning to England. Ultimately, someone 'accidentallie' touched off Smith's powder-bag as he lay sleeping one hundred miles from Jamestown on an expedition to inspect the garrison he had sent above the falls of the James River, 'which tore the flesh from his body and thighs, nine or ten inches square in a most pittifull manner'. Returning to the settlement, Ratcliffe and Archer, about to come to trial for their supposed plots, allegedly tried to have Smith murdered; that attempt miscarrying, 'they joyned together to usurpe the government, thereby to escape their punishment'. With no physician in the colony to treat his serious injuries, Smith had to return to England to receive attention; he never saw North America again. Instead, he inherited the role, along with the Reverend Samuel Purchas, of cheerleader for English expansion from Richard Hakluyt, who died in 1616 after turning his attentions away from Virginia towards the East Indies.[34]

The figure of Smith himself and the character of his accounts, because he was so prolific a published author, reflected this partisanship. Contemporary residents of Jamestown have left less adulatory versions of events, although they remained in manuscript until the nineteenth century and so generated less attention than Smith's accounts did. George Percy, another original settler and Smith's successor as president *pro tempore*, regarded him as 'an ambitious unworthy and vayneglorious fellowe, attempteinge to take all mens authoreties from them'. According to Percy, 'a discencyon' did occur between Smith and the new arrivals in Virginia from the Gates fleet, 'butt after some debate all was quyeted and pacifyed' until Smith came to fear that the seamen and passengers 'mighte growe too stronge and by a meanes to depose him of his government'. To prevent this, Smith spent considerable powder and other resources 'to noe other purpose butt to Insinewate with his Reconcyled enemyes and for his owen vayne glory', and allowed the mariners 'to Carry away whatt victewalls and other necessaryes they wolde'.

When Smith went on his inspection tour above the falls of the James River, 'a greate devisyon did grow' between him and the garrison; the captain 'perceaveinge bothe his authority and person neglected, incensed and animated the Salvages agaeinste Capteyne West [commander at the fort] and his company, Reporteinge unto them thatt our men had noe more powder lefte them then wolde serve for one volley of shott'. Returning to Jamestown, Smith, 'ageine fownd to have too mutch powder about him' in his pocket 'where the sparke of a matche Lighted very shreawdly burned him', suffered his injury. Then, Ratcliffe, Martin and Archer 'justely deprived' him, for 'Smithe wolde Rule al and ingrose all authority into his owne hands', despite the commission for the government now held by Sir Thomas Gates, as he aimed at 'a sovereigne Rule withoutt the assistance of the cowncell'. In his own manuscript justification, Wingfield charged Smith with mutiny and 'proved to his face, that he begged in Ireland like a rogue, without licence, to such I would not my name should be a Companyon'.[35]

Thus, we have both substantially different versions of events as well as substantially different characterizations of those involved in the general history of the first years of the Virginia colony. We also have an imbalance in the record due to the volume of published work of Captain John Smith, the chronology and subject matter of which have rendered it among the classics of 'early American literature'. Correspondingly, the testimony offered by the man on the colonizing scene against those behaviours and policies he opposed has tended to allow Smith's judgements of those with whom he disagreed and even fought to hold historiographical sway. Predictably, then, the Virginia Company and its officers, with their desire to show leniency rather than force towards the 'subtile' Wahunsonacock, their focus on 'unrealizable goals' of mines and ores and a 'Northwest Passage', their desire to stimulate the manufacturing of glass and potash which entailed sending more people than the colony could feed (and who proved to be traitors who consorted with Wahunsonacock to boot), have come in for long-standing and considerable criticism. Generations of historians have charged the company's directors and agents with short-sightedness; pursuing short-term rewards and returns rather than investing the patience required for the long-term building of successful colonies. Moreover, the company's belief that military discipline would generate the recreation of the metropolitan society was mistaken: 'Had they known that Virginia would absorb money over many years with no profit', according to a recent analysis, 'the colony would have been abandoned at the outset – as so many others were. From the company's point of view, the colony was nothing but a drain on its resources, eating up huge amounts of money in supplies and new settlers without ever repaying the backers' investment, much less returning a profit'. To compound the difficulty, 'Elites did not know how to organize and motivate ['ordinary' colonists] for the necessary work; they simply blamed the men for not acting as they wanted them to'.[36]

Without questioning the dire difficulties the early Virginians faced, this sort of analysis overlooks the reality that the Virginia Company – including different groups of investors within the company over the eighteen years of its existence – continued to promote, to invest in and to supply the colony, notwithstanding the endemic factionalism of the colonists and the distance between London and Jamestown which automatically aggravated difficulties in maintaining the settlement. Sir Thomas Smythe, who became the treasurer and *de facto* leader of the company from 1608 until 1618, was a prominent, wealthy, merchant who had served as lord mayor of London at the time of the Essex rebellion (which may have contributed to the difficulties he later experienced over his tenure at the hands of the faction led by Essex's second-in-command, the Earl of Southampton) and who had, correspondingly, considerable commercial and political experience, if not direct experience in creating and successfully maintaining colonies (no one did in England in the first decade of the seventeenth century). As a director of the East India Company at the same time, he would have been aware of less costly, less risky alternatives for pursuing profit than an American colony, and others which offered potentially greater rewards. Such ventures, however, did not support the public good to the same degree as the establishment of the Virginia settlement did. Unlike, for instance, sending a ship to Calicut or Bantam for silks or spices, a colony would, as Hakluyt (a fellow investor in the company) argued, advance employment, trade and commodities, and national pride in addition (possibly) to the purses of investors. Smythe and his fellow company officials, however, may not have reckoned with the remarkable sequence of bad luck their endeavour suffered, such as the sudden death of Bartholomew Gosnold, and the particularly fractious nature of their colony's supposed leadership.

The reality remains that Smythe's administration, despite its unpopularity with, for instance, Captain John Smith, and notwithstanding its colonizing inexperience, would have realized the difficulties (since Smith and others had communicated them) the colony faced in its early days.[37] Wingfield, unable to manage the other councillors, had proven unsatisfactory. Of the other original councillors, Kendall had been executed (possibly for espionage), while Smith, Martin and Ratcliffe (or whatever his name was) had demonstrated their inability to cooperate – fatal in any governmental body. Men sent subsequently to assist with governmental and military functions, such as Peter Wynn, also tended to die untimely deaths. Thus, Smythe and the Council for Virginia sent another of the number, Sir Thomas Gates, as soon as possible to try and restore order (or perhaps create it for the first time). Unfortunately, Gates, Sir George Somers and a large part of their fleet were shipwrecked on Bermuda.[38]

While this episode brought England, inadvertently, its second overseas colony (one that would be twinned with Virginia for several decades), it also allowed the disputes between Smith and the other Jamestown leaders to fester, as we have seen. Coincidentally, the behaviour surrounding the departure of Smith occurred during a period of renewed hostility with the Powhatans and, correspondingly, a shortage of food. The Indians drove away the force settled above the falls and when Ratcliffe, commanding at another new fort at Point Comfort, went to trade for provisions with Wahunsonacock, the 'slye olde kinge' captured and tortured him. A second expedition acquired an adequate amount of grain along the Potomac River, but on their return they informed the remnant at Point Comfort 'acquainteinge them with our greate wantts [and] exhortinge them' to relieve Jamestown. Instead, the garrison promptly 'hoysed upp Sayles and shaped their Course directly for England'. The well-known 'starving time', during which the settlers experienced a 'worlde of miseries' while their president and chronicler of their difficulties, George Percy, languished in his sickbed, now began. Facing the 'sharp pricke of hunger which noe man trewly describe butt he which hathe Tasted the bitternesse thereof', the colonists resorted to eating shoe-leather, rats, their horses and 'wylde and unknown Rootees', searching for which 'many of our men weare Cutt of and slayne by the Salvages' or 'did Runn away unto the Salvages', while Percy tried to maintain order by executing those who robbed the storehouse.

More lamentably, the dearth compelled some colonists to raid the graveyard and eat the corpses and to 'have Licked upp the Bloode which hathe fallen from their weake fellowes'. In one case, which became notorious, one man 'murdered his wyfe Ripped the Childe outt of her woambe and threwe itt into the River and after Chopped the Mother in pieces and salted her for his foode'. Percy, knowing that the Point Comfort fort (named Algernon's Fort after his nephew, the prospective Earl of Northumberland) had adequate food, proposed moving at least half of the Jamestown contingent there only to discovery that 'their intente was for to have keptt some of the better sorte alive and with their towe pinnesses to have Retourned to England nott Regardinge our miseries and wantts att all'. With their 'miseries now beinge att the hygheste', two pinnaces arrived bearing, at last, Sir Thomas Gates and Sir George Somers. But, with only some sixty men left of a complement of five hundred and able to 'Reade a lecture of miserie in our peoples faces and perceive the skarsety of victewalles and understande the malice of the Salvages, who knoweinge our weaknes had dyvers Tymes assawlted us withoutt the foarte', the new leaders quickly concluded that the colony had to be abandoned and Jamestown burned. Famously, however, the colonists had set off down the James River for England on 9 June 1610 when they received word that Thomas West, third Baron de la Ware, had arrived 'with many gentlemen of quallety and thre hundredthe men besides greate store of victewles municyon and other provisyon'.[39]

There can be no doubt that de la Ware's arrival not only kept the colony in place; it reinvigorated the whole enterprise on its American side. Immediately, the colony's officers organized themselves into a council, carried out a series of successful 'revenge' attacks against neighbouring Indian towns, sent out foraging expeditions to Bermuda and further north along the coast which returned with more provisions, and built a new fort at the falls. The battery of serious illnesses which he had suffered practically from his arrival at Jamestown, however, finally compelled the governor to return to England after eight months, leaving Percy again in command and martial law in place.[40]

Sir Thomas Dale then arrived on 10 May 1611 with three hundred men 'besides great store of armour, municyon victewalls and other provissyon'. The new governor 'ordeyned newe Lawes sette downe good articles which were well observed', and set the colonists to planting corn or to building boats and houses. He also led a resumption of 'invaysions & excursions upon the Salvages' who, following the departure of de la Ware, 'did fall to their wonted practyses ageine', and intercepted a Spanish reconnaissance expedition. Dale, in conjunction with Gates who had returned to the colony with a fresh supply, also established one new plantation and fort with two hundred men at Henrico (named for the prince of Wales) at the falls of the James and another at Bermuda City, as well as rebuilding Algernon's Fort, which had burnt.[41]

Perhaps inevitably, the setbacks the colony had endured over the first five years of its history seem to have generated a 'coldnesse and irresolution' among some of the investors in the Virginia Company just as they had compelled Gates and the colonists to abandon their settlement.[42] But, instead of packing in their venture, the return of Lord de la Ware to England in 1611 seems to have revitalized the company's associates just as his arrival in Virginia had succoured Jamestown. For between 1611 and 1617, the company published a series of tracts which promoted the Virginia colony. But in addition to addressing the unhappy incidents (*viz.* cannibalism and Indian attacks) with which the venture had become associated and to rehearsing the rationale for supporting Anglo-American colonization, these pamphlets now offered particular reports from eyewitnesses (survivors?) for Virginia and those who invested their purses and persons in it. All that was required, according to those who had been there, for an English colony to prosper in North America was the arrival of people with the ambition to take advantage of the opportunities which the Chesapeake presented.

Despite his illness, de la Ware reported that Virginia 'is wonderfull fertile and very rich, and makes good whatsoever hath beene reported of it', including a healthy increase in the numbers of livestock, 'the goodliest Trees for Masts', better hemp than in England, and lead and antinomy mines. It also had 'an excellent fishing Bancke' to the north and coastal islands 'that doe promise rich merchandise, and will further exceedingly the establishment of the Plantation', such as wine: 'there is no want of any thing, if the action can be upheld with constancy and resolution' on both sides of the Atlantic, as de la Ware promised for himself: 'that both the State may receive Honour, your selves Profit, and I future Comfort, by being imployed (though but as a weake Instrument) in so great an Action', especially since Wahunsonacock no longer (allegedly) posed a threat.[43]

Other writers soon followed suit. The colony's situation had improved by 1614 to the extent that Ralph Hamor, who had also lived in Virginia, could extol Jamestown's 'strong pale' with '3 streets of well framed howses, a hansom Church, and the foundation of a more stately one laid, of Brick' and 'Store houses, watch houses'. This 'Pale' contained 'a great quantity of corne ground' enough 'to maintain with but easiy manuring, and husbandry, more men, then I suppose, will be addressed thither, (the more is the pitty) these 3 yeeres'. The climate of its island, the eyewitness insisted, 'although formerly scandoled with unhealtfull aire, we have since approved as healthfull as any other place in the country'.

Moreover, new settlements had sprung up, further evidence that the dearth and Indian concerns had been alleviated and permitting, for the first time perhaps, articulation of particular future agricultural prospects; Gates, Dale and Captain George Yeardley had all built 'very fair houses' about half a mile apart from each other outside of Jamestown. Hamor 'purposely omitted' (pleading ignorance) a discussion of 'the hope of better mines, the more base, as Iron, Allom, and such like'. Instead, he focused on the 'hopefull, and merchantable commodities of tobacco, silke grasse, and silke wormes'. The first of these, had just had its 'first triall', but Hamor, from his own experience, contended 'that no country under the Sunne, may, or doth, afford more pleasant, sweet, and strong Tobacco'. As for silk-grass, the promoter averred, Captain Martin, 'who much delighteth in those businesses, hath made, exceeding fine, and exceeding strong silke, and himselfe hath replanted many of the wilde plants this yeere, the silke whereof he purposeth to returne for triall'. Helpfully, 'thousands of' the silkworms sent from England had 'grown to great bignesse'; since 'no Country affordeth more store of Mulbery trees, or a kind with whose leafe they more delight, or thrive better' the prospects for this commodity looked exceedingly bright.[44]

The leadership exercised by the veteran Essexians de la Ware, Gates and Dale, played a significant role in engineering the change of the atmosphere surrounding Virginia from one of abject desperation to one of hopeful expectation by the summer of 1614. According to Hamor, its secretary, the colony 'therefore standing now in such a goodly proportion, and faire forwardnesse of thriving, as it was never yet hitherto seen in, since it began to be first planted: cannot but soone come to perfection, to the exceeding great comfort of all well affected Christians, and no small profit of the planters [a new term in the literature], and adventurers: if it be well seconded and supplied, with a good number of able men'.[45]

Captain John Smith is the most celebrated figure of the history of early Virginia and the author of three volumes of papers related to colonization, including two editions (published in 1624 and 1632) of a history of English America.[46] The historiographical importance of Smith arose from the happenstance of the development of the United States of America, a country with a proclaimed ideology of the equal opportunity to pursue life, liberty and happiness and forged in a frenzy of anti-monarchical and anti-aristocratic spirit.[47] Smith readily fit the bill of a prototypical American: the scion of Lincolnshire yeomanry, who, according to his own account, saved Jamestown, first, by ordering, to their consternation, 'lazy gentlemen' (whom he blamed for the failures which beset Jamestown in its early years and for opposing his reforms at every turn) to work if they wanted to eat. He also ordered the settlers to disperse and move inland as the Indians did, contrary to conventional wisdom, in order to avoid the pestilential environment on James Island. To add to Smith's *ex post facto* lustre, Pocahontas dramatically saved him from execution at the hands of her father, Wahunsonacock. His career for most Americans, when they think about colonial America, constitutes the personification of egalitarian values – in the face of the allegedly entrenched hierarchical values and socio-political attitudes of his times – in the figure who succeeded Hakluyt to the role of tireless promoter of Anglo-American colonization.[48]

Yet, for all of the ink that has been spilled on whether or not Captain John Smith wrote the truth or whether or not he knew what he was writing about, or whether he founded 'America' or not, the reality remains that he played a relatively minor direct role in the expansion of English overseas interests generally (although, unlike Hakluyt, he did venture across the Atlantic) or in the settlement of Virginia in particular. As Peter Mancall has recently observed, Smith 'was not the first English explorer on the mainland; he did not play a central role in establishing the tobacco economy; he did not remain in Virginia long enough to be a crucial figure in its survival; and he did little to establish peaceful relations between natives and newcomers'; perhaps 'any claims Smith has to a significant role derived chiefly from his skill and getting it to the wider public'. As Smith himself noted, he left Jamestown (within two years of his arrival, although his American career was, admittedly cut short) without having 'suppressed those factions, and range[d] the countries for provision as he intended' and without returning to America.[49]

Even more significantly, however, a careful reading of Smith's *oeuvre* reveals that, even by his own account, the captain had a clear knowledge of – and was a full participant in – the Jacobean socio-political game. While Wingfield and Percy tarred him with the brush of factionalism, Smith preferred to portray himself as the public-spirited enemy of factions, perennially regarded as the viper ready to wreak discord and destruction in early modern commonwealths. Regardless of his intent and the historical accuracy of his chronicles, the captain, like all politically active Jacobeans, pursued the patronage of the powerful in order to further his projects, advance himself, and promote, perhaps, the public good, taking care to dedicate his publications to such worthies as Prince Charles and the Duchess of Lennox.[50]

Smith's comprehension of how his world worked had two particularly important manifestations. First, as we will see in Chapter 4, he participated in the 1617 campaign which revitalized the Virginia Company and enabled building upon the platform described by Hamor. Then, his career provides a further illustration that most of the English people who went to America in the first half of the seventeenth century (with the exception of people like de la Ware, Gates and Dale who went to provide leadership and, perhaps, to augment their estates) did so because they could not find a fit in metropolitan society whether from wanderlust, loss of career, economic disadvantage, religious differences or a combination of any or all of these motives. Like his more elderly counterpart, Peter Wynn, Smith had seen the opportunities for military adventure dry up. He had no particular ties to England – due in large part, undoubtedly, to his long tenure on the Continent following the deaths of his parents – and no lands or position. Yet, he had, somehow, come to the attention of the Virginia Company who thought his record worthy of employment and rescued him from the obscurity and, probably, penury of an old soldier.[51]

Putting Smith's voluminous 'works' to one side enables us to see the remarkable resemblance between his Virginia experience and that of George Percy. On the face of things, Percy constitutes the stereotypical younger son of an aristocrat; the very sort traditionally regarded as unable, due to the 'Old World' institution of primogeniture which denied them an inheritance, to advance themselves and so keen to try out American opportunities. Oftentimes, however, the 'New World' failed to measure up to expectations that the metropolitan hierarchy (absent elder brothers, of course) would be replicated, and the younger son returned home with his proverbial tail between his legs.[52]

In reality, the restrictions placed by primogeniture on the socio-economic position of the younger sons of aristocrats played only a partial role in Percy's move to Jamestown. Moreover, we have no evidence that he left the colony, which he led twice as its temporary president, because his fellow planters did not readily defer to him. As it happens, Percy, like his six other 'younger brothers', received substantial, if not lavish, pensions from the Northumberland estates. He seems to have gone to America in order to avoid the political cloud which had formed over his family due to the imprisonment of the ninth Earl of Northumberland (the eldest brother) upon suspicion of involvement in the Gunpowder Plot. Ill-health may have prompted his return to England; we have no evidence that he had any particular disagreements in Virginia.[53]

The career of Rolfe, however, provides the best illustration amongst these early migrants of their mindset and how they pursued their goals, although we have no evidence as to why he went to Virginia. Sailing with Sir Thomas Gates, Rolfe and his family were shipwrecked on Bermuda, where his infant daughter died, before arriving in Virginia, where his wife then died. Subsequently, he famously married Pocahontas (who also accepted baptism), thereby securing peace at last for the colony with the Powhatans. Equally famously, he 'first tooke the pains to make triall' of tobacco which, while it proved the lifeline for the colony's planters, proved as addictive to its economy and to the early English empire as it did for those who smoked it.[54]

In addition, like Smith, Hamor and others, Rolfe composed a promotional pamphlet which set out 'a true relation' of the state of Virginia, in this instance at the time of the departure of Sir Thomas Dale. This tract differs from its predecessors, however, because it constituted the first in a series of phenomena which, in a calculated way, furthered the complete transformation of the colony from a military endeavour to a plantation. The success of this manoeuvre came through cooperation on both sides of the Atlantic (as we shall see in Chapter 4) and, thus, through a patronage network: Rolfe dedicated his pamphlet to the Earl of

Pembroke, one of the key new figures in the Virginia Company and, correspondingly, a leader of an important and rising political group along with another newly prominent figure in the company, the Earl of Southampton.

Building on Hamor's tract, Rolfe stressed the fundamental need for 'good and sufficient men, as well of birth and quallyty to command: souldiers to march, discover and defend the Country from Invasions: as artificers, Laborers, and husbondmen' if Virginia was to succeed. But to encourage migration required answers to major questions:

> How is it possible Virginia can now be so good? so fertile a Country? so plentifully stored with food and other commodities? is it not the same still it was, when men pined with famine? were there not Governors, Men and Meanes to have wrought this heretofore? and can it now on the suddayne be so frutifull? surly (say they) these are rather baites to catch and intrapp more men into woe and misery, then otherwise can by imagined.

In response to these reasonable enquiries, Rolfe lauded, as Hamor had, the 'freshe and temperate' air, fertility of the soil, and the quality of the colony's harbours: 'I maie boldly avouch, scarce anie or no Country knowen to man of itself more aboundantly furnished'. What had changed, however, was an increase in livestock and fowl as well as in the nature of government from an 'aristocraticall' one, 'in which tyme such envie, dissentions and jarrs were daily sowen amongst them, that they choaked the seeds and blasted the fruits of all mens labors', in favour of a 'monarchicall' version under which the colonists 'were daily ymployed in pallazadoing and building of Townes, ympaling groundes, and other needful busynesses'.[55]

Equally importantly, Virginia had made peace with the Indians. This enabled 'every man [to sit] under his figtree in safety, gathering and reaping the fruites of their labors with much joy and comfort'. The colonists now grew maize, peas, beans, English wheat, turnips, and many other fruits and vegetables, which, along with the prodigious supply of fish at hand, assured their food supply without having to resort to the Indians. In addition to hemp and flax, 'none better in England or Holland', as Hamor had noted, silk and tobacco had undergone trials as commodities for export, the first fruits of which were on their way to England with high hopes of success, after further experience. Already, however, fears about an over-reliance on tobacco – practically before the first shipment of it to England had departed – had appeared: Sir Thomas Dale had enacted laws to deter 'Farmors' from spending 'too much of their tyme and labor' in cultivating it, 'and so neglect their tillage of Corne and fall into want thereof'.[56]

Rolfe had even more to offer to the future of Virginia than another promotional pamphlet: he had an exotic wife who even had some small fame in England, thanks to Hamor's account. Her appearance in the metropolis would undoubtedly attract attention and, thus, encourage interest in English America. Moreover, her very existence as the daughter of the fearsome Wahunsonacock now the Christian wife of a prominent colonist would speak volumes – and more effectively than any amount of propaganda – about the new realities and new prospects in Virginia. And go to England, Pocahontas and Rolfe did.

4 FATAL AND NEAR-FATAL ATTRACTIONS

> The Virginian woman Pocahontas, with her father counselor hath been with the King and graciously used, and both she and her assistant well placed at the masque. She is on her return (though sore against her will) if the wind would come to send them away. John Chamberlain to Sir Dudley Carleton, 18 January 1616/17
>
> Here is a fine picture of no fair Lady and yet with her tricking up and high style and title you might think her and her worshipful husband to be somebody, if you do not know that the poor company of Virginia out of their poverty are fain to allow her four pounds a week for her maintenance.
> John Chamberlain to Sir Dudley Carleton, 22 February 1616/17[1]

As Chamberlain, the prolific news-monger of Jacobean England, noted, Pocahontas and her 'assistant', Rolfe attended the Twelfth Night masque, *A Vision of Desire*, produced by the popular team of Ben Jonson and Inigo Jones for the Christmas season of 1616–17. Their appearance at court, accompanied by the once and future governor of Virginia, Lord de la Ware, and his wife, constituted a key item in the tour that was designed to bring renewed (positive) attention to English America and to convince people to invest their persons and their money in the Virginia Company's venture. Indeed, 6 January 1616/17 proved to be a highly significant date in the history of Jacobean England and its empire, although none of the historical actors concerned derived much joy in the end from the turn of events: for them, the results should be filed under 'be careful what you wish for' or 'the best laid plans oft go astray'. Notwithstanding, their activity secured the English toehold in North America and, by extension, the early modern English Empire.[2]

This appearance of the 'Virginia woman' and 'her worshipful husband' at court signalled a new sense of purpose within the Virginia Company. With peace with the Powhatans at last achieved and prospects for the cultivation of silk and tobacco seeming bright, the time had come to reverse the negative image of Virginia in English minds (if they held any image of Virginia at all) and to encourage those minds, in turn, to invest persons and money in the colony. This reinvigoration, as we have seen, was accompanied by the involvement with the company of a group of backers led by Henry Wriothesley, third Earl of Southampton, and William Herbert, third Earl of Pembroke. Their close associates included gentlemen such as Sir Edwin Sandys and Sir John Danvers and the merchant John Ferrar and Ferrar's scholarly brother, Nicholas, and these men came to assume a controlling role in the Virginia Company between 1618 and the company's dissolution in 1624.

Southampton, as noted in Chapter 2, had seconded the failed rebellion of the Earl of Essex in 1601. Although restored to his lands, he chafed at his position, shared with Pembroke, on the periphery of the government. He had invested in Weymouth's 1605 voyage, but had not involved himself in overseas activity to any great degree prior to the mid-1610s, being more concerned with returning to what he regarded as his rightful place in the councils of the monarch. By the time of Rolfe's marriage to Pocahontas and his successful 'triall' of tobacco in 1614, the Howard family constituted the main obstacle, as Southampton saw it, to the achievement of this goal. Of course, again from the perspective of Southampton (and Pembroke), the favoured position occupied by Howards not only deprived the king of the superior, disinterested counsel of the former Essexian, but the suspicious religious and political tendencies of these rivals endangered the welfare of the realm: as always, the public and the personal good merged. In targeting the Howards, Southampton and his faction entered a larger group under the aegis of a more powerful patron: Anna of Denmark, queen-consort of James I.

Queen Anna's reputation as a political operator has received a recent rehabilitation. Until a decade or so ago, Anna was dismissed as a feather-brained backer of expensive and frivolous court entertainments with no aptitude in or understanding of court politics. The research, however, of Leeds Barroll in Scotland (where Anna was the queen-consort of James VI for fourteen years before they moved south, but a nation still customarily ignored in English history) and in Denmark (where Princess Anna, sister of the Danish king, Christian IV, may have been exposed, at an early age, to the notion of pompous, overblown male monarchs) has revealed that Anna played a very active and substantial political role in the northern kingdom. She formed her own substantial household and attempted, often successfully, to use that household and its connections to advance her associates even against the wishes of her husband.[3]

When that husband succeeded to the English throne, Anna registered several significant and immediate successes in establishing herself as an autonomous political figure: she quickly regained control over her eldest son, Prince Henry, from her enemy, the Earl of Mar; she promptly established her own English household whose makeup did not agree with the plans of the king and his council; and she began to use that household as the nexus for political and literary patronage in England. Most significantly, a group of noblewomen, led by Lucy Russell, Countess of Bedford, and including Penelope Rich (née Devereux) and

Mary, Countess of Pembroke (née Sidney) – all members of the old Essex circle – travelled north to meet the new queen at Newcastle as she made her way to the English capital from Edinburgh. It was this group who formed the core of Anna's English network, which included their husbands, brothers and sons, as well as the leading lights of Jacobean literature and theatre.[4]

Perhaps inevitably (and, therefore, tiresomely), the gender of this 'feminine commonwealth' has led to its historiographical devaluation.[5] The evidence uncovered so far would seem to suggest, however, that, not only did these women – notably within the context of a monarchy that took great pains to codify patriarchy as its ideology – engage in political activity of the sort customarily assigned to the 'public' (*viz.* male) sphere of early modern European societies, they also shared a fully-fledged political platform (albeit a negative one) of opposition to Spain and to the Scottish retainers whom James brought south with him, which they shared, of course, with Southampton. This opposition manifested itself, especially early in the reign, in the plays and masques created by the literary talents who attached themselves to patrons within the queen's circle such as *Eastward Hoe!*[6]

As a newcomer to the English scene and as consort to the reigning monarch, however, Anna, even with the ready retinue who joined her at Newcastle, would have had to undertake a preliminary investigation of the political landscape. From 1603 until his death in 1612, Sir Robert Cecil, the successful architect of the peaceful accession of the Scottish king to the English throne, handled much of the day-to-day administration of government and, correspondingly, dominated the political scene by keeping various claimants for power at arm's length. The queen seems to have largely acquiesced in this state of affairs: Cecil served as the high steward of her estates and he took charge of the mourning when her infant daughters died, they exchanged gifts and correspondence, and she attended him 'diligently' during his final illness.[7]

Nevertheless, the record reveals that individuals with close connections to the queen-consort scored significant hits against the king and Cecil even early in the reign, in addition to the relatively light blows inflicted from the stage. Sandys, Sir Thomas Ridgeway and Sir Maurice Berkeley (members of Anna's new council) together with Southampton, Pembroke, Pembroke's client-associate Sir Benjamin Rudyerd and Sir William Strode, a relation of Sandys, led the successful fight via parliament against the effort to unite the realms of England and Scotland in the face of the deepest wishes of the monarch.[8] We also know that the Scots who accompanied James VI on his sojourn to become James I – and so had the most to benefit from union – had already, with the exception of the Duke of Lennox, earned the enmity of Anna (the Earls of Dunbar and Mar especially so). Their successful pursuit of English office and perquisites had also irritated prideful English nobles, such as Southampton, Pembroke and the

Earl of Arundel, by further crowding them towards the margins of the patronage picture. And the Scots were foreigners who might not have the best interests of England at heart – or least so Sandys and his associates relentlessly and successfully argued in the parliament of 1604.[9]

The Howards, especially Henry Howard, Earl of Northampton, fell into the same category of threat. Cecil's death in 1612 created a vacuum at the centre of the government and a bitter fight began over patronage and policy between the queen's group and the Howard family. Early on, the Howards, already better placed with the monarch, added substantially to their advantage by negotiating the annulment of the marriage between Frances Howard, daughter of Thomas, Earl of Suffolk, and the son and heir of Essex; she then wed Robert Carr, Earl of Somerset and the lover and favourite of James I, in a lavish ceremony on the day after Christmas 1613. Unfortunately for the pair and their backers, however, matters began to sour when Somerset's close friend and advisor (and opponent of his wedding to Frances), the author Sir Thomas Overbury, died in mysterious circumstances in the Tower (where the Howards had engineered his imprisonment for insulting the king prior to the annulment proceedings) in September 1615. Ultimately, Somerset and his wife were convicted of murdering Overbury by poisoning to great scandal in May 1616. Once the couple came under suspicion, the Howards found themselves in a vulnerable position; their enemies wasted little time pursuing the opportunity.[10]

While the queen's animosity towards the Howards may have stemmed, in part, from personal reasons – she quarrelled with Northampton, for instance, over the control of Greenwich Park in 1613 – she seems to have shared the suspicions held towards that family by the members of her circle – the Countess of Bedford, Penelope Rich, the Earls of Pembroke and Southampton, Sandys, Rudyerd and George Abbot, the archbishop of Canterbury – for policy reasons as well.[11] We have long known, as contemporaries suspected, that Northampton (a pensioner of Spain from the 1580s) led (until his death in 1614) the pro-Madrid wing of James I's government. Unsurprisingly, his presence in the inner circle of James I posed a long and serious concern for those who styled themselves the successors of the anti-Spanish leader, Essex, and even his famous political Elizabethan forebears, Robert Dudley, Earl of Leicester (Essex's step-father), and Sir Philip Sidney (who had courted Essex's sister prior to his 'martyrdom' fighting in the battle of Zutphen against the Spanish in 1586).[12]

Anna of Denmark did not have rabid anti-Spanish beliefs, but she did have a long-standing interest in the maritime and colonial affairs of her realms with which those of Spain often conflicted. She commissioned, for instance, the publication of William Welwood's contribution to the debate between 'Britain' and the Dutch over freedom of the seas, *De Dominio Maris* (1616).[13] Anna also maintained a close friendship with Sir Walter Ralegh, despite the historical conflict between the old colonizer and the Essexians in her circle; the basis of their friendship included Anna's interest 'from the beginning' in Ralegh's activities in Guiana and Virginia.[14] In addition, Captain John Smith recommended the visiting Pocahontas to the queen's patronage despite 'her husbands estate not being able to make her fit to attend your Majestie', warning that 'if she should not be well received, seeing this Kingdome may rightly have a Kingdome by her meanes; her present love to us and Christianitie, might turne to such scorne and furie, as to divert all this good to the worst of evill'. This horrid possibility, however, would dissipate and relations between Powhatans and English secured if 'so great a Queene should doe her some honour more than she can imagine'.[15]

Recognizing the king's proclivities, Anna and her faction set their eyes on the destruction of Somerset and they selected a young gentleman of an impoverished and obscure gentry family, George Villiers, to supplant the favourite and his allies, and they orchestrated his ingratiation with James. Helped no end by the folly of Somerset and his new wife, Villiers rose with remarkable speed through the king's bedchamber to become, in quick order, viscount, earl, marquis and duke by 1623 (the first in England since the execution of the Duke of Norfolk in 1572) before his death at the hands of the assassin Felton on a Portsmouth wharf in 1628. As it happens, he was created Earl of Buckingham at the same Twelfth Night masque attended by Pocahontas, Rolfe and the de la Wares.[16]

The death of Northampton, the increasing age of the Howard Earls of Suffolk and Nottingham, and the collapse of Somerset made Anna's group preeminent between 1615 and 1617: in addition to the continuing rise of Villiers, Pembroke became lord chamberlain, while Anna took effective charge of the English government for much of 1617 whilst her husband made his return to Scotland, presiding over a council which included Prince Charles (still just seventeen years old at the time), as well as her allies Canterbury, Edward Somerset, Earl of Worcester, and Lord Chancellor Ellesmere (stepfather of the queen's close friends Elizabeth de Vere, Countess of Derby, and Susan de Vere, Countess of Montgomery) and the outnumbered (but not pro-Spanish) Earl of Suffolk.[17]

This new political atmosphere made the time propitious for revisiting Anglo-American colonization and, as they advanced Villiers at court, Southampton and his associates turned to advancing Virginia. Hamor's tract had appeared in 1615. But, despite the firm assertion of the colony's secretary that green shoots of prosperity could be found in English America, the Southampton group remained unconvinced of the administration of Sir Thomas Smythe (the dedicatee of Hamor's account). In November 1616, Southampton, Sandys, Danvers and others demanded a review of the accounts of the Virginia Company, the leadership of which, to their minds, had spent a lot of money with little to show for that expenditure on the ground; while Smythe and the Southampton-Sandys group battled over the accounts, the latter assumed control of the company by 1618.

At the same time, as we have seen, Pocahontas and Rolfe arrived in England with their news of the promise offered by tobacco and silk cultivation along with their personification of a new peaceful phase of Indian–English relations. Rolfe's pamphlet, dedicated to Pembroke, underscored these new prospects. The couple visited Captain Smith, now the *doyen* of Anglo-American settlement, and he, in turn, sought the patronage of the queen for the Indian visitor and accompanied her on her visits to 'divers Courtiers and others', before Pocahontas died at Gravesend on the way back to America.[18]

This promotional campaign had a palpable effect. Southampton, Pembroke and their friends put their money where their mouths were and encouraged others to do the same: a remarkable number of Anna's associates held remarkable prominence on the lengthy list of 1618 investors in the Virginia Company, although the pleurisy to which she would succumb on 2 March 1618/19 prevented the queen herself from participating: the Earl of Bedford subscribed £120, Sir Maurice Berkeley £80, the archbishop of Canterbury £75, Sir Oliver Cromwell (another member of the queen's council) £65, Sir John Harington £187 10s, Viscount L'Isle £90, Southampton £350, Sandys £287 10s., Suffolk and his son (constituting the Howard presence on the list, and Suffolk had also been involved in the government of the company previously) £133 6s. 8d. and £87 10s. respectively, and Pembroke himself £400, the third highest subscription after Lord de la Ware and the Company of Grocers.[19]

Perhaps even more importantly than the acquisition of this new investment, Virginia, so long regarded with disdain (if at all), gained a positive association in English minds practically for the first time since the 'first fleet' sailed at the end of 1606. People no longer believed that those who went to Jamestown were most likely to starve to death, contract the 'bloody flux' or suffer an agonizing death at the hands of the Indians.

A transformation in colonial policy, encouraged on both sides of the Atlantic, accompanied these political changes and metropolitan sensibilities. Under the military regime at Jamestown prior to 1614, the colonists inevitably spent much of their time building and maintaining their defences, fighting and otherwise interacting with the Indians, and searching for mines and a passage to the 'South Sea'; the Virginia Company made no provision for the allocation of lands or the production of agricultural commodities and the settlers relied on the company store or their neighbours for food, obtained either by trade or force.

With the successful 'triall' of tobacco in 1612 (and the hope of other products), along with a less pressing need to devote individual and collective energy to short-term survival, the premise of the settlement had changed. In 1614, Sir Thomas Dale implemented a system whereby the colonists worked three-acre private gardens to feed themselves, to maintain the store, and 'more commodity returned to the Merchant' with some success. Martial law, deemed necessary to govern the Jamestown garrison in 1611, remained in place.[20]

Three years later, the Indian threat had receded and the character of Virginia had become more relaxed. Such a condition, if incorporated into policy, would benefit both the settlers and the Virginia Company as it would enable the former to turn their swords into ploughshares. English people, however, required positive incentives, in addition to peace and reassurances about the prospects for starvation and disease, in order to migrate: they required the opportunity for landownership, the barometer (as noted in Chapter 1) of socio-political status, and guarantees that they and their heirs would be able to enjoy their estates without arbitrary intrusions from the government. Those who acquired American lands would be, like their counterparts in England, best situated to undertake the government of their own affairs and, at the same time, to serve as the ligaments between the central government and their locality. If prospective migrants could be convinced that they could achieve a status and security beyond them in an overly crowded metropolis, the Southampton-Sandys group recognized, they would be moved to meet Virginia's people shortage.

Thus, upon taking control of the Virginia Company from Sir Thomas Smythe's administration in 1618, Southampton, Sandys and the Ferrar brothers – with the latter trio assuming responsibility for its day-to-day oversight – applied a new broom.[21] First, after setting aside one hundred acres of land for each of the 'ancient Adventurers and Planters' who had arrived in the colony at their own charge as well for those who had arrived at the charge of the company prior to the end of 1616, they awarded each newcomer arriving in Virginia at their own charge fifty acres (for a shilling rent). Moreover, they devised the expediency of indentured servitude which would provide labour for the company's lands while enabling those who could not afford the cost of passage across the Atlantic the chance to avail themselves of American opportunities: those people would work for seven years and receive half of the profits from those lands (the other half going to the governor).[22]

In addition, the company's new officers provided guarantees of those estates. They repealed martial law and 'to settle such a forme of government ther as may bee to the greatest comfort of the people and wherby all Iniustice greuance and oppression may bee prevented and kept of as much as possible from the said Colony', created a general assembly, modelled on parliament and consisting of the governor, the council and 'two Burgesses elected out of eache Incorporation and Plantation'. This assembly, later venerated somewhat erroneously as the 'first legislative assembly that ever convened on the American continent', duly convened on 30 July 1619. Two years later, the company modified the colony's government to resemble the English model more closely: it created a permanent council of colonists, appointed in London, to run day-to-day affairs as the Privy Council did while the general assembly would meet annually (but 'no oftener') 'with free power, to treat Consult & conclude as well of all emergent occasions concerning the publique weal of the said colony' and to enact appropriate laws for the review of and ratification by the company's quarter courts in the metropolis.[23]

With the colony's officials now declaring its readiness to receive prospective migrants and to treat them as English subjects with, perhaps, a better chance to advance themselves then at home, Virginia suddenly 'boomed': the Reverend Samuel Purchas, Hakluyt's successor as colonizing propagandist, reported that 'twelve hundred persons and upward' went to the colony in 1619 'and there are neere one thousand more remaining of those that were gone before'.[24]

The first reports of the effects of the new regime waxed promisingly. A proud Sir Edwin Sandys reported to Villiers (now marquis of Buckingham) that 'more hath been doon in my one yeare, wth less then Eight Thousand pounds, for the advancement of that Colonie in People & store of Commodities, then was doon in Sr Thomas Smiths Twelve yeares, wth expence of neer Eightie Thousand pounds'.[25]

Unfortunately, and infamously, these initial developments – and the hopes and expectations they generated on both sides of the Atlantic – collapsed spectacularly and this relatively massive influx of people, while it preserved the English presence in North America (and, consequently, the platform for the English Empire), generated unforeseen and horrible costs. First, many of these newcomers died shortly after their arrival. According to our best figures, some 3,500 to 4,000 people came to Virginia from England between 1619 and 1623, bringing the population of the colony to a height of between 4,500 and 5,000, although, even according to the company's defenders, 'notwithstanding the late Massacres [about which more below] and the great mortality which hath ensued', it contained only some 2,500 inhabitants. According to another account, prepared privately, Virginia had about 700 people in 1619, '3560 or 3570 Persons' were transported in 1619–21, but only 1,240 surviving after the 'Massacre'. An additional 1,000 people arrived in 1622, but 'manie dyed by the way and it appeareth by some l[etter]s that by the sword and sicknes there are perished aboue 500 since the massacre', which left no more than 1,700 inhabitants in the colony. The muster prepared for the government in 1625 indicates a population of 1,218.[26]

The vast majority of these migrants, as English people, came, at least in relation to African migrants, of their own volition to some degree. While we have no direct evidence, such as a helpful diary or clutch of letters, as to their motives for crossing the Atlantic, we can surmise, both from the literature the Virginia Company disseminated to attract them and by the social realities they created on the ground, that, aside from those who may have, naively, regarded America as a lark or who had little or no alternative, they hoped to achieve the ownership of their own lands and the prosperity and status the income produced by those lands would generate and to build their own communities in approximation of the world, including the significant presence of women, they had left behind (but to which they might, as a number of them did, return). This world was, as noted in Chapter 1, neither socially hidebound nor did it constitute some sort of idyll: people competed for wealth and status and, correspondingly, bred resentment and envy in both the 'Old World' and the 'New'.[27]

One of the resources for which early modern socio-political aspirants, wherever they might have been, had to compete was agricultural labour to generate landed income. With Virginia having become a recognizably agricultural colony, would-be planters there had to compete for servants. They also tapped into an unforeseen – so far as the company was concerned – labour source: Africans, 32 of whom resided in the colony out of a total population of 928 by the spring of 1619.[28] Then (and more famously), towards the end of August that year, John Rolfe reported to Sir Edwin Sandys, a Dutch man-of-war with an English pilot arrived at Point Comfort. To Rolfe's evident chagrin, this rover, which had lost its companion in the West Indies, had 'brought not any thing but 20. and odd Negroes, which the Governor [Sir George Yeardley] and Cape Merchant [Abraham Peircey] bought for victualls'. Rolfe was more concerned about the news of a possible Spanish attack on the colony then the purchase of these Africans and Sandys's summary of the letter makes no mention whatsoever of the incident, but this note indicates that, while this constitutes the first (and, consequently, now famous) mention of Africans in English Virginia, the colonists had a ready familiarity with the concept of purchasing 'Negroes' and, indeed, slavery already existed on Bermuda by 1616.[29]

A massive flood of ink has been spilled debating the 'origins' of slavery and its sibling, racism, in what came to be the 'land of the free', the United States.[30] The African population in Virginia in 1625 numbered only 23 people (including two children born in North America), and we cannot be certain about their status; at least some of these blacks seem to have been freed at the end of a term of servitude as whites were.[31] Rolfe's report and other circumstantial evidence we have indicates, however, that the English had a clear understanding of slavery and the slave trade by this time. In another episode, which also took place in 1619 and also involved a Dutch privateer (perhaps the same one as that which visited Point Comfort in August), the ship's captain gave Captain Kendall, the deputy governor of Bermuda, 'fourteen Negroes' in exchange for 'a small consideration', noting that he would otherwise have to throw them overboard 'for want of water and Victuall'. According to a complaint, which was included in the legal dispute between factions in the Virginia and Somers Island Companies led by Southampton and the Earl of Warwick (as will be detailed further below), Warwick's agent, the new governor of Bermuda Captain Nathaniel Butler, unlawfully seized the 'said Negroes' from Kendall on the grounds that they belonged to a ship of Warwick's.[32]

Thus, slavery slipped without concern onto the Virginia scene. This really should not be surprising despite the language of liberty which English people were fond of invoking. In the first place, in the early seventeenth century, no one conceived of the 'liberties of Englishmen' as applying universally. Even in England itself (as noted in Chapter 1), those who lacked 'independence', as derived from landownership, also lacked rights although, at least in theory, the presumption of innocence, for instance, applied to them as English subjects. Non-English people ('aliens') lacked, by definition, the 'liberties of Englishmen' unless and until they received denization.[33]

Then, a distinctive system of slavery in which non-whites only were enslaved had been practised in America practically since the arrival of Columbus in the Caribbean at the end of the fifteenth century. By the time of the founding of Jamestown, over a century later, planters throughout the territories colonized by Europeans had made the enslavement of Africans and Indians habitual. Correspondingly, the transatlantic slave trade had become a familiar and lucrative concept: the infamous vessel which brought 'the 20. and odd Negroes' to Virginia had seized the cargo in an attack on a Spanish vessel. These people had been captured originally in war, possibly between the Portuguese in Angola and the Kingdom of Ndongo before the Dutch raider captured them in turn on the Atlantic.[34]

Having, at best, servant status meant that Africans arriving in Virginia provided, from the perspective of planters now in a position to advance their estates vigorously, a bonus of long-term bound labour at this time of labour shortage. In England, landlords used servants habitually on their estates as they required workers in place at certain times of the agricultural year, especially harvest, to ensure that those estates produced the requisite income. In return, servants received security in the form of lodging, board and, possibly, a small stipend, depending on the competition and their own skills. When the new year began (on 'Lady Day', 25 March, under the old-style calendar), masters and servants around England would venture to neighbouring market towns and negotiate deals for the entire year.[35]

This system – both as precedent and since no realistic alternative existed – was naturally translated to America. In 1619 Virginia, both blacks and whites filled the demands for bound workers. But, like those who provided their sociopolitical model in England, ambitious Virginians manufactured all sorts of pretexts and schemes to prolong the servitude of their workforce and to erode the ties of reciprocity upon which the maintenance of the social fabric depended, according to various commentators (as noted in Chapter 1). More servants, in short, meant, in conjunction with land, more status and wealth – a formula as applicable to the 'New World' as the old – and by 1625 a recognizable group of successful social climbers had emerged, including the Virginia Company's merchant, Abraham Peircey, who topped the table with 40 servants, former governor Yeardley with 36 (both Peircey and Yeardley, the reader will recall, had acquired some of the Africans who came to the colony in 1619), Samuel Mathews with 23, Captain William Tucker with 18 and George Sandys (brother of Sir Edwin) with 16.

The white servants of these men, if, for instance, caught fornicating, running away or, ultimately, consorting with blacks saw their terms of service increase. African migrants, who had no legal rights and who had no legal connections beyond their owners, whose persons had already been bought and sold, the enslavement of whose counterparts from Brazil to Mexico provided a ready example, and who lacked, at least in the immediate term, any familiarity with their new surroundings, made candidates for permanent servitude in the revitalized English colony, although it took most of the seventeenth century for those in charge of Virginia and subsequent colonies (and their successors) to work out clearer rules governing slavery.[36] As the African population became established, they responded to this situation in the same manner as their counterparts in other colonies did.[37]

The manner of the introduction of Africans to Virginia also has significance in that it reminds us both of the early Dutch presence in the Chesapeake and the early integration of the English colony into the activities, particularly commercial, of people of other nationalities, especially the Dutch, in the Americas. That a Dutch privateer with a cargo of slaves should turn up at Point Comfort in the summer of 1619 appears to have generated no particular excitement (or alarm). By this time, of course, the Dutch Republic, as part of their long and widespread conflict with the Habsburg monarchy, had developed commercial and political interests around the globe. Now, in anticipation of the end of the Twelve Years Truce (1609–21), which had interrupted what proved to be an Eighty Years War (1568–1648), Dutch forays had begun to probe further north from the Caribbean; by the 1620s, as we shall see, their appearances at the Point Comfort roadstead would breed disquiet within the English imperial administration, and happiness for the planters seeking a market for their tobacco.[38]

In another bitter irony, the increase in the colonial population, its growing commercial activity, and the corresponding increase in its need for land and other resources led, despite the improved self-reliance of the colony, to renewed and more demands – made in a high-handed way – for food from the Indians. This pattern continually recurred – while naturally fostering deeper loathing and suspicion on both sides of the 'frontier' which ultimately coalesced – as the English encroached further into the interior of North America. Fearing the threats to their hunting grounds from the expansion of English plantations and to their culture from the Virginia Company's plans to establish a 'college for the training up of the Children of those Infidels in true Religion moral virtue and Civility' at Henrico, the Powhatans, now led by Opechancanough, felt obliged to destroy the colony. Although unsuccessful in achieving this goal, the 'massacre' in 1622 cost Virginia approximately a quarter of its population, including the deputy in charge of the 'college' and leading advocate of accommodation with the Indians, George Thorpe. In addition, the attack devastated the college itself (and the surrounding Henrico plantation), along with the fledgling iron works, and the Charles City and Martin's Hundred plantations.[39]

Finally, the combination of the demographic disaster which befell the migrants and the destruction wrought by Opechancanough and his warriors provided the basis for a series of withering attacks and counter-attacks staged between, on the one side, the Southampton-Sandys-Ferrar administration and its supporters and, on the other, the supporters of its predecessor Sir Thomas Smythe and by a group led by Robert Rich, soon to succeed to the title of second Earl of Warwick. This bout of factionalism became so intense, so disruptive to the company and its management of the colony, and, consequently, such a threat to the future of Virginia that the king had to step in, dissolve the company, and, at least temporarily as it was envisioned, assume direct control of the situation.

Unfortunately, in terms of the record, the heat generated by this episode of factionalism (as in the case surrounding the career of Captain John Smith) permeates much of the documentation of what happened at Jamestown after the promise of 1616–17 and makes it exceedingly difficult to ascertain with entirely satisfactory clarity who was doing what and for what purposes. But, in addition to the reality that the company self-destructed on the rocks of finger-pointing and blame, the character of this record demonstrates the degree to which the parties concerned regarded their involvement in overseas interests as central to their reputations, as well as that Virginia, despite all of its problems, had gained enough importance – economically and in terms of national prestige – that it was deemed worth saving.

In yet another irony, although the disastrous course that the Southampton-Sandys group unwittingly adopted seemed to have set Virginia (and Bermuda) on an even keel, they managed to ignite a huge furore which engulfed the Virginia Company and, almost, the colony. With reputations, estates, empire and wealth (in no particular order) at stake, the parties to whatever had transpired in the recent history of the colony found plenty of blame to cast on their enemies. After Southampton and Sandys assumed the direction of the company's affairs, they sought permission from its quarter court to conduct an enquiry into the management of Sir Thomas Smythe. They secured this approval by successfully soliciting an alliance with Warwick and his associates who had joined the Virginia and Somers Island Companies.

Warwick, twenty-nine years of age in 1617 and yet another Virginia figure with a connection to the second Earl of Essex (as Essex's nephew), had big plans for himself and for English overseas interests. In conjunction with his cousin, Sir Nathaniel Rich, he became a pre-eminent figure in the English Atlantic world; in addition to his involvement in Virginia and Bermuda, he bankrolled 'privateering' and colonization in the Indian Ocean, the Caribbean and New England. Indeed, piracy provided much of the basis for the deep hostility which had developed between Warwick and Smythe. First, Warwick's pirates had generated a huge controversy with the East India Company (and a loss for Warwick whose ships the company seized in retaliation) and its governor, Sir Thomas Smythe, when they attacked a ship carrying the mother of the Mughal emperor on her *hajj*. Then, the governor of Bermuda, supported by Smythe (treasurer of the Somers Island Company as well) imprisoned Robert Rich, brother of Sir Nathaniel, thereby infuriating the Rich faction. Smythe also seems to have taken exception to the marriage between his son and Isabella Rich, Warwick's sister.[40]

In enlisting the support of Warwick against Smythe, Sandys may have thought he could guide the younger man or that Warwick would accept the leadership of his uncle's staunch friend, Southampton. If so, he seriously miscalculated his man. Warwick and his supporters did second the demands for an audit of Smythe's books and helped Sandys succeed Sir Thomas as treasurer of the Virginia Company, in exchange for Sandys's support of the Rich man, Nathaniel Butler, as governor of Bermuda. Smythe's lieutenant, Alderman Robert Johnson, received the censure of the Council of Virginia, consisting of Southampton, Warwick, Sir Thomas Gates, Sir Nathaniel Rich and Southampton's clients Sir John Danvers, George Thorpe, John Wroth and John Ferrar, for the 'vndecent & vncivill but very iniurious' language he used towards Sandys in front of the court (to its 'contempte & indignitye').[41]

Their association, however, served to admit Warwick's privateering operations, though his agents Sir Samuel Argall, a Virginia veteran, and Daniel Elfrith, into both colonies. Their activities, inevitably directed against Spanish shipping, violated the peace between England and Spain and, thus, placed the charters of their governing companies in serious jeopardy from the wrath of *Rex Pacificus*; realizing this, Sandys sought to bring Argall to book, thereby enraging Argall's patron, Warwick, to the extent that he switched sides over the summer of 1619, almost as soon as the alliance had been perfected, and joined Smythe and his supporters.[42]

Thus, in 1623, Smythe's lieutenant, Alderman Johnson, brought 'a very bitter and grievous petition against ye Gouernemt and carriage of ye Company these last ffoure years' to the king and Butler contributed an 'Vnmaskinge of ye Colony'. According to Butler, the colonists had planted themselves in places 'subjected to all those inconveniences and diseases which are soe commonly found in the moste Unsounde and most Unhealthy parts of England', along a 'Mayne River' too shallow to accommodate the boats of ships, so the settlers had to wade into it to collect goods 'and therby gett such violent surfetts of colde uppon colde as seldom leave them until they leave to live'. Even worse, those 'sent over' customarily arrived in winter with no accommodation or assistance available 'so that many of them by want hereof are not onely seen dying under hedges and in the woods but beinge dead ly some of them many dayes Unregarded and Unburied' while the 'Antient Plantations' of Henrico and Charles City had been abandoned. Ten thousand people had been 'transported thither', but 'through the aforenamed abuses', only two thousand still survived. For those survivors, food was sold at an exorbitant price, housing could only approximate 'the meanest Cottages in England', the defensive situation was deplorable, the government 'not onely ignorant', but wilfully so. Moreover, the much-vaunted iron and glass works 'were utterly wasted' and 'in a small hope'; thus, 'Tobacco onely was the buisnes'. If the situation did receive a remedy, Butler claimed, 'in sted of a Plantacion it will shortly gett the name of a Slaughterhouse, and soe justly become both odious to our selves and contemptible to all the worlde'.[43]

Moreover, Johnson's petition alleged that the government of Smythe and his associates had been 'discreet & milde' so that 'they know not how itt is of late years come to pass yt vnitie and peace here att home is turned to Civill discord and Discention and divers of the antient Adventurers and Planters conceive themselvs many waies iniured and oppressed'. Moreover, under that government, relations with the Indians had been quiet 'wheras of late there hath been a Massacre and Hostillytie between the Natives and our Colony of Virginia', while the colony had produced various commodities, including iron, caviar, soap, potash, masts and 'that most desyred worke of Silkwormes, whereas in the latter years the foresaid Comodities do not appeare'.[44]

Johnson and Samuel Wrote, the former Southampton-Sandys client turned, as so often happens, vigorous enemy, made even more telling allegations before the company's court that Sandys and the Ferrars had derived undue personal benefit in the form of salaries and other perquisites from the lotteries the company had received licence to conduct and other operations. Such an engrossment, if the charge was proven, was bad enough in itself, but it also exposed the trio to charges of hypocrisy: they had always insisted that they had taken the high moral road in their dealings while accusing their enemies, such as Captain Argall, of a habitual lack of scruple. Adding further credence to this allegation, Sandys had tried desperately in parliament to prevent the Crown from revoking its permission to conduct lotteries departing from his customary and 'patriotic' opposition to monopolies – suspiciously so, in the minds of his enemies.[45]

The supporters of Sandys responded with a vigorous defence both in the court of the Virginia Company (the leadership of which they controlled) and in public. To the charges of impropriety made by Johnson and Wrote, Sandys's allies Southampton, Lord Cavendish, Danvers and Sir Edward Sackville, at a meeting at the end of the following month, warned Wrote that he had behaved insolently towards Southampton and Cavendish, and that he had improperly denied the company's jurisdiction over his behaviour in court, while upholding the propriety of Sandys and the Ferrars.[46]

In addition, the company published a broadside in May 1622 which set out the state of the colony in 1621. According to this document, it sent 1,300 'men' and 80 cattle to Virginia and another 250 'men' to Bermuda; this figure apparently did not include the 'Italians and others' making beads for trade with the Indians as well as glass or the 'young maids [who] haue bin sent to make wiues for the Planters'. The company claimed that 24 ships and 500 mariners visited those colonies. In addition, the prospects for vines, mulberry trees, indigo, cotton, iron manufacturing and naval stores, among other commodities, looked very bright, as evidenced by the list of investors at the end of the tract. The impact of this report, however, may have been reduced by the intervening 'massacre' two months previously.[47]

Both sides rushed to attract supporters and, thus, prospective supporters rushed to ingratiate themselves with whichever side would offer them the best situation. One Captain John Bargrave, who had a long-standing suit against the Smythe administration, was naturally attracted to the Sandys camp, but, perhaps because of the political cloud surrounding Sir Edwin following his behaviour in the recent parliament, he hedged his bets. In April 1622, Bargrave denied that he had any issues with Sandys's administration and informed Sir Edwin 'that all the petitions to the King against the Companie' came from Smythe, who 'directeth to get them referred to him & his frends'.[48]

Even so, Sandys sought reassurances of support from Bargrave, which he duly received through a published 'disclaimer', in which the captain proclaimed that, since the Southampton group had taken control of Virginia, 'the Businesse of the Plantation could not have been menaged wth more industrie or integritie then during that time it hath been'. On the other hand, Smythe had assumed 'absolute power of Governing both the Plantation and the Company according to his will'; consequently, 'no Lawes were made to prevent faction and packing of Coorts, nor no order kept of menaging businesses in publique Coorts lawfully assembled'. Bargrave wanted his readers to make no mistake: he objected to Smythe's 'abuse' of government, not the corporate form of colonization.[49]

A month after this pamphlet appeared, however, the captain visited Sir Nathaniel Rich at Warwick's house. Drawing on his 'long acquaintance' with Sandys, Bargrave had drawn up 'a paper on the psent Gouermt of Virginia' which he now showed to Rich. In this document, Bargrave claimed that, as 'there was not any man in the world that carried a more *malitious* hart to the Gouermt of a

Monarchie' and apparently a Brownist sympathizer to boot, Sir Edwin, under the guise of company business, was actually moving 'to erect a free state in Virginia'; serious charges for a prominent figure already in trouble with James I for his 'patriotic' behaviour in the recent parliament, culminating in his arrest on 16 June 1621 and five-week imprisonment.[50] Unfortunately for Bargrave, however, he seems to have been more used than user. While Sandys and Rich gladly received the heavy ammunition he provided them, the captain's persistent complaints against Smythe, 'which seemes to have no other end then to blemishe his Reputacon', finally triggered the wrath of the king, who ordered the Privy Council to dismiss his petition.[51]

In a similar vein, although not at the same socio-political level, Rich exploited the letters of Richard Frethorne, a settler at the devastated Martin's Hundred, which described his 'most miserable and pittiful case both for want of meat and want of cloathes'. In the aftermath of the Indian attack, Frethorne lamented to a Mr Bateman, no one could plant and 'att every Plantacon all of them for the most part were slaine and theyr houses and goods burnt'. When a supply ship did arrive, 'they fell to feedinge hard on our prouision that itt killed them that were ould Virginians as fast, as the scurvie & the bloody fluxe did kill vs new Virginians'. Frethorne pleaded with his parents to 'release me from this bondage, and saue my life' from starvation, or the return of the Indians. Frethorne's situation was undoubtedly desperate, but his reports, which found their way, for reasons that are unclear, into the hands of Rich, became cannon fodder in the fight with Sandys. Perhaps his parents – a family of some means since they had a literate son who could entertain some prospect of prompt redemption from his indentured servitude – sought Sir Nathaniel's help; perhaps they or someone else thought these documents could help discredit Sandys. Either way, the relationship between the Frethornes and the Riches remains unknown, as does the place of these documents in the debate over the present state and future of Virginia at this time. Thus, we might entertain some question as to their complete reliability as an account of the colony a year after the 'massacre', although we do know that Richard Frethorne died in the colony some time within the year after he wrote his letters.[52]

The dissemination of these 'sundry disorders and abuses' finally exhausted the patience of James I. On 9 May 1623, the king created a commission, including justice of the Court of Common Pleas Sir William Jones, Sir Nicholas Fortescue, Sir Francis Gofton, Sir Richard Sutton, Sir William Pitt, Sir Henry Bouchier and Sir Henry Spiller, and endowed them with plenary powers to investigate Virginia's affairs, including the review of the various charters issued to the Virginia Company and to hear witnesses.[53] Sandys and his associates, while they officially welcomed the commission and its enquiry, almost immediately ran afoul of it for casting 'unnecessary invectives and aspersions upon the person of the Earl of Warwick and others' in their response to Johnson's petition and the 'unmasking': within four days of the creation of the commission, the Privy Council placed Sandys, the Ferrars and William, Lord Cavendish under house arrest for the duration of its investigation for their 'provocation'.[54]

Within a year, this entity had concluded that 'most of' the colonists were sick from famine or killed 'by the native Savages', while 'those that were living of them lived in 'miserable and lamentable necessitye and Wante' even though they inhabited a 'fruitfull and healthfull' place which 'yf industrie Were vsed yt Woulde pduce many staple and good comodities'. That it had 'yeilded fewe or none' over the previous sixteen years was the fault of 'governors and Company here'. Armed with these findings, the government brought a *quo warranto* proceeding which dissolved the company's charter and returned its privileges to the king.[55]

Thus, on 15 July 1624, the king established another commission to set up a new government for Virginia. The make-up of this body reveals the comprehensive victory of the Smythe-Warwick faction over their discredited rivals: in addition to the Earl of Manchester, lord president of the council, other high officials and the two secretaries of state, it included Smythe, Alderman Johnson and Rich themselves, along with their close associates Sir John Wolstenholme, Argall, Butler, Wrote and John Pory. None of the leaders of the Southampton-Sandys group received an appointment to the commission.[56]

Consequently, while Virginia may now have been 'royal', the personnel of its government looked remarkably familiar; indeed, the very first meeting of the 'Commissioners for Virginia' took place at the home of Sir Thomas Smythe, just as the first meeting of the Virginia Company had done eighteen years before. Across the Atlantic, the membership of the council 'in' Virginia also maintained a fundamental continuity into the 'royal' period: Sir Francis Wyatt remained governor, while the list of councillors included a litany of holdovers, including the former governor Sir George Yeardley, George Sandys, Ralph Hamor, John Martin, Samuel Mathews, Abraham Peircey and William Claiborne.[57]

Correspondingly, despite the end of company rule for the colony, it remains very unclear to what degree, if any, 'royalization' constituted a change either in imperial method or the nature of colonial society: factions competed with one another and the winners kept their places (on both sides of the ocean), until they, in turn, were edged out, as happened as a matter of course in the political world of early seventeenth-century England. Moreover, the same names continued to dominate the Virginia – and imperial – scene after the royal takeover of Virginia. Did, then, 1624 really constitute the end of an era?

Smythe and Sandys (not to mention James I himself who died in March 1624/5 and Captain John Smith who died in 1632), members of an older generation, passed from the scene shortly after the dissolution of the Virginia Company.

But Warwick, Rich and others from the next generation of colonizers certainly stayed on, and – as we shall see in Chapter 5 – became involved in new projects as well. Moreover, a number of these men, such as Wolstenholme, the Sandys partisan Sir Edward Sackville, who joined the company towards the end of its life, and Sir John Danvers, even continued to advocate for a return of company government as the best means of resolving the colony's continuing problems. In 1641–2, another Virginia veteran, George Sandys, who had returned to England as agent for the colony, petitioned parliament, to the consternation of the planters, for the restoration of the company. The colonial government, including long-time planters such as Mathews and George Menefie, decried Sandys's presumption and protested vehemently against his proposal which would cause them to 'degenerate from the Condition of our birth naturaliz'd under a Monarchical Government'. This 'Intollerable Calamity', in turn, would permit the company to monopolize trade to the grief of the planters, as well as deprive the colonists of their yearly assemblies ('warranted to us by his Majesty's gracious instructions') and trials by jury, and, perhaps, most importantly, it would call into question the legality of the land grants made to the colonists.[58]

Much of the attraction of Virginia for participants in the English Empire in the 1630s and 1640s, as we shall also see in Chapter 5, continued to arise from the tobacco trade. But others who had been deeply involved in the affairs of the Virginia Company, especially those who had incurred disappointment in the company's history, and who retained their interest in the colony after its dissolution, regarded the continued attachment to the cultivation of the weed as the primary threat to the colony's future. To these minds, tobacco constituted, at best, a short-term, but necessary, economic evil which the planters would cast aside as soon as they developed more durable and useful staple crops; at worst, it was a useless and noxious commodity, the enduring and unseemly preoccupation with which continued to stunt the diversification and growth of Virginia's prospects and to give colonization a bad name.

Yet, despite a barrage of entreaties over the years after the end of the company from Virginia's friends and a series of protestations of willingness – even desperation – to wean themselves off tobacco issued by the planters, the production of tobacco remained the centre of life in the Chesapeake. As Sir Francis Wyatt, back in the colony for a second term as governor, noted in 1640, 'we have been (in a manner) wholly taken up about the regulation of tobacco, the excessive planting whereof hath been so great a hindrance to the growth of the colony'. For this year, because they had grown too much, the Virginians had been 'forced to a strict way of destroying the bad, and half the good which was propounded to us and desired by the principal merchants about London, as the only means to raise the price'.[59]

Concerns about the effects of tobacco led to the publication of a number of brief histories of Virginia in the 1640s and 1650s. These authors donned the mantle of Captain John Smith, promoting the 'natural advantages' of the place, including its proximity to great rivers and Chesapeake Bay for shipping and its suitability for the production of all sorts of useful and popular commodities. In particular, they invariably recommended silk, an exotic, highly desirable and worthwhile alternative to tobacco: reports appeared on a regular basis at least from the time of the Southampton-Sandys takeover as to the eminent suitability of Virginia for the flourishing of mulberry trees, the food of the essential silkworms.[60]

The circle of the Ferrar brothers, vestiges of the old Southampton-Sandys regime, provides a clear illustration of both the continuity of the people interested in Virginia (and colonization generally) and the promotion of silk. Thus, even though the shock of the debacle with the Smythe and Rich factions had compelled Nicholas Ferrar to retire to the religious retreat he founded at Little Gidding, Huntingdonshire, until his death in 1637, he, along with his brother, John (d. 1657), maintained contacts within the colony, receiving reports of its progress and, still, on occasion providing advice.[61] As company officers, they had worked hard to develop and diversify the colony's economy and sent vignerons and silk-men to start work there; unfortunately, disease, starvation (to which, arguably, their own 'peopling' policies contributed, as noted above) and the Indian attack had put paid to these endeavours. Even so, they and their cousins, the Wodenoth brothers, promoted silk-works in print and continued to encourage the planters to turn to silk (and wine production). After the Restoration, Sir William Berkeley, long-time governor and resident of the colony, seconded these views.[62]

By the middle of the seventeenth century, after almost a half-century of colonization activity, however, nagging questions remained. First and foremost, why, given all of the advantages and prospects listed again and again by its promoters, had Virginia, especially after over twenty-five years of royal government, continued to lag behind the hopes and expectations of the colony's backers on both sides of the Atlantic? Then, in a related vein, why had the colony's planters remained ever-dependent upon tobacco, despite the commonly recognized wisdom of pursuing alternative commodities to the better benefit of people and governments on both sides of the Atlantic, the eminent suitability of its climate for producing those commodities, and the exhortations and promises to do better, to produce alternatives and to realize, at last, the promise of the country?

Those in England who proclaimed they had always acted with Virginia's best interests at heart did not place the greatest part of the blame for its shortcomings on the planters: they knew as well as anyone the settlers had undergone great trials to survive, let alone achieve a modicum of prosperity; they understood the regrettable purpose tobacco had served in kick-starting the colony's socio-economic development, and they also, as noted above, had tobacco-growing friends in America. But they could identify a villain, whose ill will and nefarious labours had, to their minds, done more than anyone else to undo this 'pious and glorious work' when it had been on the verge of bearing wonderful fruit – rather than tobacco smoke: the ambassador of Felipe III of Spain to the court of James I, Diego Sarmiento de Acuña, Count Gondomar.[63]

It bears testimony to Gondomar's diplomatic brilliance that, while he cannot, of course, take the credit for hampering the Virginia colony (although he did scupper Roger North's 1620 attempt to colonize the Amazon), the degree of access he enjoyed to the English king, as well as to the favourite, Villiers, and the heir to the throne, Prince Charles, made him a long-time bogey figure in the minds of 'patriotic' English political figures of an anti-Spanish hue. For many contemporaries who reflected upon England's place in the world after 1613 (when Gondomar first arrived in England), the Spanish ambassador had seemed to appear at every important juncture, exercising his wiles over an ageing, weak, effeminate monarch while English interests suffered in the Palatinate (where Habsburg forces had driven away James's daughter and son-in-law, the elector, and ensconced themselves in 1621) and in America (where the Spaniards arrested and hanged 'pirates' with seeming impunity). It seemed that so far from protecting the honour of his family and his realm, as a monarch should, James had fallen sway to Gondomar to the extent that he planned to marry his son and heir, Prince Charles, to the Spanish Infanta, thereby effecting the introduction of dreaded popery at a stroke and bringing England under 'the Spanish yoke'. This calamitous result was avoided, seemingly, only through direct divine intervention. On the other hand, surely the diplomat was responsible for engineering the crippling factional divisions within the Virginia Company which had brought about its dissolution, especially at a time when the Southampton-Sandys party, which had played a lead role in advocating relief for the Palatinate, had managed to resuscitate the colony to the point of promising a real threat, at last, to Spanish interests in the Americas?[64]

Remarkably, this conspiratorial view retained currency even after over almost a generation had passed since the deaths of James, Gondomar, Sir Thomas Smythe, the Earl of Southampton and Sir Edwin Sandys. Its endurance suggests that at least some contemporaries who actively sought the promotion of what they regarded as English interests in the first half of the seventeenth century developed and retained some bitterness over what they regarded as missed opportunities – opportunities which those at the wheel of colonization continued to miss either wilfully or negligently. The 'patriots' blamed these failures on the perfidy of Spain, especially in conjunction with the fecklessness of English governments, which had proven all too successful in checking the ambitions of English patriots and creating deep embarrassment for the nation. When, if ever, would this situation change?

5 AN EMPIRE OF 'SMOAK'

Amongst many other weighty Reasons, why *Virginia* has not all this while made any progression into staple Commodities, this is the chief. That our Governours by reason of the corruption of those times they lived in, laid the Foundation of our wealth and industry on the vices of men; for about the time of our first seating of the Country, did this vicious habit of taking *Tobacco* possesse the English Nation, and from them has diffused it self into most parts of the World.[1]

Here arrived one Sir Edmund Plowden, who had been in Virginia about seven years. He came first with a patent of a county Palatine for Delaware Bay, but wanting a pilot for that place, he went to Virginia and there having lost the estate he brought over, and all his people scattered from him, he came hither to return to England for supply, intending to return and plant the Delaware, if he could get sufficient strength to supplant the Swedes.[2]

Despite these contemporary laments and the colony's erratic career, the permanent establishment of Virginia did provide the platform for the furtherance of English territorial ambitions, for the negotiation of the relationship between the metropolitan government and its colonies and, as we shall see in Chapter 6, for the development of Anglo-American colonial societies. As we have seen in the case of Virginia, a manifest degree of imperial impetus for overseas colonization did come from the Crown, even in 1606. Moreover, in addition to continuing to issue charters to the various entities which sponsored an explosion of colonial ventures between 1624 and 1663, various English governments, always with a close eye on their revenues, tried to bring the tobacco trade under closer control, culminating in the enactment of the first 'Navigation Acts' in 1651.

At the same time, the history of empire offers a further illustration of the extent of the grasp – and the limits of the reach – of the English state prior to the restoration of Charles II, particularly thanks to the fluid character of that state, especially prior to 1642. Indeed, this fluidity was accompanied by the inability (or refusal, in some cases) of the English political nation in the reign of Charles I (1625–49) to reconcile differing views which developed over the extent of monarchical power and the character of the Church of England, and were inevitably intertwined with and further aggravated by the pursuit of personal and political agendas and changes in circumstance. These factors caused the collapse of that state during the 1640s, followed by a brief dalliance with republican government, and the accession of Oliver Cromwell as Lord Protector in 1653, before the Stuarts returned in 1660 in the wake of the tumult which followed Cromwell's death in 1658.[3]

As of 1622 – fifteen years after the arrival of the first English settlers at Jamestown island and twenty years before Charles raised his standard at Nottingham and summoned his loyal subjects to join him against the 'rebels' who had taken control of the parliament – this empire included two colonies which had spun off from the Virginia effort, in addition to the original: Bermuda, founded in 1609 (as noted previously), when part of the fleet led by Sir Thomas Gates was wrecked on the island, and the settlement of the Scrooby Brownists who ensconced themselves at Plymouth in present-day Massachusetts in 1620. Both of these endeavours began with colonists recruited by the Virginia Company to settle in their bailiwick but who wound up elsewhere accidentally or on purpose.[4]

While Bermuda maintained close links with Virginia and even shared *de facto* a government for its first decade, the Plymouth settlers, by virtue of their distance from the other English settlements, the uncertain legality of their colony, the distinctive socio-political character of their leadership and a general lack of interest in their activities on the metropolitan scene, remained essentially autonomous once their ship, the *Mayflower*, arrived off the coast of 'New England'. In terms of comprehending the history of early modern England and its empire the colonizing experiences of these 'Brownists' have little importance other than to demonstrate that, like their contemporaries, they used patronage connections when they sought to advance their desires: in this case, relocation from their exile in Leiden to an English-speaking place; otherwise, they feared, 'their posteritie would be in great danger to degenerate & be corrupted'.[5]

This clutch of 'Brownists', in accord with the views of similar groups as noted in Chapter 1, insisted on the primacy of the injunction of the gospel to 'Render therefore unto Caesar, the things which are Caesar's; and unto God the things that are God's' (Matthew 22:21). This view, of course, proscribed the idea of a church headed by a temporal sovereign as in the Church of England, and holding to it put them at odds with the views of almost all of their contemporaries, as well as statute, thereby rendering them outlaws. They and their story, however, came to assume an importance out of all proportion to their significance because their beliefs and experiences seemed to resonate with what came to be identified as the ideals of the United States, after that nation came into existence over 150 years after the 'Pilgrim Fathers' alighted on their 'New World' rock. Having achieved independence through a war provoked in large part by the attitude of George III and during which they adopted the new intellectual currency of the day of inherent rights to 'life, liberty and the pursuit of happiness', Americans, especially in New England, readily identified with the 'escape' of the 'Pilgrims' from the 'Old World tyrannies' of monarchy and established church in furtherance of 'religious freedom'. Moreover, the establishment of seemingly peaceful relations with neighbouring indigenous folk, as manifested by the assistance the Plymouth group received from Squanto (the accidental survivor of the smallpox epidemic which ravaged southern New England in 1617) and, of course, the celebration of the 'first Thanksgiving' (in actuality, a customary 'Old World' harvest celebration), along with the creation, through their Mayflower Compact, of a seemingly egalitarian, proto-democratic society in the North American wilderness, made the historical tableau complete.[6]

More importantly, at least in terms of the seventeenth century, however, was the rapid deterioration of relations between England and Spain in the last years of the reign of James I due to the collapse of negotiations for a marriage between Prince Charles and the Infanta, Maria Anna. The anger of the heir to the throne (and, not coincidentally, the royal favourite, George Villiers, Duke of Buckingham, who had accompanied Charles on the trip) at the treatment he had received from the Spanish court on his secret visit to Madrid in 1623 compelled the removal of the checks which the now ageing *Rex Pacificus* had placed on English activities in the Americas and enabled building on the colonial initiatives of Virginia and its offspring. The West Indies in particular – for so long a no-go zone – was now fair game for colonizers.

From 1624, with the arrival of a party of settlers on the island of St Christopher (like the 'Pilgrim Fathers', originally bound for Virginia), the government chartered a series of 'private' endeavours to the Caribbean, both in the form of joint-stock companies such as the Providence Island Company, whose colony existed from 1630 until the Spaniards sacked it in 1641, and proprietors such as James Hay, Earl of Carlisle, who acquired Barbados, ultimately the most successful seventeenth-century English colony in terms of population and wealth, in 1627. These ventures constituted part of an even larger series of settlements which advanced English territorial claims from Maine to Madagascar during the first half of the seventeenth century.[7]

Each of these projects arose, as their earlier counterparts had done, from the activities of people with different connections to the government who presented their plans for official licensing rather than as a result of what we would call state policy today; we have no record of any governmental direction of colonizing enterprise prior to Cromwell's 'Great Western Design' in 1655. Since those involved had a variety of reasons, both 'public' and 'private', for engaging in overseas colonization, the endeavours they sponsored inevitably assumed diverse characteristics. Indeed, the jerry-built character of the English government in the first half of the seventeenth century enabled even individuals who did not necessarily share the Protestant and commercial sensibilities of John Dee, Richard Hakluyt, Samuel Purchas and other early champions of the expansion of English colonies, but with the means and interest, to labour to advance the English Empire.[8]

Moreover, the ability of these individuals to bring state power to bear for their purposes – and, all-too-often, cross-purposes – reflected the limited ability of the early Stuart government to direct its various elements to cooperate, let alone coordinate, with one another even when it – and they – had the will to do so. Having developed from mixed motives, the pursuit of early modern empire for the English, like so much else in the seventeenth century, produced decidedly mixed results.

Even the most successful episode in this history – at least in terms of demographics – manifests both the patchwork character of the early English Empire and the consequences generated when an empire was pursued through the government rather than by the government. For the Massachusetts Bay Company, which began its operations in 1628 and received its charter from Charles I on 4 March 1628/9, not only came into existence outside of the warrens of Whitehall Palace, it oversaw the 'Great Puritan Migration', which constituted the largest systematic movement of English people to America during the seventeenth century. This influx, which boosted the white population of New England from 1,800 in 1630 to 13,500 a decade later, formed the demographic basis for the colony of Massachusetts Bay and its offshoots, Rhode Island and Providence Plantations (through the expulsions from Massachusetts of Roger Williams, Anne Hutchinson, Samuel Gorton and their numerous followers) as well as Connecticut in 1636 and New Haven in 1638; they also spread across the sound to Long Island. Its numbers overwhelmed both the older Plymouth colony, to the chagrin of the Brownists there, and the scattering of inhabitants who had planted themselves under the pre-existing patent held by Sir Ferdinando Gorges.[9]

Yet, this imperial advance came, ironically, through the efforts of people with notoriously less than fervent loyalty to the government and church of Charles I. Indeed, many of the migrants to 'the Bay', especially the leaders of this 'errand into the wilderness', proclaimed (sometimes loudly) that they had decided to undertake the dangerous Atlantic crossing to New England because of their deep dissatisfaction with the religious and political state of England in the 1630s and their fears of oppression at the hands of the ecclesiastical government of William Laud, bishop of London from 1628 to 1633 and archbishop of Canterbury from 1633 to 1645. Moreover, John Winthrop, who led the first wave of migrants, famously encouraged his listeners to think of their new home as a 'citty on a hill' whose 'shining light' would serve as an example to those they had left behind.[10]

In addition, the aristocratic and mercantile supporters of New England (as well its Caribbean counterpart, the Providence Island Company) who remained in the metropolis included the parliamentary leader John Pym, John Hampden, Robert Rich, second Earl of Warwick, and William Fiennes, Viscount Saye and Sele. By the late 1620s, Warwick, as noted in Chapter 3, had already had an extensive career supporting colonization and piracy; he had happily assumed the leadership of the anti-Spanish party once held by his uncle the second Earl of Essex. Pym and the others shared Warwick's view of Spain as the enduring threat to the security of the English state and reformed religion.

Disturbingly, however, 'popish' tendencies seemed to be increasing at home, especially after Charles I succeeded to the throne. The reign had started promisingly enough with war against Felipe IV and frequent parliaments, but these gatherings had broken down amidst rancour and suspicion, the war (also pursued against France) had gone underfunded and had been led disastrously (by Buckingham until his assassination, to popular delight and the king's deep dismay, in 1628): after the dissolution of the parliament of 1629, Charles (in)famously pursued 'new counsels'; the realm's greatest court would not meet again until 1640 while those regarded as promoters of popery and tyranny – Arminianism, universal ship money levies – gained greater access to the king's ear.[11]

This left those concerned about the policies of the government, especially in terms of religion, without a forum to express their concerns; their enemies accused them of using the Providence Island Company as a cover for seditious activity. In addition, a number of these aristocrats and merchants famously fought governmental attempts to acquire additional revenues through 'novel' means such as the Forced Loan of 1626–7 and they resisted, through devices such as the Feoffees for Impropriations, corresponding religious 'novelties' which threatened 'True Religion'. In 1642, they assumed a prominent place in the parliamentary cause against the king when the civil wars broke out. Moreover, many of those aforesaid migrants, such as the regicide cleric Hugh Peter, returned to England to participate in the civil wars against the forces of the monarch (whom they came to style as 'Antichrist').[12]

For its part, the government waxed and waned in its efforts to bring the New Englanders closer to heel. The ever-ascending Laud, who assumed a leading role in imperial government when he became head of the new Committee for Foreign Plantations in 1634, was especially keen to compel colonial nonconformists to submit to his regulations and the noxious 'Arminian' theology which underpinned it. Thus, the government began to require migrants to swear the oaths of supremacy and allegiance and ships' captains to promise that they would conduct daily services as stipulated in the Book of Common Prayer. Yet, many of those who held seemingly suspect views readily satisfied the official searchers of their religious and secular orthodoxy (if only through bribery or forgery) and received the necessary certification to emigrate. Moreover, enforcement of governmental policy remained intermittent and distracted: even the king occasionally encouraged the departure of the disaffected to New England.[13]

The resistance of the New Englanders and their supporters to Charles and Laud has cemented their place as early champions of liberty against monarchical tyranny in the Whiggish comprehension of history, and as examples of the rise of the merchant class overthrowing (at least temporarily, since, for instance, the House of Lords was restored in 1660) the feudal powers of the Crown and the aristocracy in the Marxist historiographical formulation. To American historical sensibilities, especially popular ones, the Hampdens and the Pyms, along with the 'religious refugees' created by the 'persecution' of Charles and Laud, served – and, despite correction of this misapprehension, continue to serve – as heroic progenitors of American liberty whose beliefs and behaviour began to bear full flower as their heirs, the Patriots, resisted imperial novelties in the run-up to the American Revolution.[14]

Yet, the enduring power of these characterizations makes it all the more remarkable, in retrospect, that the Massachusetts Bay and Providence Island Companies, both with membership lists crammed with thorns in the sides of Charles I and his father, should receive charters to undertake overseas settlement (and, ideally, for those memberships to profit from these ventures) from that monarch. It is also remarkable that, for all their alleged pre-civil war fears of the government and its policies, especially in terms of religion, these people would undertake to enlarge the dominions of their sovereign. Did the perceived need to create havens for the 'oppressed godly' and their sense of themselves as divine agents cancel the seeming irony which colonization entailed that, at least in theory, these ventures – and the investigations the New Englanders conducted of the interior as their Chesapeake counterparts did – advanced the power of the Antichrist by extending his realm? Or did the supporters of New England and Providence Island believe that, while the Atlantic constituted an escape route for the 'godly', it provided a barrier to the authority of the king and his servants? To what degree and where did 'worldly desires' (personal profit) fit into their thinking? The difficulties of the 1620s and 1630s, as David Cressy has noted, including dearth in 1629 and 1630, the return of the plague in 1625 and again in 1636–7, as well as the failure of the East Anglian cloth trade, may well have entered the mix of factors which prospective migrants, even 'godly' ones, considered when deciding whether or not to move to America.[15]

Moreover, despite their alleged disaffection from the government of state and church, the 'godly' on both sides of the Atlantic remained enmeshed in the socio-political fabric of Caroline England and they remained willing, at least in the 1630s, to use their patronage connections (which, despite the decline of the influence of 'godliness' at court at this time, remained apparent) to further their own interests and to outmanoeuvre their opponents. Ironically, we get a good look at the normality of their political behaviour from an incident long celebrated in 'American history' as a manifestation of the proto-independence of the 'Puritans' from 'Old World' thinking and institutions.

The episode in question revolves around the demand made by Laud and his Committee for Foreign Plantations in July 1634 that the Massachusetts Bay Company surrender their charter to the committee for review. Fearing that the committee would revoke the charter and establish a royal government over their colony, company officials had the document conveyed to Boston safely away from the clutches of the archbishop while Governor Winthrop and his officials readied the colony's defences. In the meantime, John Endecott, the founding governor of Massachusetts Bay, cut the cross of St George (a 'relic of Antichrist') out of an English flag, which generated a debate in New England over the propriety of displaying this popish image as a national emblem; this ended with deprivation (for one year) of office and censure for Endecott and the agreement to fly the king's flag (probably, as Francis Bremer, Winthrop's biographer suggests, the quartered flag of the arms of England, Scotland, Ireland and France).[16]

According to the hagiographical comprehension of this event, the sacred charter provided the base 'on which the freemen of Massachusetts succeeded in erecting a system of independent representative liberty' as their 'public mind' began 'ripening for the practice of democratic liberty' and a recognizable 'germ of a representative government' appeared within a couple of years of the founding of Boston. The removal of the charter to Massachusetts preserved the liberty of the colony, and by extension that of the nation yet to be: the light emanating from the 'city on a hill' would continue to shine out to the rest of the world.[17]

Stripping this incident of the glosses, which anachronistic notions of American exceptionalism have applied over the centuries, we learn (again) that the lens of early modern English politics, albeit of the religious stripe, provides the best perspective for comprehension of 'American' history. For the attack on the charter of the Massachusetts Bay Company actually arose out of the dispute between the company and Sir Ferdinando Gorges and Captain John Mason, who had received a patent to 'New England', along with Buckingham, Warwick, the Duke of Lennox, the Earl of Arundel, the Marquis of Hamilton 'and diverse others' from James I and his council of New England on 10 August 1622.[18]

Yet another veteran of the Essex circle, Gorges had long maintained an interest in New England. Indeed, he had been a member of the old Virginia Company of Plymouth (he was from the West Country), the twin of the Virginia Company of London whose Saghedoc colony in present-day Maine ran afoul of the winter of 1607–8. Despite this interest and his periodic attempts to perfect the rights granted by the 1622 patent, however, Sir Ferdinando and his partner, Mason, found themselves having to see off the pretensions of the interloping Massachusetts Bay Company. Understandably, they sought out allies in this battle.

Given the religious and political character of that company, the Gorges-Mason group had little difficulty in securing powerful friends, although they also had powerful opponents, notably their former partner, Warwick, who had abandoned the 1622 venture and joined the New England Company, predecessor of the Massachusetts Bay Company in 1628. Moreover, the behaviour of officials in 'the Bay' had made the colony enemies, such as the trader Thomas Morton, whom the Boston magistrates banished twice on the grounds of selling guns to Indians, who habitually returned to England to heap scorn on both the moral pretensions of the New Englanders and the prospects for their colony as well as to promote the 'schismatickall' character of their system of religious government to the indignation of Winthrop.[19]

Laud, for one, was quite willing to act upon these reports. When Gorges, who had assumed control of the Council for New England, challenged the claims of the Massachusetts Bay Company, the archbishop's commission issued a *quo warranto* against the company's charter and the king appointed Gorges 'governor of New England' in 1637 in the midst of the furore, as Charles McLean Andrews noted in his account of these events, caused by unprecedented royal demands for the payment of ship money by shires with no coastline. Defeat, however, sprang from the jaws of victory for Sir Ferdinando: he and Mason had built a ship to convey them in style to New England to take up their place as proprietors, serve the *quo warranto*, secure the dissolution of the Massachusetts Bay Company and enjoy their own patent; unfortunately, their ship sank and the government had no resources to assist them with a replacement. Then the Scots rebelled against the Prayer Book, sparking, in the end, civil war.[20]

The view from the opposite end of the Caroline religious-political spectrum reveals the same imperial scene. Those Roman Catholics engaged in colonizing activities, had, like their 'godly' counterparts, to curry favour with patrons, secure chartered rights, recruit migrants, provide them with supplies and provide leadership for the problems which a settlement inevitably encountered. They also had to so while operating under an even greater – almost automatic – cloud of suspicion which their proscribed religion generated in the minds of many of their compatriots. Papists, like Brownists and 'Puritans', had eschewed the 'natural allegiance' (reinforced by parliamentary statute) they owed to their sovereign, and therefore threatened the natural order of things. Catholics were 'worse', however, since they insisted on rendering obedience to a foreign potentate, and one who laboured ceaselessly, it was believed, to turn back the years and restore Roman Catholicism in England and, correspondingly, to 're-enslave' the English people. Notwithstanding this, an Elizabethan Catholic, Sir George Peckham, had been involved in America, while, on the other hand, the prominent Jesuit Robert Parsons had come out against the notion of English Catholics supporting colonization as it assisted the position of a 'heretical' government. Parsons's view seems not to have received unanimous approval, as a number of English Catholics continued to sponsor colonizing ventures (including Virginia) in the early part of the seventeenth century.[21]

The character of Catholic involvement in overseas settlement increased dramatically, however, during the relatively benign reign of Charles I when two colonial enterprises – one the well-known and successful establishment of Maryland, the other an obscure failure to colonize the area between the Delaware and Hudson Rivers – came into being under papist auspices. Both of these episodes reveal how a coterie of English Catholics viewed American settlement as a means of demonstrating to their fellow subjects that they could reconcile their religion, with its prescribed loyalty to the pope, with the loyalty they owed to their sovereign. The presence of Dutch (especially) and Swedish colonies in the area after 1624 fuelled desires among English people on both sides of the Atlantic to secure this area against foreigners.[22]

Remarkably, notwithstanding the promise of public benefit these ventures held out, like their counterparts, they received no state encouragement aside from the patents granted to the adventurers. Indeed, the execution of the idea was undertaken primarily and extraordinarily by people who were not only unconnected with the government – although the first Lord Baltimore had served as secretary of state for several years before his conversion to Rome – but who were barred legally from public life because of their religion. One can scarcely contemplate the prospect of, say, Huguenots petitioning Louis XIII or *conversos* applying to Felipe IV for such colonizing grants.

In pursuing this vision, Catholic colonizers negotiated, with some success, a political arena rife with ideological, religious and personal opposition just as other would-be colonizers did. But, despite adhering to their obnoxious religion, the undertakers of Maryland and New Albion, like their 'godly' counterparts, did have friends and other connections who were sympathetic – if only on a personal level, but sometimes on an imperial one – to their efforts and who held positions from which they could lend practical support. This enabled them to secure charters, which contained significant powers, to acquire ships and to start, at least, the expensive and risky business of colonization.

The successful Catholic colony of Maryland was founded by Cecilius Calvert, second Lord Baltimore, just after the death of his father, George, who had laid the groundwork for the venture, in 1632. A Yorkshireman, Sir George Calvert served James I as secretary of state from 1619 until his resignation, having run afoul of Prince Charles and Buckingham for retaining his pro-Spanish proclivities and continuing to favour the Spanish Match, in February 1624/5. At that time, he received the Irish title and lands of Lord Baltimore, before apparently suffering a crisis of faith and converting to the Catholicism of his childhood, possibly at the urging of Sir Toby Matthew, and retiring from public life.[23]

Even before his resignation from office and his change in creed, Secretary Calvert had become interested in the settlement of Newfoundland. By 1621, he had received a land grant from the Newfoundland Company and had dispatched a colony. Its leader, Captain Edward Wynne, reported favourably on the area's climate (either he deliberately misled Calvert or missed the realities of a Newfoundland winter) and the secretary of state decided to pursue the venture to the extent that he acquired a patent with proprietary powers to the whole area, which he called 'Avalon', on 7 April 1623.[24]

Following his enforced departure from office, Calvert went to Newfoundland himself in 1627, taking along two priests. He returned the following year, but encountered and fought off a French force (England and France were at war at the time). This victory, however, marked the beginning of the end for Avalon: disputes over the prizes taken went to court; then reports appeared in England that Calvert not only had priests in his colony where Mass was said, but that forcible conversions of Protestants were taking place. Then, the onset of winter disabused the settlers of the salubriousness of the climate and hit their food supply drastically. On 19 August 1629, he abandoned his plans for Avalon and, after due deliberation, decided to relocate his people to the Chesapeake.[25]

Originally, like other founders of English colonies, Calvert intended to settle in Virginia. The government there, however, tendered the oaths of supremacy and allegiance for swearing by its prospective new inhabitants and it refused to accept the amended version, amenable to papists, which the former of secretary of state proposed to substitute. Unable, consequently, to reside in the existing colony, Calvert was obliged to go to Charles I and request a grant outside of Virginia's jurisdiction, although he died before he could secure it. Cecilius duly acquired the patent to the land and accompanying palatine powers of government between Chesapeake and Delaware Bays on 20 June 1632. In due course, the *Ark* and *Dove* carried the first settlers, including a brace of Jesuits, to Maryland, where they celebrated the first Mass in Anglo-America.[26]

While the Calverts were changing their minds about the prospects for 'Avalon', their close friend, the Hampshire gentleman and lawyer Sir Edmund Plowden, had begun plans to establish another English Catholic colony between the Delaware and Hudson Rivers. Unfortunately for these plans, while Plowden had substantial resources at his disposal and he articulated a remarkably clear sense of purpose, he lacked both the degree of political capital and the necessary mechanism for the ready recruitment of prospective migrants which his colonizing contemporaries, including the Calverts, possessed. Sir Edmund and his associates had to circumvent powerful opposition to his project by taking advantage of the composite character of the monarchy of Charles I: they obtained their proprietary rights to American lands located between thirty-nine and forty degrees north latitude from a patent granted by the kingdom of Ireland.[27]

As, at least nominally, its own kingdom, Ireland offered a procedural route, in theory, around this opposition. Furthermore, the lord deputy in Dublin, Sir Thomas Wentworth, recognized the potential of New Albion to himself, to the Irish kingdom (and, therefore, again to himself) and to the Caroline state generally. Although Wentworth, an ally of Pym and other 'patriots' in the parliaments of the late 1620s, became one of the most notorious advocates of centralizing state authority in Charles I's monarchy and was a fierce persecutor of recusants, he had a number of reasons of his own for creating an Irish avenue for colonization. In addition to maintaining personal friendships with a number of papists, including Matthew and the Calverts, the lord, like his Catholic friends, supported closer relations with Spain, which he regarded as a model of order and strength.[28] Correspondingly, and, in conjunction with a small but influential group of Caroline officials, he felt the urgent need to blunt the emerging threat of the Dutch, whose 'chaotic' republican system served as a poor example of government, and whose mercantile activities, which often conflicted with English interests both in the Channel and overseas, seemed unbridled.[29]

Moreover, as lord deputy, Sir Thomas quickly developed a particular interest in bolstering the importance and revenues of the kingdom of Ireland. Success in managing Ireland – the political graveyard for so many of the deputy's predecessors – would enhance his own prestige with the king. The colonial tobacco trade would provide a source of increased Irish customs revenue and generate corresponding Irish economic and political weight as well as increased prestige with the king for the official who could pull it off.[30]

The proposed location of the colony, moreover, would have held further appeal for the lord deputy, who also supported the Maryland colony. New Netherland provided the base for merchants who visited the Chesapeake and diverted both tobacco revenue and Indian trading partners from the English economy. Cutting off Dutch pretensions to the Delaware River area and pressuring the obnoxious Dutch presence on Manhattan Island from the south through the successful establishment of the Irish colony would have reduced – ideally eliminated – this nuisance and further advanced the position of Dublin and its lord deputy.[31]

The support of Wentworth would also have helped to shield New Albion from the threat posed by powerful anti-Spanish figures. Some of these people viewed the ongoing continental war as the prelude to the final overthrow of the 'Papal Antichrist' and so supported the Dutch and other Protestants involved in that conflict. Conversely, some regarded continuing Habsburg pretensions to universal monarchy as a threat to 'liberty' and 'true religion'. Others, such as the colonial supporters Edward Sackville, fourth Earl of Dorset, and Henry Rich, first Earl of Holland and brother of the Earl of Warwick, favoured France, the historic enemy of Spain, for political and personal reasons.[32]

While these figures retained substantial influence, at the time of the conception of New Albion those supporting friendship with Spain and hostility towards the Dutch had some encouragement that they were gaining ascendancy. Between 1630, when war between Spain and England ended, and 1635, when his hopes of Madrid finally foundered on the rocks of the Peace of Prague, Charles I, whilst maintaining official neutrality in the Thirty Years War, saw Spain as sympathetic to his enduring hopes for the restoration of his nephew, Charles Louis, to the Palatinate. At the same time, greater concerns began to emerge about a balance of power in the English Channel and the possible loss of the Spanish Netherlands to a French-Dutch combination.[33]

Plowden received his first patent on 24 July 1632 and a second more detailed one two years later. These grants included the right to settle the land and to form a government independent of other colonies (notably Virginia), to transport convicts and 'vagabonds' to their patent, to recruit and transport migrants of other sorts, to collect customs revenue for ten years, to build forts, as well as to create laws (consonant with the laws of England and Ireland), aristocratic titles and chartered towns. Sir Edmund himself became lord palatine and obtained the same powers to oversee the whole operation, just as Charles I had granted them to Lord Baltimore for Maryland, to James Hay, Earl of Carlisle, for Barbados, to Sir Robert Heath for Carolana, and to other colonizing proprietors.[34]

Sir Edmund did not arrive in North America to take up his grant until 1642. Shortly after the Dublin government issued the second New Albion patent, legal concerns developed over its power to grant colonizing powers of this sort within an English empire. Thus, Plowden and his associates petitioned for ratification of their grant by the English Privy Council. The 'motives and reasons' they supplied in support of their request expressed an imperial sensibility absent from documents generated from contemporary ventures, including Massachusetts Bay, Providence Island and Barbados, as well as Maryland and Carolana.[35] For while they reiterated the commercial attractions of the proposed colony in a Hakluytian sense, such as the 'two great rivers bigger than the Thames with good harbors fair timbers [and] masts' and the prospects of the inevitable silk, wine, oil and other exotic and valuable commodities, the case of New Albion had important geopolitical implications. Indeed it was, Plowden and his associates insisted, a *'great matter of state* to have it planted' (emphasis added), for 'it strengthens & comforts' the widely separated colonies of New England and Virginia and 'will prevent the encroaching of Dutch and other aliens who else by settling there may drive all the English out of America'. Thus in order to preserve the English presence in the Delaware and to repel foreign interlopers, New

Albion's leaders requested additional powers, including the authority to impress fifty shipbuilding artisans.[36]

The delay, however, proved fatal to the venture as the period after 1642 was a particularly inauspicious time to start an English Catholic colony: the king had departed his capital, his government, which included several suspected Catholics (such as the secretary of state Sir Francis Windebank), had lost much of its authority, Ireland was in rebellion, civil war had broken out, and parliament readily blamed the papists for these calamities. Unsurprisingly, when Plowden arrived in Virginia and his small party proved impotent for dealing with New Sweden, expected reinforcements failed to arrive. Compelled to return to England, the would-be Earl of Albion never crossed the Atlantic again.[37]

More of the seventeenth-century colonizing activities of the English produced the New Albion result than the Maryland one. Yet between 1622 and 1652, a year after the Rump Parliament enacted the first set of 'Navigation Acts' and a year before that parliament (and the English Republic) was forcibly dissolved by Oliver Cromwell, they had managed to extend their settlements into Connecticut, Rhode Island, present-day New Hampshire, Long Island and Maryland and set their sights firmly on the areas surrounding the Delaware River and south of Virginia despite initial setbacks; groundwork, at least in retrospect, for expansion continued to be laid despite the enduring risks entailed in new settlements and the opposition of Indians and other Europeans. Significantly, many of these initiatives arose from the colonies – perhaps due to the distractions the civil wars presented to potential colonizers, such as Sir Edmund Plowden, in the metropolis in the years between 1642 and 1651.[38]

In addition to the continual, if fitful, growth of colonial branches from Virginia and, after 1635, Massachusetts Bay, an imperial structure of sorts began to emerge in the aftermath of the establishment of tobacco as a profitable commodity. Early Stuart government – ever conscious of its precarious fiscal situation and, correspondingly, always on the lookout for new revenue opportunities – took a keen interest in colonial tobacco production, notwithstanding the personal aversion to the weed of James I, as soon as the profitability of the crop became evident at the end of the 1610s.[39]

The leading treasury official of this period, Lionel Cranfield, Earl of Middlesex, a Virginia investor as well as a prominent London merchant, had a brief to overhaul the Jacobean financial system, to increase revenue, to cut expenditures and to ensure a reliable income stream. Given that this reform programme conflicted with the rampant pursuit of office, wealth and power by the royal favourite, the Duke of Buckingham, its prospect for ultimate success may have been slim, despite official backing from the king. Notwithstanding, Cranfield tried to bring the colonial trade under regulation through the device of a contract whereby winning bidders would receive the 'farm' for the customs generated by all of the tobacco imported into England. In accordance with early modern custom, they would keep all of the money they made minus the cost of their farm paid to the government. In 1619, he negotiated an agreement with Sir Thomas Roe, a long-time advocate of overseas activity, and the merchant Abraham Jacob by which they paid the treasury £8,000 in exchange for the right to receive 6*d*. per pound in customs and an additional 6*d*. per pound as an imposition upon imported tobacco.[40]

By 1620, tobacco had become apparently so important to the future of Virginia and Bermuda (and, by extension, the future of the English Empire) that all attempts to curtail its production fell to dust: at the end of 1616, the importation and resale of 2,300 pounds of Virginia tobacco ('and diverse other comoditYes') had yielded £125 3*s*. 4*d*. in customs revenue; just two years later, a trade of almost 50,000 pounds of tobacco had brought £3,332 6*s*. 4*d*. in customs. In 1621, 73,777 pounds of Virginia and Bermuda tobacco arrived in London.[41] When the king himself issued a proclamation forbidding its production, the planters pleaded with the Virginia Company to petition for its rescission, 'seeing the issue of the plantation dependeth on the [cultivation] of yt'.[42]

Confronted by the fears of ruin expressed by the planters and the amount of money at stake, James gave up on prohibition and Cranfield turned again to taxation and from 1621 through 1623, as the Virginia Company suffered the series of body blows (some self-inflicted) noted in Chapter 4, his papers set out the debate over the relative advantages of permitting a free tobacco trade as opposed to 'farmers'. For a while, the lord treasurer, who was a friend and neighbour of Sir Edwin Sandys at the time, seems to have thought seriously of giving the company the tobacco contract. This solution might have solved the company's enduring revenue shortages, enabled it to control the price of Spanish ('Varinas') tobacco, for which English smokers retained a preference over the Virginia variety, and made it responsible for keeping the customs money steadily flowing into the exchequer.[43]

These negotiations, however, broke down in the face of allegations that Sandys and the Ferrar brothers had received exorbitant salaries, accompanied by charges brought by their enemies of their general mismanagement of the company and the colony (all discussed in Chapter 4). In concert with the lack of enthusiasm for monopolies (whipped up by Sandys, ironically) that had developed at the same time, Cranfield abruptly decided to suspend further dealings with the company until the completion of the enquiries into its behaviour and summarily dismissed the attempts at defence presented by Sandys and the Earl of Southampton. Denied this potential income, the Virginia Company continued to haemorrhage red ink until the king put it out of its misery. Sandys, Southampton and their associates did gain a healthy measure of revenge, however, when they joined Buckingham in his attack in parliament in 1624 on Cranfield's own conduct: charged with taking bribes, gross mismanagement and unlawfully accumulating power, he was impeached, imprisoned in the Tower and fined £50,000; although released by the king (whose profligacy he had been unable to curb), he departed to an embittered retirement and the flocking of his creditors.[44]

The removal of Cranfield (followed by the death of James I the following year) did not mean an end to Crown attempts to control the tobacco trade. The grandest of these plans must have been the appointment, in 1632 under the Great Seal, of the diplomat and keeper of the state papers Sir William Boswell and the Huguenot gentleman Pierre de Licques as hereditary receivers-general for Virginia and the West Indies. De Licques had put forward 'an advice in writinge and readinge to be putt in execution concerning [those] plantations', the nature of which, unfortunately, remains unknown. This plan (whatever it may have been) would generate within 'fowre or five yeares', to the undoubted pleasure of the monarch, 'a Revenue of fifty thousand pounds sterling per Annum' and create 'a greate increase in traffique and profitt to our Subjects'. Over that same five-year period, de Licques evidently claimed that he would be able to maintain five ships of the Royal Navy and he and Boswell agreed to provide the king with a newly built 'lustie tall Ship' of at least five hundred tons every year after the five years had passed. In addition to their new office, Boswell and de Licques were to receive a fifth of all of the profit generated by their plantation.[45]

To be sure, neither of the patentees ever took up their position as receiver-general nor did their plans ever go beyond the paper stage (although they certainly impressed the king) nor did they build any ships for Charles I. Moreover, we know next to nothing about de Licques, although the patent identifies him as a 'chevalier' from Picardy.[46] Consequently, it seems easy to dismiss the whole idea as a flight of fancy. This may, however, be premature. The first, and ultimately insurmountable, obstacle to the perfection of this plan was the posting of Sir William Boswell to an embassy in the Netherlands by the autumn of 1632.[47] Even so, he did not give up immediately on his American project as he received in the Netherlands further propositions, which he heartily recommended to a Mr Bernard, from de Licques for the 'collection, transportation, provision & employment for the poore of England' in the West Indies, a 'designe for the advancing & establishment of the plantacons' on the Earl of Carlisle's islands (Boswell was a client of the earl's), and a 'memorial with advise' for plantations on the mainland. Unfortunately for these plans, they may have gone astray while the king (and Carlisle) visited Scotland. In the event, Boswell remained on ambassadorial duty at The Hague until his death in 1649.[48]

The government of Charles I entertained other ideas for its colonies and for tobacco, aside from the stillborn Boswell-de Licques project, including the one put forward by William Anys which Thomas Cogswell has discussed in a recent article.[49] In the aftermath of the demise of the Virginia Company, something had to be done about the government of Virginia and paradoxical problems of colonial over-reliance on tobacco and the revenue generated by the commerce in the weed. Thus, for instance, to consider (again) these vexing questions, in 1631 the king created a commission 'for the advising & settling of some course to be established for the advancement of the plantation of Virginia' with the power 'to consider how the estate of that plantation stood formerly' and to recommend what commodities might be produced there, so that 'it may be better advanced for the future'. He naturally turned to those with long experience with the colony dating back to the Virginia Company's government, including Edward Sackville, fourth Earl of Dorset, Sir John Danvers, Sir Robert Killigrew, Sir Thomas Roe, Sir John Wolstenholme, Sir Francis Wyatt and the Ferrar brothers.[50]

The Crown, on a constant lookout for ways to increase its revenues, retained its preference for the establishment of a monopolistic contract. Since the contract would have guaranteed the planters with a market and a set price for their commodity and provided the prospect of a reasonably certain delivery of customs revenue to the Exchequer, the idea seemed to make considerable sense, especially given the inefficient financial system and correspondingly notoriously poor fiscal straits under which the Caroline regime operated. Since, at least in his first years as king, Charles I tried to work out fiscal issues in a parliamentary way, this meant that the governor would consult on the contract with the provincial council and its House of Burgesses just as their metropolitan counterparts, king and parliament, consulted on subsidies. Unfortunately, this series of meetings, which continued from 1627 into 1638, produced the same dismal results – at least in terms of agreement between the parties – in Caroline Virginia that they did in Caroline England.[51]

It probably did not help matters that the prickly and self-important John Harvey became governor. This ship's captain seized the chance for advancement offered by the development of overseas empire to hitch his star as firmly as he could to the socio-political centre of the early Stuart world, the monarch. Harvey entered Virginia's affairs as early as August 1623 when he accepted an appointment – possibly obtained through the offices of the diplomat Sir Dudley Carleton – to the commission appointed by the Privy Council to investigate the nature of the damage inflicted on the colony by the Indian attack of the previous year. While rendering this service, he identified himself as a soldier in the Virginia Company faction headed by the Earl of Warwick, discussed in Chapter 4, when he provided a preliminary report to Sir Nathaniel Rich.[52] He also composed a 'briefe declaration' for the government which discussed the colony's defensive situation and its relations with the 'Salvages' and noted the 'generall desire' of the inhabitants 'to bee immediately under the government and protection of his Majestie'. Having become convinced of Harvey's 'experience', as well as his 'fidelitie prudence and sufficiency', the government rewarded him with membership of the Council for Virginia, a knighthood and, on 12 September 1628, the governorship of the colony.[53]

When Harvey assumed his Virginia government, his fellow councillors included the planters William Claiborne and Samuel Mathews. Although this pair, both of whom arrived in the colony prior to the royal intervention of 1623, evidently shared Harvey's belief in the colonial route to improved status and wealth, they formed their connections with different patrons who tended to have less direct associations with the government. Claiborne, for instance, enlisted in the Virginia Company faction led by Sir Edwin Sandys and the Earl of Southampton, whose disputes with the Rich group, again discussed in Chapter 4, paralysed the company and whose management of the colony culminated in the Indian attack of 1622 and royal intervention.

A native of Kent, Claiborne obtained the important office of surveyor of Virginia from his powerful neighbour, Sandys. He arrived at Jamestown in 1621 and proceeded to use his position, in customary early modern fashion, to advance himself by acquiring lands and involving himself in the Indian trade. To the latter end, by 1632, Claiborne, Mathews and the latter's in-law, Abraham Peircey, had founded a lucrative establishment on Kent Island in northern Chesapeake Bay. At the same time, Sandys having by now retired from public life (Sir Edwin died in 1629), Claiborne forged a new connection with another company veteran, the powerful Dorset, who, probably not coincidentally, held substantial lands in Kent.[54]

Mathews, like Harvey, came to Virginia as a member of the 1623 commission of enquiry. Following the customary practice, he used the land he received for his services and two helpful marriages, especially to the daughter of Peircey, who had been the chief factor (or 'cape merchant') of the Virginia Company, as the platform for advancement. Having sunk his stakes in colonial society, he acquired corresponding political power. The perpetually spiralling income stream and status mixing office, estate and income from trade with the Indians and with London maintained Mathews as a redoubtable force in the colony until his death in 1657.[55]

Despite his experience in the colony and although they seem to have had no previous differences, friction between Harvey and these men began to manifest itself after he became governor.[56] In April 1631, Harvey complained to his friend Carleton, now secretary of state, about the behaviour of his council, especially Mathews and Peircey. Despite the king's 'gracious letter for the strengthening of my commission which I have often showed them', they continued 'this malignity against me' since he could 'discern nothing in them but factions, seeking to carry all matters, rather for their own ends, than either seeking the general good or doing right to particular men'.[57] Some three weeks later, the parties proclaimed themselves 'unanimously reconciled', while acknowledging themselves 'ever bound' to the Commissioners for Virginia. The councillors further promised Harvey 'that we have no other intentions then upon all occasions to do him the service honor & due desert which belong unto him as his Majesty's substitute'.[58]

This 'reconciliation', which proved temporary, seems to have further inflated the governor's sense of his position. Unfortunately, while he regarded himself as the personification of royal authority in Virginia, it is, at best, unclear whether anyone else entirely shared this view. On the one hand, his letter to Coventry suggests that he appears, not unnaturally, to have expected the planters to render him what he regarded as his due obedience. Yet, at the same time, he remained equally frustrated in his dealings with his superiors who never seem to have provided him with the trappings of office which, Harvey believed, were not only due to him as the agent of royal authority but also would have helped him to exercise that authority.

Matters came to a head because Charles I created the Maryland patent for Lord Baltimore. Prior to 1632, this new colony had constituted the northern part of Virginia where Claiborne and Mathews had set up their semi-autonomous trading post; the Virginians now found themselves squatters in their neighbour's territory. Charged with carrying out royal instructions to lend such assistance as he could to the Maryland settlers, Harvey welcomed the Marylanders upon their arrival in America and supplied them with boats and other necessaries. Unfortunately this attitude, in the eyes of Claiborne, Mathews and their associates, constituted an unacceptable attack on their political and economic interests and rekindled their animosity towards the governor.[59]

By 1635, the plotters had secured their own powerful friends in London who, according to Harvey, 'nourished' Mathews – 'the patron of disorder' – and his party.[60] In addition to Dorset, these friends included others long prominent in Virginia affairs who now sat on the advisory Commission on Virginia, such as Sir John Wolstenholme and Sir John Zouch, as well as Samuel Vassall and Maurice Thompson, counterparts of Wolstenholme and Zouch at the head of the capital's merchant community. Trying to arrest Mathews for treason, the governor himself was seized and conveyed back to England to answer the charges of his enemies.[61]

The positions occupied by these patrons – although we have no firm evidence that they had foreknowledge of the coup against Harvey – enabled the Claiborne-Mathews faction to grasp the chance to arrest Harvey and return him to England. In taking this initiative, the rebels naturally took considerable pains to emphasize their 'miserable condition' brought on by the governor's 'tyrannical behaviour' which had compelled them to overthrow him. In particular, Mathews claimed in the justification he quickly sent to Wolstenholme via Zouch (who was present in the colony at the time of the coup and who Harvey identified as an instigator of his difficulties), Harvey had detained letters to the king and Privy Council respecting the tobacco contract. Moreover, the governor had abused the council and the burgesses, completed a 'dangerous peace' with the Indians, and claimed 'the power lay in himselfe to dispose of all matters as his Majesties substitute'. Perhaps most worryingly, Harvey had failed to follow 'his Majestie's express command' and upheld the seizure by the Marylanders of Claiborne's 'Pinnasses and men with the goods in them'. Thus, in order to preserve themselves from 'the oppressions of the Marylanders' and the governor, the Claiborne-Mathews group had to act.[62]

Harvey's enemies did not rest there; they also wasted no time bringing a case against him in the Star Chamber along with a petition to Charles I to have Baltimore's patent revoked. But, since the king had made the Maryland grant and since Harvey was the representative of royal authority in Virginia, the petitioners had to tread carefully. Thus, their pleadings characterized the behaviour of Baltimore and Harvey as grave threats to royal authority, social order and the prosperity of their colony: the governor, in particular, had disobeyed royal instructions and 'refused to administer the oath of allegiance to any belonging to Maryland'. This behaviour had inevitably encouraged 'the Romish Religion and Popish Priests are permitted freely to reside in Virginia'. At the same time, Harvey had cooperated with Baltimore's agents 'to interdict the pl[aintiffs'] trade, without the limits of Maryland'. He also assisted the Marylanders in the struggle over the patent, 'forbidding the planters trade there, and taking away commissions formerly granted', as well as prosecuting Claiborne 'with all violence'. According to the complaint, he had also failed to prosecute one 'Rabnett of Maryland' who allegedly had claimed 'that it was lawful and meritorious to kill an Heretic King', made 'a doubtful peace with the Indians', governed in accordance with secret instructions, interfered with the due process of law, barred trade in Delaware Bay and 'permitted trade to Dutchmen' without taking a bond, all without the consent of the Virginia Council. They also warned that the division of Virginia 'into several governments' would 'give a general disheartening to the planters' and serve as 'a bar to that trade, which they have long exercised'.[63]

Unfortunately for the petitioners, the court of Star Chamber declined to give them relief: it allowed Lord Baltimore to keep his patent and ordered that the planters in both colonies 'shall have fair traffic and commerce' with each other and 'sincerely entertain all considerations and assist each other on all occasions, in such manner as becomes fellow-subjects and members of the same state'; thus, Harvey returned to his post.[64] The governor then tried to exact revenge upon his opponents by packing them off to England to answer for their 'mutiny'. Unfortunately for him, the mutineers quickly secured their liberty, apparently for lack of a plausible alternative, thanks to their connections to the Virginia commissioners – helped by an illness suffered by the governor's representative, and the distance and expense required on the part of Harvey to pursue the case – and they used the opportunity provided by their presence in the metropolis to lobby the Privy Council for a replacement governor, which duly came in 1639.[65] They then returned to Virginia in time to frustrate Harvey over the propositions in their parliament. Harvey suffered comprehensive defeat: deprived of his office, unable to secure recompense for the debts he had incurred while in office, and left to the tender mercies of the Claiborne-Mathews faction who 'persecuted [him] with much malice' and sequestered his estates, he died in misery and obscurity.[66]

While Harvey had managed to defend himself successfully before the Privy Council, his embarrassments continued in the meantime. Not only did he fail consistently to receive proper remuneration for the expenses he had incurred as governor (including the hosting of guests), but the government failed to provide him with a seaworthy vessel when it returned him to Virginia in 1636. Thus, as with Sir Ferdinando Gorges – who, like Harvey, seems also to have over-estimated the capacity (and perhaps the ultimate commitment) of Charles I and his ministers to empire and, correspondingly, his own position – his ship sprang leaks as it left harbour. This engendered both a humiliating return to port and an admiralty lawsuit over wages due brought against the governor by some of the mariners involved.[67]

Harvey's difficulties arose from his miscalculation of royal support for his position, which may have naturally arisen, in turn, from the diffusion of authority that existed in the government of Virginia and in the English Empire at this time. By virtue of his office, he should have constituted the primary point of contact between the Privy Council and the locality. It remained unclear, however, just how much authority – and respect – a colonial governor commanded at this time. The former ship's captain might have regarded himself as the vicegerent of the king – the equivalent of the Lord Deputy of Ireland – but it was by no means clear that anyone else shared this lofty view of his position. The creation of Dorset's Commission on Virginia and the Commission on Plantations (with its own Virginia subcommittee), moreover, created alternative channels that enabled the Claiborne and his friends to outflank even those who held royal office. In order to cement his position, Harvey had to curry favour with these commissioners – many of whom were his enemies – as well as Secretary Windebank. But, since we have no record of any correspondence between the governor and those bodies – as opposed to the battery of letters he and his friends sent to Windebank now contained in the National Archives at Kew, he seems not to have recognized this reality.[68]

Not incidentally, the existence of these overlapping and semi-autonomous institutions of colonial administration stemmed from the character of the central administration. The king remained reliant on a bewildering array of officers – justices of the peace, members of parliament, sheriffs, receivers and escheators of Crown lands, attorneys in the Court of Wards (such as John Winthrop) – some of whom held their places directly from the central government, but others of whom gained their places from powerful local patrons and, so, were not beholden to the Crown for their positions. Additionally, of course, the pursuit of the fruits of office provided a *raison d'être* for faction. The lack of clear policy direction from Whitehall, as in the case of Caroline Virginia, gave additional room for autonomous operation to these networks, despite the best efforts of the king's ministers.[69]

Customarily portrayed as 'symptomatic of a profound disorganization of European society in an American setting' that revealed, in turn, 'a new configuration of forces which shaped the origins of American politics', the defeat of Harvey thus actually demonstrates the political sophistication of his enemies despite the apparent material and cultural shortcomings in their 'Old World' backgrounds. It also illustrates the early and thorough integration of leading Virginians into the early modern English socio-political world. Yet, their experiences have provided ready support for the prevalent characterization of early Virginian society and politics as a manifestation of the formation of a peculiarly American socio-political scene that arose from the acquisitive, individualistic, character of the settlers and from the new opportunities afforded them by the relative availability of American land. The Virginians then opposed attempts on the part of higher authority to bridle their control of their local situation, thereby creating both a 'divergence between political and social leadership' and a social structure that was 'by European standards strangely shaped'.[70]

In the first instance, the behaviour of all of the parties concerned demonstrates their continued commitment to the cultivation of patronage and clientage links on both sides of the Atlantic Ocean to further their ambitions as well as their political acumen by successfully acquiring these connections.[71] Unfortunately for Harvey, his patrons proved either unwilling or unable to provide the means for him to wield greater authority, despite their assurances to the contrary, while those of his enemies readily lent assistance to their colonial clients. Harvey's unfortunate career sheds helpful light on the character of the English Empire at this time as it demonstrates that the reach of the Caroline government – whether styled 'imperial' in the overseas sense or 'state formation' in domestic terms – all too often exceeded its grasp. The distance from Whitehall, especially in the colonial case, compounded the continuing inability of king and ministers to reconcile the conundrum of balancing monarchical authority and prestige with policy issues, the liberties of subjects (as exemplified by parliamentary gatherings) and the ongoing manoeuvres of factions. These phenomena – as well as the divergent institutional setup that existed for colonial administration – further diluted kingly authority and, thus, helped to widen the socio-political cracks that came to rend the king's realms on both sides of the Atlantic.[72]

Harvey's unfortunate career also demonstrates that the reach of the Caroline government – whether styled 'imperial' in the overseas sense or 'state formation' in domestic terms – all-too-often exceeded its grasp. The distance from Whitehall, especially in the colonial case, compounded the continuing inability of king and ministers to reconcile the conundrum of balancing monarchical authority and prestige with policy issues, the liberties of subjects (as exemplified by parliamentary gatherings) and the ongoing manoeuvres of factions. These phenomena – as well as the divergent institutional set-up that existed for colonial administration – further diluted kingly authority and, thus, helped to widen the socio-political cracks that came to rend the king's realms on both sides of the Atlantic.

Yet, in the short term – and despite the setbacks he had suffered – Harvey remained confident in his position. During his enforced absence in England, he prepared a memorandum on the state of the colony. His views no doubt affected by his 'thrusting out', Harvey lay the blame for the colony's failings partly on 'irregular government', chiefly arising 'from some covetous and grasping disposition that strives to plant such vast and excessive quantities, and that also so base and ill conditioned, that for some particular gains they hazard the common good of the whole plantation, and bring such low esteem and value upon their tobacco'. This behaviour, and the attitude that underpinned it, brought minimal return for both the planters and the government.[73]

Having received this advice, Charles I now announced his intention to act on it, with Harvey to return (once he found a proper ship) to Virginia and place a firmer handle on the reins. Having had the previous attempts to regulate the tobacco trade via the contract mechanism rebuffed, the king directed the Virginians to consider propositions he had prepared to address their particular situation as well as conditions they shared with their counterparts in the Caribbean, on Bermuda 'or elsewhere'. He also banned trade 'with any Dutch ship that shall either purposely or casually come into any of your plantations'. Failure to fulfil these directives, either by the Virginia government or his colonial subjects, the memorandum warned, would result in the intervention of the Privy Council.[74] Thus, on 20 February 1637/8, the House of Burgesses, 'called by his Majesty's appointment', convened to consider five 'Propositions' offered by Charles I for the reformation of their colony's tobacco trade.[75]

The king's message, which tracked the language of a memorandum that Whitehall sent to Jamestown in April 1637, reminded the Virginians, as if they needed to be reminded, of the problems generated by their continuing and excessive devotion to tobacco cultivation. Unlike their counterparts on St Christopher, Barbados and the other English islands in the Caribbean, who had 'already begun with cotton wools and other good and useful commodities' in order to wean themselves away from the weed, Virginians continued to neglect 'to plant corn and grain sufficient for the support of the colony, whereby you are brought into so great straits and hazards'. Thus, they had to rely on the Indians, the Dutch 'and other strangers' for essentials. This situation, according to Whitehall, permitted these suppliers to 'take advantage upon your necessities, and by the equal brunt of wines, victuals and other commodities, make a prey of the tobacco and crop of the plantations, not only to our subjects great loss in their livelihoods but to the prejudice of our such duties and profits that should redound unto us upon the same'.[76]

It is perhaps painfully obvious that no colonial delegations ever met to consider the reformation of the tobacco trade, while this 1638 session proved to be the final time in the history of the British Empire that a monarch ordered the summoning of a colonial assembly for the consideration of imperial issues. Indeed, the tobacco question festered throughout the seventeenth century.[77] The Virginians never seem to have acted upon any of the king's propositions for regulation other than to offer counter-proposals, centring on the maintenance of free trade which, they insisted, would provide the best basis for furthering the prosperity of their colony. They also doubted the other tobacco-producing colonies would cooperate in the formulation of a general policy. Harvey dismissed these assertions, finding that 'you have rather studied to serve your own ends then his Majesty's commands' both by contradicting previous agreements made by the burgesses on limiting tobacco production and by doubting royal promises with respect to the compliance of other colonies. If this remained the extent of their compliance, the governor saw no alternative to dissolving the assembly and conveying 'your disobedience' to the king.[78]

Despite their concerns about the propositions, the Burgesses passed an act (now lost) that regulated the quality and quantity of their tobacco for the next year 'wherein according to my best understanding, [they] met with many of the abuses which were therein committed heretofore'. The issue of a contract for the staple, however, 'sticks still', and the governor found 'no inclination in the colony to embrace it': the planters feared such a restraint on their trade would put them in the 'hard condition' of their counterparts on Bermuda who had to accept whatever rates their company gave them.[79]

Yet, even this resistance did not entail opposition to the concept of awarding a monopoly ('contract') for the importation of Virginia tobacco *per se*. For even as they raised their objections to the royal propositions in their parliament, 'the principal planters of Virginia and others that have long continued in that plantation' offered a 'humble remonstrance' on the contract issue directly to Charles I and his ministers that they felt would satisfy all of the constituencies concerned, which memorial stemmed from a proposal offered by Sir George Goring, another of the commissioners appointed to oversee Virginia's affairs in 1631, and other 'agents' of the king to 'give us 1600000 weight of tobacco' at 6*d.* per pound.⁸⁰ This anticipated sum, 'which amounts to £40000 sterling and 8d per pound in England', the planters regarded as 'really for the advancement and the future good of the plantation' since it promised them, first (and apparently foremost), an additional income of '4d per pound which yearly amounts to £26666 13s 4d'. This increased private benefit would further the public weal as it would 'save half our labour in that bewitched commodity of tobacco, and convert our endeavours to better uses', including manufacturing iron, potash, salt, saltpetre, hemp, pipe staves and flax, growing vines, orchards, gardens and grain, as well as pursuing 'discoveries and trade with the Indians'. The pursuit of these industries would, in turn, generate the building of 'commodious habitations & towns'.⁸¹

Nothing, however, seems to have happened with this proposal and discussions about the contract idea then disappear from the record. In the meantime, Virginians vigorously pursued the status quo. Two years later, they had seen Harvey out of his office for the second time; his successor, Sir Francis Wyatt, who had also occupied the post at the end of the Virginia Company's rule, advised Whitehall that the planters had returned yet again to the vexing issue of tobacco overproduction 'whereof hath been so great a hindrance to the growth of this colony'. At this point, the problem had compelled the destruction of 'the bad, and half the good' of their crop in order to raise the price of the weed to an acceptable level. 'Although the physic seem sharp', Wyatt hoped 'it will bring the body of the colony to a sound constitution of health, then ever it enjoyed before' so as to justify the action against 'any refractory person' who should question it.⁸²

It remains unclear to what degree the failure to resolve the tobacco issues to the satisfaction of the central government constituted an imperial failure. After all, the early Stuart governments pursued a litany of policies, many concerning issues more significant and closer to home than Virginia, which foundered upon opposition raised both in and outside of parliament despite closer proximity and the devotion of far greater attention and effort to them: the attempt to unite England and Scotland (1604), the 'Great Contract' to inject some system into the generation and collection of the royal revenue (1610), the pursuit of war and diplomacy with Spain and France (1624–9). Since the government proved unable – although not necessarily incapable of doing so – to put its revenue stream on a systematic basis in the metropolis, should we be surprised that it could not do so across the Atlantic?⁸³

The most significant of these instances had a direct effect on the outcome of the Crown's efforts to reform the Virginia tobacco trade in 1638. Charles, in conjunction with his Scottish bishops, introduced the Prayer Book of the Church of England into the Kirk at the same time that the tobacco propositions were making their way to Jamestown. Many of the subjects of his northern kingdom objected and famously entered into a 'National Covenant' on 19 February

1637/8 (as it happens, the day before the Virginia 'Assembly' met to consider the royal proclamations on tobacco) to resist this new religious policy, about which the government had not consulted them. The 'Covenanters' warded off all attempts to reduce them to obedience, captured Newcastle and compelled Charles to pay them an annuity. This disaster, in the end, obliged the king to call the first meeting of the English parliament for eleven years in April 1640, a gathering which, after a dissolution and a new meeting of the great court the following November, provided the platform for civil war.[84]

Students of English history in the period between of the start of the sitting of the Long Parliament to the 'happy Restoration' of Charles II in May 1660 have had no more success than contemporaries did in reaching a consensus of understanding of what exactly happened and why it happened.[85] Some things, to be sure, were and are clear. First, forces loyal to Charles I fought those loyal to the parliament (minus those of its members who joined Charles I or retired to the country during the course of the conflict) between 1642 and 1649 in England, Wales, Ireland, Scotland and America before the parliamentary forces, in large part thanks to the efforts of the New Model Army which formed during the fighting, triumphed. Those troops achieved empire on an unprecedented scale in the history of England: they subjugated both Scotland and Ireland (a dream of English governments dating back, at least, to the reign of Edward I (1272–1307), and achieved the first English military victory outside of Europe (and the first recognizable victory anywhere against a foreign enemy since the temporary capture of Boulogne in 1544) by seizing the island of Jamaica from Spain in 1655.

During the same period, the royalists were defeated, while Archbishop Laud went to the block on 10 January 1644/5, as did, finally, the king on 30 January 1648/9. In addition, the parliament stripped the Church of England of its bishops 'root-and-branch' and abolished the House of Lords (March 1649). The 'Cavaliers' also lost their collective place in local government and thus, to a degree, their social status as suspect persons; their estates were fined, they had to post bonds for their good behaviour. Men of a 'godly' bent, often (but not necessarily) possessing less landed income, took their place. After 1649, many aristocrats and gentlemen who had supported the parliamentary cause, such as Warwick, who had commanded the navy, withdrew from public life alarmed at the radical course English society seemed to be taking. For what had begun as a dispute over the character of kingly power and the governmental and theological character of the Church of England had led to the proliferation of all sorts of new religious and social views, thanks in part to the collapse of the press licensing system which had accompanied the collapse of the government in 1642. Radical groups such as 'Diggers', 'Levellers', 'Antinomians' and, most alarmingly,

'Ranters', not only emerged into the public light but took the chance to proffer a 'world turned upside down' to a wider audience through the printing press.[86]

We cannot, however, calculate with much confidence the degree to which these views registered with those who were exposed to them. Correspondingly, we cannot determine with any precision how revolutionary English society became in the mid-seventeenth century. We do know about the alarm which the publication of these views generated. The fear that they might gain popularity, along with the seeming inability of the Rump Parliament to take decisive action on any important matter, especially the payment of arrears to the army (these phenomena may have been linked), led to the takeover of the government by Oliver Cromwell and his supporters in 1653 and – following the death of the 'Lord Protector' in 1658 and the unwillingness of his son and designated successor, Richard, to wield power – to the return of the Stuarts (albeit without some of their previous prerogatives, such as the Court of Wards), the House of Lords and the bishops. It also marked the return of the royalists to their places in the 'Cavalier Parliament' and in local government; those who had seethed on the sidelines for over a decade during the 'revolution of the saints' lost little time in exacting their revenge by turning back the clock.[87]

What did all of these tumults mean for the English Empire in America? First, as noted above, the New Model Army succeeded in advancing English territorial control where its predecessors had notably failed. In addition to capturing Jamaica, Cromwell's government managed to compel the obedience of those colonies where royalists had assumed control of the government, such as Virginia and Barbados, by sending a force from England. A couple of years earlier, the republic had confronted the Dutch threat by enacting the Navigation Acts in 1651, which compelled colonists to convey their commodities to England and which foreshadowed the outbreak of the first of three seventeenth-century Anglo-Dutch Wars (1652–4, 1664–7, 1672–4). Despite war and general official hostility, however, trade between English colonies and ships of other nations continued in defiance of the Navigation Acts – since the colonists customarily received a better price from the interlopers – although, by the definition of the activity, we cannot establish the degree of smuggling with any precision.[88]

Even so, the metropolitan government fell a good way short of its imperial objectives. Even the 'Great Western Design' of 1655 demonstrates the continuing limited scope of English imperial enterprise and the continuing importance of local cooperation for 'central' success in the mid-seventeenth century: the attempt to capture Santo Domingo, the nerve centre of the Spanish Empire, failed thanks largely to the meagre offerings of men and supplies which the Barbados planters tendered compounded by the effects of disease, which wracked the attackers, and the strength of the Spanish defences. As they would do with the Dutch in 1674, the English had to settle for a consolation prize: Jamaica.[89]

In a similar vein, when the Cromwellian government took the direct route and prohibited the cultivation of colonial, as well as domestic, tobacco in 1654, the planters and their merchant allies immediately went to work seeking a repeal of the ban. Samuel Mathews informed Cromwell that it would result in 'the utter ruin of most English plantations in America, to the great prejudice of adventurers and traders, who usually vended great quantities of English manufactures yearly' while hindering navigation and greatly reducing customs revenue. Moreover, another petitioner contended, echoing Hakluyt, that the colonies had furthered the export of English goods, increasing customs, 'and England eased of many thousand idle and dissolute persons whose continuance here was a burden, but their labors there, have been and still are very advantageous to the improvement of these plantations'; without the cultivation of 'superior' colonial tobacco, all of these advantages would quickly disappear along with the investment already made in the colonies. The government had to backtrack: 'smoak', for all of the hand-wringing and decrying it provoked on both sides of the Atlantic, had provided the foundation of the English Empire and it had proven impossible, at least by the mid-seventeenth century, to wean its planters to other commodities to a satisfactory degree.[90]

While the Interregnum produced indifferent 'imperial' results, it is not easy to find much socio-political 'revolution' taking place in Anglo-America between 1649 and 1660. In the first place, colonists continued to value metropolitan contacts, as we shall see in Chapter 6. On occasion, colonial affairs provided fodder for metropolitan disputes: the prolix Presbyterian lawyer William Prynne used the religious controversy which broke out between his co-religionists and independents on Bermuda to support his contention that, while episcopacy equalled tyranny, the encouragement of the proliferation of 'sects' threatened the proper order of things.[91]

Very little change occurred in the social order of the colonies. Those people who had made their way to the top tended to remain there despite the sometimes fierce ramifications of metropolitan affairs. In Barbados and its mainland offshoot, Surinam, men such as Sir Thomas Modyford and Francis, Lord Willoughby of Parham, knew they had to tack their political sails to the prevailing winds to stay ahead in the race to socio-political leadership. Moreover, the basis of the colonial fighting that did take place, as in Maryland, tended to arise from local issues, rather than from a ready affinity for either parliamentarians or royalists; colonists tried to use the civil war to their advantage as they had previously sought to use other events in England. In doing so, they showed remarkable adaptability in finding new patrons with whom they curried support in republican, Cromwellian or, after 1660, monarchical governments. That a number of these patrons were able to tack successfully as well did not hurt.[92]

6 SOME MEASURE OF SUCCESS

But we humbly conceive and hope that there is and will appear to be so much of reason and justice, and so much of his Highness interest to dispose of the government enclosed, that there will be sufficient cause for his Highness to dispose of the government of Maryland (in case it belong not to Virginia) otherwise then to put it into the hands of such a one, when if once confirmed, will undoubtedly be as ready to slight and oppose ye authority of his Highness, as ever he was to slight and oppose ye authority of ye parliament, which he hath manifestly and boldly done, and that with a very high hand

Sir, your former propensness to take cognizance of the business makes us presume thus to trouble you, and it being of such a public concernment in relation to his Highness interest and ye good of these profitable plantations we hope you will please to excuse our boldness, and to further the determination and dispatch of this long tedious dispute, that so those plantations may be settled under ye present government, and that we may return to our relations and occasions from which we have been so long detained.[1]

The Planters, some of them, have not only dealt unjustly and inhumanely with the poor heathen Indians; but to the farther dishonour of this Nation, and the greater scandal of our religion professed by them, they did lately commit a most hainous outrage, and bloody fact upon some of their own English Nation, that had seated themselves in Mary-land; & that not upon a suddain provoked, boyling of their own blood, but, (so far as circumstances could demonstrate their intention) out of a Cain-like thirsting after their brethrens blood, and a sordid coveting of their estates.[2]

On 13 March 1676/7, the long-time Virginia planter William Claiborne had a great concern on his mind, but which had nothing to do with either his advancing age (he died later that year) or with 'Bacon's Rebellion' which had recently wracked his colony. Rather, Claiborne's preoccupation remained his 'utter undoeing' at the hands of the late Cecilius Calvert, second Lord Baltimore, who had, some forty years before, 'expelled' him from Kent Island which, Claiborne claimed, he had 'discovered & planted' by authority of the governor of Virginia fifty years before. In addition to causing the petitioner great personal loss, by 'takeing away his Estate to the value of above Ten thousand pounds sterling in Goods Catle Servants & many Plantations thereon', Baltimore had, Claiborne assured Charles II, generated 'a great greivance of the Country'. Having served on Virginia's council of state 'to your Majesties Grandfather: & after also secretary of state to your father of Glorious Memory', he had no doubt of receiving the king's 'speedy justice in so Lamentable a case'.[3]

This petition proved to be the final salvo fired in a bombardment which had started practically as soon the colonists sent by Baltimore set foot in the Chesapeake in 1634. The basis of Claiborne's grievance – the loss of his Kent Island outpost to the new colony – and the disruptions the pursuit of his claims generated have naturally attracted interest, especially in terms of the early history of Maryland. But the methods and attitude (including language) he, and men like him, adopted in furthering his agenda tell us even more; for they demonstrate how people went about pursuing social, political and economic success in the early decades of the English Empire. We learn that, despite the serious setbacks Claiborne, in particular, received over Kent Island and elsewhere, the scope of opportunity for socio-political advancement certainly increased for those with the resources of character and capital to pursue them. Correspondingly, the extent, geographic as well economic, of ambition which an English person could conceive, also certainly increased – and the William Claibornes of this world certainly helped here as well.[4]

The courses to which Claiborne and those like him readily resorted certainly contributed to social tumult. Thus, they encouraged the sense, held by both contemporaries, such as the Reverend Lionel Gatford cited above, and subsequent historians, that early English America, excepting 'communal' New England, was a Hobbesian, seething, lawless sort of place where the predatory tendencies of the leading planters received freer rein in new environments and encouragement towards 'savagery' from working and living in proximity to Indians and 'Negroes'.[5] And there can be no denying the frenzy – both physical and literary – which infused, for instance, the Baltimore-Claiborne dispute and which spilled over into more public arenas even though the Maryland proprietor had wanted peace with Claiborne. Baltimore instructed his colonial agents, even before they arrived in the Chesapeake, to inform the Kent Island planter of the creation of the new colony, 'to lett him know that his L[ord]ship is willing to give him all the encouragement he cann to proceede', and 'to shew him all the love and favour'. If the Virginian refused to meet with them, they were to leave him alone for a year, although Baltimore also wanted a report on Kent Island, including its relationship with Virginia.[6]

Claiborne, for his part, had no interest in this 'encouragement' to advance his plantation under Baltimore's auspices and rebuffed these overtures. Indeed, he 'incensed the Indians against' Maryland, warning them that the newcomers were Spaniards and 'contrived divers other malitious plots and conspiracies against them'. Then, his partner Samuel Mathews, 'the incendiary of all this wicked plot of Cleybourne's', had the 'boldnesse' to question the legitimacy of the Maryland grant as it might have been 'surreptitiously procured'.[7] Then, as discussed in Chapter 5, the Kent Island associates had no hesitation in moving against the nominal agent of royal authority in Virginia, Sir John Harvey, when he rendered assistance to the Marylanders: the governor's expectations of due obedience to his orders and further favour from the Crown turned to dust, despite his links to the government, at the hands of his enemies.[8]

In addition to crushing Harvey, Claiborne apparently ignored the directions of the court of Star Chamber and Charles I to patch up his differences with the Marylanders and to live quietly with his fellow subjects. Instead, his behaviour obliged Baltimore to submit another petition to the king to declare his rights and to note that 'it will appear that the said Claiborne and his servants are guilty of piracy and murder': despite having 'no legal right to his unjust pretenses' to Kent Island, the Virginian had encouraged 'the Indians to destroy two of your petitioner's brothers, with divers gentlemen and others of your Majesty's subjects and by many other unlawful ways to overthrow his plantations'. Meanwhile, Harvey had jailed Claiborne on the latter's return to the colony 'for his contemptuous & mutinous carriage towards the government there, and rebellious departure from thence' after he had submitted dubious allegations in support of his claims against the Maryland patent. Yet, despite Baltimore's request for 'justice' in the form of a bar to any cession of his patent, and another finding in favour of the Maryland proprietor by the Commissioners for Plantations (which found that Claiborne had been granted his licence to trade at Kent Island from the government of Scotland and, thus, it had no validity in English territory), no action against the Virginian was forthcoming. Instead, Claiborne continued to make further allegations of wrongful conduct from the Marylanders against the Kent Islanders and to work on undermining Harvey.[9]

The outbreak of civil war in 1642 provided Claiborne and his allies with a seemingly splendid opportunity to strike again at the detested Maryland patent. A fear and loathing of 'popery' constituted a – perhaps the – central component of the concerns that were raised about the character of the government of Charles I. These worries became especially aggravated following the outbreak of rebellion in Ireland in 1641 to the extent that, as we also saw in Chapter 5, members of parliament circulated a 'protestation' promising to defend the realm and the king's person. Then, when that royal person, instead of placing himself under its 'protection', went north and formed an army, the parliament issued its own call to arms and further investigations into Catholic activity. As a 'professed recusant' with an Irish title, Cecilius Calvert was a marked man; could England really acquiesce in the idea of an American 'receptacle for Papists, Priests, and Jesuits' where, far away from the defenders of order, they tyrannized good Protestants within the colony and inevitably laboured towards the overthrow of king, state and religion elsewhere? In short, did not the preservation of England and its empire (and, after there was no more monarch in 1649, the state) mandate an end to this absurd threat and the return of 'Maryland' to Virginia and of Kent Island to William Claiborne?[10]

The Claiborne group took a variety of approaches to ensure that a 'yes' answer to this question was forthcoming: they continually lobbied their connections in the metropolis; they fought a long pamphlet war with Baltimore's supporters; and they took to real battlefields. In doing so, they employed little scruple over who they supported in the civil wars, taking care only to try to stay on the winning side amidst all of the tumult.

In 1642, Claiborne received the office of treasurer in Virginia for life from Charles I.[11] With the defeat of the royalists at Marston Moor on 2 July 1644, however, the prevailing wind began to blow with increasing force from the parliamentary direction, and the Kent Islanders steered accordingly. Taking advantage of fears of popery in Maryland, they joined with one Richard Ingle – a ship's captain who had escaped charges of treason against the king, ill-advisedly brought against him by Baltimore's deputy-governor, and then returned to the Chesapeake with parliamentary letters of marque – in a miniature civil war. In the course of 'Ingle's Rebellion', Claiborne regained control of his island while Leonard Calvert, the lord proprietor's brother and governor of Maryland, fled to Virginia.[12]

Although the parliament restored Baltimore's position by the end of 1646, the continuing success of the parliamentary cause in England fanned the hopes of the Kent Islanders. The defeat of the royalist army at Preston in August 1648, which ended the 'second civil war', the ensuing 'Pride's Purge' of parliament, and, finally, the trial and beheading of Charles I all signalled a more radical turn of events and an accompanying desire to crack down on popery further. These events also presented a practical opportunity. For in response to the execution of his sovereign, which he, for one, regarded as a horrid and unnatural act, Sir William Berkeley, whom Charles had appointed governor of Virginia in 1641 and who had maintained his government throughout the civil wars, declared his support for the new 'king', Charles II, as did several other colonial governments. Unable, of course, to countenance resistance, the forces of the new English Republic, which had demonstrated their continuing strength by ending armed royalism in Britain (at the battle of Dunbar in Scotland on 3 September 1650 and the battle of Worcester in England exactly one year later) subdued the rebellious colonies; Virginia, where a number of 'Cavaliers' went into exile after their defeat, surrendered to a parliamentary fleet on 12 March 1651/2.

Circumstances had changed and, to a degree, the cast of characters had changed.[13] But despite the departure from the scene of some familiar faces, notably the Earl of Dorset who had helped them with Harvey, Claiborne, Mathews and their allies continued, as they had done in their defeat of Harvey, to solicit the favour of metropolitan patrons and they went to England again at the end of the 1640s. Some of these potential partners may have been old acquaintances, such as the Virginia Company relict, regicide and now member of the Council of State Sir John Danvers, who maintained a lifelong interest in the colonies.[14] Others, however, were certainly new men, especially, after another parliamentary purge and establishment of the Protectorate, Oliver Cromwell himself and John Thurloe, Cromwell's secretary of state. Unlike Berkeley, who grounded his post-1648 behaviour in an enduring belief in monarchical government and a deep dismay at the proceedings taken against Charles I, the Kent Island partners, despite holding their offices from a royal warrant, had no qualms about accepting the regicide and the successors to kingly government.

Moreover, these successors, as the creation of fervent Protestants, seemed likely to be especially hostile to a Catholic colony. The Long Parliament had already enacted even tougher legislation against Catholics in 1643, both in terms of proscribed behaviour and belief and punishments for recusants: popery was not only abhorrent in and of itself; most of its practitioners had been ardent royalists. The Commonwealth and the Protectorate thus proceeded to put fierce pressure on Catholic estates. On 24 April 1655, for instance, Cromwell denounced priests and ordered justices of the peace to compile (on a form provided by the government) lists of recusants living within their jurisdictions. Another crackdown, including the introduction of new, more draconian legislation in parliament, took place the following year.[15]

The Interregnum governments, for their part, liked the argument made by the Virginians and their partners in London that a proper relationship between metropolis and colony should entail the removal of the difficult Governor Berkeley and the barring of foreigners from colonial trade. Thus, Claiborne, along with his associates, including Richard Bennett and Thomas Stegge, received commissions for 'the reduceing of Virginia' to the Commonwealth on 26 September 1651. The commissioners then negotiated the surrender of Virginia and the departure of Berkeley to (temporary) retirement from public life the following March, as noted above. Bennett assumed the governorship.[16]

These manoeuvres, which entailed local agendas at least as much as 'revolutionary' and metropolitan behaviour, enabled a full-scale assault on Baltimore's position. In the Chesapeake, as is well known, the dispute between anti-proprietary (now backed by the Virginia government) and proprietary forces escalated into the victory of Baltimore's opponents at the 'Battle of the Severn' of 25 March 1655 before a truce was negotiated on 16 September 1656 while the Cromwellian government investigated the whole affair. In the metropolis meanwhile, a corresponding paper war broke out with allegations and counter-allegations of atrocities flying from the pens on both sides as surely as their counterparts across the Atlantic fired shot at each other. For the stakes were just as high: a military victory would bring advantage, of course; but that advantage required ultimate confirmation from the government; which, in turn, meant that the government had to be persuaded of the righteousness and benefits of one's position. Public debate of this sort, including finger-pointing, had been a hallmark of Anglo-American colonization practically since its inception, as we have seen, and it would continue long after the Interregnum.

Undoubtedly, anti-popery provided much of the fuel for the opponents of Baltimore, at least within Maryland (despite the proprietor's continued insistence on religious toleration): their military victory on the Severn forced the hated Jesuits out of the colony, and the fears of slaughter at the hands of the papists as well as the prospects of a redistribution of seized Catholic lands (as happened in Ireland) may have encouraged rebellion against the proprietor. It is difficult, however, to dismiss the suspicion that, for the Claiborne-Mathews group, religion, like republicanism, constituted more of a pretext – both for aligning their party with the Commonwealth and for encouraging civil war in Maryland. After all, their grievances dated from the 1630s and Claiborne was still pressing his claim twenty years after the final recognition of Baltimore's rights; 'popery' seems not to have received much mention in these petitions submitted to kings forty years apart.[17]

Regardless of the motives of the anti-Baltimore group, the Protectorate, failed to meet their expectations – possibly because Cromwell, always concerned about the legitimacy of his regime, insisted on using the law rather than 'anti-popery' as the governing rule. In this case, the government compelled the restoration of the Maryland proprietorship in exchange for Baltimore's permanent guarantee of religious toleration and the right of any Marylander who wished to do so to depart the colony within one year.[18]

Despite this disappointment, Claiborne's career must rank as among the most significant in the development of the early English Empire. From his Chesapeake base, his interests and connections stretched to England, naturally, but to the Caribbean and West Africa as well. In May 1638, while his case against Baltimore was still before the Virginia Commissioners of Charles I, the Virginian received a grant to Ruatan Island off the coast of present-day Honduras from the Providence Island Company. Naming his colony Rich Island, after the Rich Earls of Warwick and Holland, who were leading participants in the Providence Island venture, Claiborne maintained his Caribbean endeavour until the Spanish captured it in 1642 (Providence itself having been seized the previous year).[19]

Ships belonging to Claiborne and his partners, the London-based merchants William Clobery and Maurice Thompson, arrived off the 'Gold Coast' of West Africa in the mid-1630s in search of gold and 'elephants teeth'.[20] By this time, the English had become increasingly active in trade with Africans. As with colonization, however, inexperience and internecine bickering hampered initial efforts. In 1636, for instance, the crew of Claiborne-Clobery-Thompson fell into a dispute with the master of another English vessel, George Lamberton, over the value of gold and 'elephants teeth' brought back by their men from 'Guinea' which generated a suit before the high court of Admiralty. The English traders also had difficulty finding commodities which would appeal to African partners; they ultimately had to sell the cheese they had brought, naively, for this trade to other Europeans.[21]

All of these men belonged to a coterie of mid-seventeenth-century English adventurers who developed a range of interests and associations which spanned the Atlantic Ocean and penetrated even farther afield. In addition to Claiborne and Clobery, this group included aristocrats, such as the Earls of Warwick and Holland, as well as men who had a combination of mercantile, political and landed interests, such as Thompson, Lamberton, Samuel Vassall and Sir John Yeamans. In pursuing and maintaining various economic ventures, they, as we saw in Claiborne's case, forged patronage and clientage networks, lobbied with officialdom to gain advantages – corporate and colonizing charters, office, commercial concessions – and readily resorted to litigation and to violence in order to gain advantage. We might regard them as the heirs of the earlier generation of 'imperial' undertakers, including Sir Thomas Smythe, the Earl of Southampton, Sir Edwin Sandys and John Rolfe, in terms of their wider orientation, their involvement and interest in faraway places and their corresponding willingness to outweigh the risks entailed in early modern overseas opportunities with the prospects of reward. In doing so, they substantially strengthened the web of English overseas interests which had begun to be spun in the sixteenth century and, consequently, stretched the reasonable prospects for the advancement of those interests even further.[22]

Some of these figures, including Claiborne, received attention in Robert Brenner's mammoth examination of the activities of 'new' seventeenth-century English merchants whose behaviour, according to Brenner, led to the profound political changes of the mid-seventeenth century. As Brenner notes, Thompson, seems to have had his fingers in every pie from India to Africa to Canada to the West Indies from around 1625 until his death in 1676. On his way to becoming one of the wealthiest and most important merchants of his day, Thompson lived for a time in Virginia and developed commercial connections in the Dutch Republic. Indeed, the tobacco trade constituted the cornerstone of his interests, but he also made a lot of money by shipping provisions to Providence Island and other colonies and by transporting African slaves to the West Indies. Ultimately, he became a governor of the East India Company and his son, John, was created Baron Haversham in 1673.[23]

Lamberton, a 'godly' merchant, like Thompson and Vassall, made his base in New Haven Colony when it was founded in 1638, where he was one of four planters whose estates exceeded £1,000. As we have seen, he could be found off the Gold Coast looking for gold and ivory and squabbling with the representatives of Clobery and Thompson.[24] Also interested in furthering the Indian trade, Lamberton led a New Haven-sponsored colony to the Delaware River valley (noted briefly in Chapter 5) in 1643, having explored the region, acquired land from the Indians and established a preliminary settlement over the preceding two years. Unfortunately, these efforts came to naught when the new governor of New Sweden, Johan Printz, arrested him on charges of inciting the Indians to attack the Swedish colony and for trading without a licence duly issued by the Swedish government. The New Sweden court (which included Dutch members) fined the Englishman for the latter offence and expelled him from their territory.

The administration of these 'foul injuries' (John Winthrop's view) sparked a diplomatic incident between New Sweden, New Netherland (Winthrop accused the Dutch colony of 'joining with the Swedes'), and New England; New Haven, with the support of Connecticut and Massachusetts Bay, continued to probe the area while the colonial governments endeavoured to secure the removal of the obnoxious foreign presence. Lamberton, however, did not live to see any English imperial triumph in the Delaware region: in January 1645/6, he and a number of other prominent New Haven colonists perished when the colony's ship carrying them along with £5,000 of peas, wheat, 'West India hides', beaver pelts 'and plate' went to the bottom of the Atlantic en route to London.[25]

Samuel Vassall, the descendant of Huguenot émigrés to London and, like Claiborne and Clobery, an occasional partner of Maurice Thompson, became one of most vociferous defenders of mercantile interests against the 'novel' efforts of the Stuart monarchy to increase its revenues. He was imprisoned a total of sixteen times and claimed £20,000 in damages for refusing to pay the Forced Loan of 1626–7 and for resisting the payment of impositions, tonnage and poundage, as well as ship money. At the same time, he expanded his own activities from the Levant and the East Indies to North America. An original patentee of the Massachusetts Bay Company and of Rhode Island and Providence Plantations (along with Warwick, John Pym and Oliver Cromwell), he also became involved in trade, including for slaves, with West Africans.[26]

Like Claiborne, Vassall also tried founding his own colony, acquiring, in 1630, the patent rights to 'Carolana', the region between Virginia and Spanish Florida, from Sir Robert Heath, the original grantee. While we have no record of Claiborne's Ruatan endeavour, we have, perhaps from Vassall's perspective, a relatively decent amount of information about 'Carolana' and an early effort to extend the English presence in North America southward: an investigation of the suitability of the coast of present-day South Carolina was made, and, in 1632, colonists supplied with provisions were sent there, but the ship arrived in

Virginia instead, where many of them died, and the ramifications of the debacle, inevitably, carried to the high court of Admiralty (again). The court ordered Vassall to pay the captain of the colonizing vessel £611 1s. 4d.; when he was not forthcoming, he was committed to the Fleet. This unhappy experience, however, did not put him off of the idea of colonizing the area: after the Restoration, thirty years later, he led a settlement, which conflicted with the rights of the Carolina proprietorship, at Cape Fear in present-day North Carolina. Unfortunately for his aspirations, this endeavour became a victim of the distractions presented by Second Anglo-Dutch War and the Great Fire of London (1666) before his death in 1667.[27]

Although, unlike the other cases discussed here, Sir John Yeamans was a royalist during the civil wars, his career assumed a similar colonial and transatlantic character. Born in 1611, the son of a prominent Bristol brewer and merchant, Yeamans arrived in Barbados by 1638 and entered that colony's legislature in July 1639. He returned to England, though, at the outbreak of the civil wars and served the cause of Charles I as a colonel. At the same time, he expanded his Barbadian landed and commercial interests in partnership with Benjamin Berringer.

After the execution of the king, Sir John returned to Barbados, where, despite maintaining their staunch support of Charles Stuart, he and Berringer continued their rise towards the top of the island's society, a process which, by this time, entailed devoting lands to the production of sugar and the acquisition of slave labour. Following the capitulation of the island to the Commonwealth in January 1651/2, Yeamans compounded with the new regime and remained involved in the provincial government while his partner returned to England.

Having weathered the series of political tempests that, as we have seen, the Interregnum generated throughout the English-speaking world, Sir John's star began to ascend again following the Restoration. As it did so, it attracted considerable controversy and opprobrium – this disputatiousness in itself seems to have been a hallmark of the lives of the ambitious in the seventeenth century. First, he married Margaret Berringer, the widow of his partner, in 1661, thereby taking sole control of their joint venture. His marriage, which occurred just ten weeks after the death of Mr Berringer, has attracted the most mud, both from contemporaries and historians. Although the evidence remains sketchy, the rapidity of Mrs Berringer's remarriage, compounded by the newlyweds' fight to vacate a will made by her first husband in England in 1656 in favour of his family there, caused all sorts of rumours and innuendo to flourish in the hothouse environment of Barbadian politics: having maintained an adulterous relationship with Margaret while her husband was still alive, Yeamans supposedly killed Berringer in a duel that arose out of jealousy – or he poisoned him – although no evidence exists to support any of these allegations of murder.[28]

Four years after his marriage, in 1665, Yeamans, notably unlike some of his counterparts under discussion here, was the recipient of a baronetcy from a grateful Charles II for his loyalty to the Stuarts in the 1640s and 1650s. Yet, like the others, Sir John did become involved in efforts to extend English territorial claims, with which the leaders of an overcrowded Barbados had developed a keen interest by this time, on the North American mainland. The Lords Proprietor of Carolina, whose operations received royal imprimatur in 1663, recognized the degree of his influence on the island: they solicited his good offices in recruiting settlers and obtaining supplies there and then appointed him lieutenant-general in charge of the abortive 1665 attempt to settle Cape Fear which came into conflict with Vassall's New England-oriented operation in that region.

Undeterred by this failure, the Carolina proprietors turned to Sir John again in 1669 to assume a similar role in a new settlement venture they had envisioned for the more southerly Port Royal area; as further recognition of his importance and interest, he received the title of landgrave in the aristocracy created under the fundamental constitutions that the lords had devised for their province. Yeamans, however, had to delay his departure for the new colony, ultimately founded at Ashley River, as he had accepted a royal commission to lead the English team charged with negotiating colonial boundaries on the island of St Christopher with the French – a further recognition of his status. He finally completed these duties in 1672 and duly arrived at Charles Town, where he had sent an entourage, including slaves, to prepare a plantation in advance. He spent the last two years of his life overseeing the building the twin foundations of his new estate and his new colony.[29]

All of these examples manifest a substantial degree of similarity in terms of social and political attitude and behaviour despite their differences in matters of religion and in civil war politics. In addition to seeking social, material and political advancement overseas, these men and the rest of their cohort on both sides of the Atlantic shared a broad sensibility – one that remained preeminent until, at least, 1776 – over the proper character of social formation so long as that formation did not interfere unduly with their own ambitions. Even though important differences certainly existed between these colonies (and between the 'Old World' and the 'New') in terms of geography, personal background of the inhabitants, demography, climate and religion, and even though some of these engineers, such as Thompson and Vassall, did not reside permanently in America, a fundamental belief in a socio-political hierarchy in which status derived from the income produced by landed estates remained the benchmark of belief and, thus, advancing one's estate to gentry status remained the primary goal of the ambitious.

At best – at least for those concerned about the character of American distinctiveness, let alone exceptionalism – the degree to which the views and behaviour of those who concentrated their attentions on overseas colonization differed from those who did not remains an open question: factional competition, political plotting, the cultivation of patronage and the thirst for advantage within the official hierarchy remained endemic throughout the early modern English-speaking world despite continuing hand-wringing over the decline of morals and, correspondingly, of society.[30]

At the same time, despite the pleading of the Hakluyts of the world, early modern English governments remained content to delegate responsibility for overseas activity, especially colonization, to 'private' concerns, as it did for most things. And, as we have seen, the impetus for colonization, as with most matters of 'public policy', except religion, warfare and diplomacy, came from outside of Whitehall. Then that monarchy failed; but, ironically, England continued to acquire more territory as it widened its commercial networks and corresponding economic opportunities during almost two decades of socio-political convulsion. The birth of the Protectorate out of those ashes certainly entailed a stronger English state upon which the governments of the later Stuarts built. Yet, responsibility for affairs beyond Europe and its waters, notwithstanding the creation of the 'Lords of Trade and Plantations' in 1675, remained the purview of entities such as the East India Company and the Carolina proprietors. The strength of England, even after 1652, may have been overstated despite the nation's noticeable military improvements cited in Chapter 5 above.[31]

The enduring ambiguities of the 'imperial' situation in the middle of the seventeenth century maintained, paradoxically, a number of important socio-political continuities on both sides of the Atlantic. First, despite the ever-increasing scope of commerce and, thus, importance of merchants, landed income remained both the benchmark of socio-political status and, as the determinant of gentlemanly status, the ultimate goal even for men like Maurice Thompson. Certainly, the promoters of migration to the various colonies continued to recognize this and pitched their recruiting efforts accordingly.[32] Theoretically, then, this land-based hierarchy continued – as it had done for centuries – to provide the means for exchanging deference and condescension – the reciprocity of responsibilities, allegiances, rights and obligations – between the social orders, as articulated most pointedly, but scarcely exclusively, in the manorial systems devised for the colonies of Maryland (1634) and South Carolina (1669) by the proprietors of those colonies.[33]

The endurance of this emphasis on landed income meant that William Claiborne, George Lamberton, Sir John Yeamans and their cohort, by virtue of their positions, continued to serve, as John Rolfe, for instance, had in the latter half of the 1610s, as the points of contact between the governmental and imperial centre – so long as they rode whatever particular political waves emanated from the metropolis – and the localities, just as their counterparts in England continued to do. They also controlled local offices in similarly 'metropolitan' fashion.[34]

Thus, as inhabitants of an empire in which, paradoxically, the imperial centre was often distracted and sometimes non-existent, this group set out the stakes of the social and political development of early modern Anglo-American colonies just as they engineered the expansion and character of English colonial interests. At any point, the central government needed to secure the cooperation of local leadership – even as men jockeyed for entry into and position within that leadership – whether in Berkshire or Barbados and, correspondingly, those local leaders customarily achieved a sort of collective recognition, in addition to their respective individual status, as county gentry. As such, these gentries could – and did – offer grievances and resist, as in the case of the tobacco contract and Virginia discussed in Chapter 5, if they found the government unresponsive to or, worse, aggressive against their interests. But, again paradoxically, the most successful gentlemen – such as the careers sketched here – never restricted their interests to only one locality and, when it suited, became a part of 'the state' as well. Colonials like Rolfe, Claiborne, Yeamans and Lamberton, in extending their influence across the Atlantic as well as around North America and the Caribbean, emulated the example set by the Earls of Dorset and Warwick.[35]

The pursuit of estates in Anglo-America in itself, however, generated two major problems. First, the desire to obtain as much fertile land as possible led to the 'straggling' of plantations and settlements, despite the warnings from Virginia Company officials, colonial governments and other colonizing officials about the lack of security in this sort of arrangement, even as the pressures which colonization brought to bear on indigenous societies, compounded by the devastating effects of epidemic disease, compelled those societies to strike back.[36] These warnings proved prophetic as Indians continued to make devastating attacks on English colonies until the second decade of the eighteenth century: following the disaster of 1622, Opechancanough, now some ninety years old, oversaw another bloody assault on Virginia (perhaps not coincidentally as 'Ingle's Rebellion' was brewing) which killed over five hundred colonists on 18 April 1644 and lasted two years before the old werowance was captured, then murdered by his guard.[37] Thirty years later, 'King Philip' and a confederacy of New England peoples destroyed towns and farms from the Connecticut River Valley to Plymouth sending the 'godly' into a trough of despair about their covenant with their god before the refusal of the Mohawks to assist Philip left him short of numbers and provisions.[38] Between 1715 and 1722, the Yamassee people turned on their former South Carolina trading partners; with their allies, they devastated that colony, driving the survivors of their attack inside the gates of Charles Town before they were rescued by assistance from the Cherokees and from neighbouring colonies.[39]

The second problem for aspiring Anglo-Americans, which they shared with their counterparts in the metropolis, was the acquisition and control of the requisite labour force to turn land – in and of itself useless – into an income-producing estate. As noted in Chapter 4, by the early 1620s, the Virginia planters had begun to supplement their indentured servants – a device which already constituted an 'improvement' on the metropolitan system of servant labour, since the servants served a far longer term than in England and could find those terms increased if they committed various offences – with Africans, although indentured servitude remained the primary means of obtaining labour in Anglo-America at least until the 1680s and an important means (at least on the mainland of North America) throughout the period prior to the inception of the United States.[40]

Correspondingly, by the 1630s, the English, if they had not been fully familiar with the concept of slavery beforehand, had not only become accustomed to employing 'Negroes' on their plantations, but had manifestly begun to seek out their acquisition as slaves: a Captain Thomas Newman of the *Happy* out of Gravesend had instructions, in 1636, to attack Spanish shipping in defence of Providence Island; if he took any prizes 'with Negroes', he was to 'put them into some of our own colonies in Virginia the Leeward Islands, or any other places which you shall find fitting for our profit, having regard to our former instructions concerning such Negroes as shall be fit for our use'.[41] At the same time, in addition to the English traders active on the Gold Coast noted above, the Guinea Company (whose membership included Clobery) had involved themselves in the transatlantic slave trade.[42]

With slavery for 'Negroes' (and for Indians captured in war[43]) having become an accepted part of reality in English America by the 1630s, the significant questions for masters came to be how to acquire slaves and how to 'manage' them. Slavery provided the great advantage of permanent servitude; but the absence of the prospect of freedom along with the barbarous circumstances of their enslavement meant – paradoxically – that there was little, if any, motivation for slaves to work to the satisfaction of masters. Moreover, the extent of the frustration and desperation of the slaves at their circumstances meant that, no matter how much masters tried to sugar-coat the ethnically based version of 'Old World' reciprocity between social orders, the prospect that the slaves would try to alter their circumstances whether by escaping, conspiring to revolt or committing suicide remained all too apparent.[44]

Thus, by the 1630s in Virginia and on Bermuda, Barbados, Providence Island and other island colonies, masters had adopted a labour system which had long ceased to exist in the metropolis. In 1647 on Barbados (twenty years after the colony's founding), according to the early chronicler of the place Richard Ligon, people of African ethnicity comprised 'more than double the numbers of Christians'. Given this demographic reality – which outpaced the African–European ratio elsewhere in English America – the island's planters, probably more so than their counterparts elsewhere by this time, had worked out something of a 'management' method. In addition to practical measures for extracting obedience (and work) from slaves, this early version of the plantation system readily incorporated purported characterizations of 'Negroes' and the corresponding belief that slaves would not resist their bondage, despite clear evidence to the contrary. Inevitably, the slaves responded and negotiation over the character of enslavement continued.[45]

Thus, when several of Colonel Walrond's 'best Negroes' killed themselves ('in a very little time') in the belief that they would be resurrected 'and that they shall go into their own Countrey again, and have their youth renewed', the planter ordered the head of one of the corpses cut off and displayed on a pole. He then summoned his slaves to view the head and asked them if it did not demonstrate 'the main errour' of their thinking; 'convinced by this sad, yet lively spectacle', according to Ligon, 'they changed their opinions; and after that, no more hanged themselves'. In 'acknowledging' Walrond's argument and in other aspects of their behaviour as he observed them, Ligon thus found 'strong motives' to believe 'that there are as honest, faithful, and conscionable people amongst them, as amongst those of Europe, or any other part of the world' – although 'there be a mark set upon these people, which will hardly ever be wip'd off, as of their cruelties when they have advantages, and of their [general] fearfulness and falseness'.[46]

Correspondingly, then, notwithstanding the discovery of a plot of servants 'to fall upon their Masters, and cut all their throats, and by that means, to make themselves only freemen, but Masters of the Island', Ligon proclaimed no such fears existed that 'the Negroes' would 'commit some horrid massacre upon the Christians'. He cited three reasons for this sanguinity. First, the colony had laws prohibiting slaves from touching weapons (although in itself this legislation suggests the existence of fear). Then, he asserted 'that they are held in such awe and slavery, as they are fearful to appear in any daring act; and seeing the mustering of our men, and hearing their Gun-shot (than which nothing is more terrible to them) their spirits are subjugated to so low a condition'. Finally, their diverse origins – 'some from Guinny and Binny [the Gulf of Guinea and Bight of Benin], some from Cutchew [Cacheo, Upper Guinea], some from Angola, and some from the River of Gambia' – meant they spoke different languages and 'one of them understands not another'.[47]

Many masters, as April Lee Hatfield has discussed, had commercial and familial ties which extended beyond their particular colonies and they moved around the Atlantic seaboard and across the ocean, as we have also seen in the present account. These realities facilitated communication and similarity in the way various colonies tried to 'manage' slaves. Although Barbados did not create the first comprehensive 'slave code' of laws until 1661 and did not designate slaves as chattel property until 1668 (models followed by every other English colony south of Connecticut), punishments for slaves such as whipping, branding and slitting of noses, some of which had been applied to whites, had become routine practice.[48]

At the same time, the West Indian planters became involved in sugar cultivation and increasingly so during the period of the civil wars. The wealth generated by the production of this commodity in Brazil and in other parts of the Caribbean was well known. Once it was introduced into the English colonies in the 1640s, the Barbadians developed a sweet tooth as quickly as their counterparts on the mainland had become addicted to tobacco, especially since the island 'sot-weed' had proven unsatisfactory: the islands quickly became denuded of vegetation and almost all of their acreage devoted to the new staple. The character of the work and the hot climate, coupled with the limited availability for land, thanks to the size of the islands, however, meant that fewer and fewer English people migrated there after sugar became entrenched (although the transportation of convicts and prisoners of war, especially of Irish and Scots defeated in the civil wars, continued).[49]

The pursuit of sugar wealth did make Barbados the most populous and wealthy of England's colonies in the seventeenth century. By 1676, the island, only 166 square miles in size, contained a population of approximately 52,000 inhabitants, including almost 32,500 enslaved blacks (more than the rest of the English colonies combined at the time). Sugar also laid the groundwork for the career of Yeamans, whose 'full share of the ruthless opportunism so characteristic of the great planter elite', has come to typify, in the view of most modern students of early modern Anglo-America, the emergence of a distinctive socio-political character of West Indian planters within the history of English colonization.[50]

Thus, according to Ira Berlin's characterization, the socio-economic character of Barbados and the other English West Indian colonies changed dramatically from origins in which 'slavery was just one form of labor among many' and slaveholders, who constituted 'just one portion of a propertied elite', treated 'all subordinates' relatively equally. After the 'sugar revolution' of the 1640s, 'slavery stood at the center of economic production, and the master–slave relationship provided the model for all social relations'. To a somewhat lesser degree, a similar 'process' played out in Virginia after the 'tobacco boom' of the 1620s but without counterpart in more northerly colonies. Consequently, slaveholders became 'the ruling class' and slaveholding became the status to which 'nearly everyone' – even slaves – aspired to belong. By the 1680s, slavery became the preferred labour system from the Chesapeake south to Barbados: those whites who could not compete departed for greener pastures while the planters increased their slaveholdings and plantations and cemented their control over their societies.[51]

But the chronology and thus the emphasis of this analysis miss the mark, since the forms of slavery and servitude which came to develop in America between 1620 and 1650, while crucial to understanding early Anglo-American history, underpinned an enduring socio-political substance which had been readily transplanted from the 'Old World'. Looking at the development of early English America from the 'top down', we see a group of societies necessarily shaped by the character of the migration of people to them. According to the smattering of records we have, those migrants, such as Ligon, decided to 'undertake to run so long a Risco from England' because their lives in the metropolis had become insufferable.[52]

Nevertheless, most of these migrants subscribed to a belief in a land-based hierarchy and its corresponding 'virtues'. The political and meteorological environments of these places, of course, had an impact on the implementation of this frame, but so did the haphazard attention paid by the metropolitan government for the early period of the English Empire in America (and for most of the colonial period of North American history): just as it declined or proved unable to take much initiative in 'empire-building', it neither granted many titles to leading Anglo-Americans nor did it do anything to encourage the growth of an American-based titled aristocracy. Nor, unlike their Spanish counterparts, did the English colonies contain weighty representatives of metropolitan-based entities, such as bishops: their governors – pointedly not viceroys or lord deputies – served one province, while each colony, by virtue of its own charter, enjoyed the power to charter in turn universities, towns and other institutions.[53]

Moreover, those, such as Sir John Harvey and Sir Ferdinando Gorges, who did receive knighthoods before journeying to America and who believed they held vicegerent authority often failed to receive the support they believed was due their station from either colony or metropolis. On the other hand, their enemies, whilst not receiving express validation of their status through the acquisition of a title, managed quite well – socially, economically and politically – on both sides of the Atlantic. While the general absence of what were regarded as the natural leaders of society created a synapse in the normal points of contact between centre and province and made it relatively difficult for successful Anglo-Americans to secure official patronage of the sort their counterparts in the shires – and even Ireland – obtained, people like William Claiborne did what they needed to do to achieve political security in their positions, as we have seen: 'negotiation' between early modern socio-political aspirants occurred around and through the state as much as it did between 'periphery' and 'centre'.[54]

Given the endurance of the expectation that localities, especially distant ones, should have primary responsibility for their own affairs, given the paradoxical involvement of all sorts of people – even the state itself – in early modern English 'empire-building', and given the inevitable tendency of the Claibornes of the world to favour their own interests, it seems remarkable that any sort of meeting of the minds about an imperial relationship came to exist between the imperial 'centre' and the socio-political leadership of its colonies. Yet, at the same time as the Claibornes endeavoured to manage their colonies, they invariably kept tabs on events and personalities 'at home' and made certain to keep in contact with those in a position to render assistance to colonial clients; patrons, for their part, with commercial or landed interests in the colonies, found a transatlantic connection useful as well. Meanwhile, the English government – for bureaucratic, fiscal and philosophical reasons – remained generally content to hover on the fringes of this situation, at least until the perceived need developed, first, to copy the monarchical tone of Louis XIV, and then, ironically, to check the perceived pretences to universal monarchy of the 'Sun King'.[55]

Thus, every English colony had a group which could pass for a ruling gentry by 1658; and, in every case, a 'civil society' with a metropolitan-style political culture formed within the first five years – and customarily sooner – of a colony's existence (Virginia, coming first, took the longest to shed its garrison skin).[56] While these colonial elites certainly lacked the wealth and power of their metropolitan counterpart, they continued to copy its behaviour: from the construction of their houses to the construction of their politics, these 'New Worlds' clearly derived in a collective fashion from the 'Old'. Yet, at the same time, access to the top of the Anglo-American pyramid – which was certainly broader than its European counterpart – seems to have stayed relatively fluid; although the degree of this fluidity, especially when compared to the 'Old World', is a question more generally presumed than analysed.[57]

The tantalizing lack of clarity on the issue of worlds, in turn, leaves open the enduring question of the historiography of early modern Anglo-America: if, as we now well know,[58] early modern Europeans tended to move around quite a bit and, equally undoubtedly, many of them moved to (and from) remote places, even to the extent of creating an 'Atlantic world', how 'new' were the societies that these migrants created? Moreover, scholarly supporters of the idea of a fundamental distinctiveness – not to mention popular celebrants of peculiarly American 'freedom' and 'equality' – must address the substantial number of quintessential early American cases, such as Sir John Yeamans – or George Washington, for that matter – where patronage and other connections, along with landed income, played the same sort of role in socio-political advancement as they did in Europe, and often buttressed by the peculiarly American phenomenon of race-based slavery. While the idea of an 'Atlantic World' devised by modern historians does provide a commendable bridge over the artificial historiographical gap that has developed over the centuries between Africa, the Americas and Europe, the complete absence of the notion from the historical record renders it equally anachronistic: early modern people certainly crossed boundaries, extended their activities to remote places and came into contact with new and different cultures, but, for the most part, they, like William Claiborne, returned to familiar surroundings at the end of the day.[59]

On the other hand, those who decry the 'inequality' of early America as a progenitor of the socio-economic shortcomings of the later United States must confront the paradoxical realities that faith in the socio-political frame provided by landed income and the opportunity to acquire the status and wealth underpinned by estates, as manifested by the repeated advertisement of readily available North American land after 1607, continued to resonate with prospective migrants. It also remains at least arguable that a substantial number of these arrivals advanced themselves where they would not have been able to do so in Europe. Moreover, at the least, even those who did rise spectacularly did not abandon their faith in the system so readily. At the same time, they all too often (and, perhaps, all too readily) resorted to the American expedient of race-based slavery – for generating landed income, for elevating and presenting status, for serving as the bedrock of their societies – a situation which, of course, became even more prevalent with the passage of time. In doing so, then, slave owners found an expedient not only for achieving their socio-economic ambitions, but also for supporting their claims to political power and their presumptions to participate in what passed for imperial government.[60]

This perceived window of opportunity continued to widen through the seventeenth century and the people under discussion here both helped with this widening and in manning the engine room which, accordingly, generated profound changes in the culture and society of England as well as, of course, elsewhere. The pace and greater scope of the chase for new and more profitable commodities in itself constituted such a change, while the wake created by the successful introduction of those products into English society could overwhelm the original ripples caused by their arrival: the eighteenth-century effects of the rapturous reception of tea along with the drink's most illustrious consumer, the restored Charles II, in 1660 ranged, most notably, from the massive increase in the demand for slaves for sugar production to the creation of a designated late-afternoon 'tea-time' to the increased involvement of women in public political life to the further extension and growth of 'market economies' to global war.[61]

Inevitably, some of these changes came to resemble increasingly modern sensibilities. But did, for instance, increased mercantile activity and the corresponding increase in importance of commerce in England, as well as the acquisition and formation of overseas colonies, further an empowering sense of individualism or did they cause a further fraying of the social fabric with fearful consequences, or somewhere in between? Did they create a more egalitarian set of social structures and a 'freer' people altogether in a 'New World'? Or did they unleash untrammelled exploitation and barbarity upon indigenous people, those of African descent, and less fortunate or less competitive European migrants? Or did much of this behaviour fall somewhere in between?

Since these characterizations – and the phenomena which led people to adopt them – have long existed in some form, it is difficult to say; although the versions of metropolitan society which developed in Anglo-American colonies suggest that the fears that overseas migration would cause further unravelling may have been inapposite: it may have been the quality of the fabric itself which was suspect. Correspondingly, does not the history of the early English Empire in America suggest that the natures of the societies which developed across the Atlantic differed in degree of scope amongst themselves as well as between them and the 'Old World' rather than representing the creation of something fundamentally new (let alone improved)? For status, wealth, competition, exploitation, power and a desire for order had crucial and sometimes conflicting parts in all of these places, notwithstanding the various socio-economic differences which formed – some, to be sure, quite palpable. Do the results generated by the behaviour of seventeenth-century English people involved in empire, then, not also suggest that the depth and character – 'progress' – of those changes which occurred will remain, at best, open questions?

NOTES

The following abbreviations are used throughout the notes:

Bodleian	Bodleian Library, University of Oxford.
CO	State Papers, Colonial Office Series, the National Archives of Great Britain, Kew, Richmond, Surrey.
CSPC	W. N. Sainsbury (ed.), *Calendar of State Papers, Colonial Series, 1574–1660, preserved in the State Paper Department of Her Majesty's Public Record Office* (London, 1860).
Hall, *Narratives*	C. C. Hall (ed.), *Narratives of Early Maryland 1633–1683* (New York: Charles Scribner's Sons, 1910).
HCA	High Court of Admiralty Papers, the National Archives of Great Britain, Kew, Richmond, Surrey.
MHM	*Maryland Historical Magazine*.
RVC	S. M. Kingsbury (ed.), *The Records of the Virginia Company of London*, 4 vols (Washington, DC: Library of Congress, 1906–35).
Smith, *Writings*	J. Smith, *Writings with Other Narratives of Roanoke, Jamestown, and the First English Settlement of America*, ed. J. Horn (New York: The Library of America, 2007).
SP	State Papers, Foreign Series, the National Archives of Great Britain, Kew, Richmond, Surrey.
Tyler, *Narratives*	L. G. Tyler (ed.), *Narratives of Early Virginia 1606–1625* (New York: Charles Scribner's Sons, 1907).
VMHB	*Virginia Magazine of History and Biography*.
WMQ	*William and Mary Quarterly*.

Introduction

1. J. Smith, *A True Relation of such Occurrences and Accidents of Noate, as hath Hapned in Virginia, since the first Planting of that Collony, which is now Resident in the South part thereof, till the Last Returne* (1608), in Smith, *Writings*, pp. 5–40, on p. 5.
2. E. S. Morgan, *American Slavery, American Freedom: the Ordeal of Colonial Virginia* (New York: W. W. Norton, 1975), which substantially revised the views of T. J. Werten-

baker, *Virginia under the Stuarts, 1607–1688* (Princeton, NJ: Princeton University Press, 1914).

3. A. U. Abrams, *The Pilgrims and Pocahontas: Rival Myths of American Origin* (Boulder, CO: Westview Press, 1999) (my thanks to Lauric Henneton for this reference); R. H. Rives, 'The Jamestown Celebration of 1857', *VMHB*, 66:3 (1958), pp. 259–71; J. M. Lindgren, '"Whatever is Un-Virginian is Wrong": The APVA's Sense of the Old Dominion', *Virginia Cavalcade*, 38 (1989), pp. 112–23; D. J. Kiracofe, 'The Jamestown Jubilees: "State Patriotism" and Virginia Identity in the Early Nineteenth Century', *VMHB*, 110:1 (2002), pp. 35–68. The career and character of Smith became a centrepiece of this dispute, which required investigation into Ottoman and Habsburg records to resolve, see P. L. Barbour, 'Captain John Smith's Route through Turkey and Russia', *WMQ*, 3rd series, 14:3 (1957), pp. 358–69.

4. See 'The Significance of the Frontier in American History' (1893), in F. J. Turner, *The Frontier in American History* (New York: Henry Holt, 1920). The centenary of the 'frontier thesis' in 1993 sparked a frenzy of reconsideration, e.g. P. N. Limerick, 'Turnerians All: The Dream of a Helpful History in an Intelligible World', *American Historical Review*, 100:3 (1995), pp. 697–716.

5. B. Bailyn, 'Politics and Social Structure in Virginia', in J. M. Smith (ed.), *Seventeenth-Century America: Essays in Colonial History* (Chapel Hill, NC: University of North Carolina Press, 1959), pp. 90–115; E. S. Morgan, 'The First American Boom: Virginia, 1618 to 1630', *WMQ*, 3rd series, 28:2 (1971), pp. 169–98; J. P. Greene, *Pursuits of Happiness: The Social Development of Early Modern British Colonies and the Formation of American Culture* (Chapel Hill, NC: University of North Carolina Press, 1988); L. G. Carr, P. D. Morgan and J. B. Russo (eds), *Colonial Chesapeake Society* (Chapel Hill, NC: University of North Carolina Press, 1988); J. H. Merrell, 'Some Thoughts on Colonial Historians and American Indians', *WMQ*, 3rd series, 46:1 (1989), pp. 94–119; D. K. Richter, 'Whose Indian History?', *WMQ*, 3rd series, 50:2 (1993), pp. 379–93; P. H. Wood, '"I Did the Best I Could for My Day": The Study of Early Black History during the Second Reconstruction, 1960 to 1976', *WMQ*, 3rd series, 35:2 (1978), pp. 185–225; L. G. Carr and L. S. Walsh, 'The Standard of Living in the Colonial Chesapeake', *WMQ*, 3rd series, 45:1 (1988), pp. 135–59; L. G. Carr and L. S. Walsh, 'The Planter's Wife: The Experience of White Women in Seventeenth–Century Maryland', *WMQ*, 3rd series, 34:4 (1977), pp. 542–71; K. M. Brown, *Good Wives, Nasty Wenches, and Anxious Patriarchs: Gender, Race, and Power in Colonial Virginia* (Chapel Hill, NC: University of North Carolina Press, 1996). One of these studies, perhaps not coincidentally written by an Englishman, did track the movement of transplanted English social norms to this part of North America, see J. P. P. Horn, *Adapting to a New World: English Society in the Seventeenth-Century Chesapeake* (Chapel Hill, NC: University of North Carolina Press, 1994).

6. P. C. Mancall, 'Introduction', in P. C. Mancall (ed.), *The Atlantic World and Virginia, 1550–1624* (Chapel Hill, NC: University of North Carolina Press, 2007), pp. 1–26, on p. 2. For a discussion of 'boundary-crossers' and 'cosmopolitans', see A. Games, 'Atlantic History: Definitions, Challenges, and Opportunities', in *American Historical Review*, 111:3 (2006), pp. 741–57; A. Games, 'Beyond the Atlantic: English Globetrotters and Transoceanic Connections', *WMQ*, 3rd series, 63:4 (2006), pp. 675–92; A. Games, 'England's Global Transition and the Cosmopolitans Who Made it Possible', *Shakespeare Studies*, 35 (2007), pp. 24–31. For a discussion of an Atlantic perspective, see B. Bailyn, *Atlantic History: Concepts and Contours* (Cambridge, MA: Harvard University Press, 2005); K. O. Kupperman, *The Jamestown Project* (Cambridge, MA: Harvard Univer-

sity Press, 2007); R. Appelbaum and J. W. Sweet (eds), *Envisioning an English Empire: Jamestown and the Making of the North Atlantic World* (Philadelphia, PA: University of Pennsylvania Press, 2005); A. L. Hatfield, *Atlantic Virginia: Intercolonial Relations in the Seventeenth Century* (Philadelphia, PA: University of Pennsylvania Press, 2004); D. Armitage and M. Braddick (eds), *The British Atlantic World, 1500–1800* (New York and Houndmills, Hampshire: Palgrave Macmillan, 2002).

7. I. Berlin, *Generations of Captivity: A History of African-American Slaves* (Cambridge, MA: Harvard University Press, 2003); P. D. Morgan, *Slave Counterpoint: Black Culture in the Eighteenth-Century Chesapeake and Lowcountry* (Chapel Hill, NC: University of North Carolina Press, 1998).

8. For Armitage's characterizations, see Armitage and Braddick, 'Introduction' and Armitage, 'Three Concepts of Atlantic History', in Armitage and Braddick (eds), *The British Atlantic World*, pp. 1–7, 11–27. For the 'unhelpfulness' of these types of 'Atlantic history' and other 'recent historiographic trends concerned with early modern America', see 'Introduction: Connecting and Disconnecting with America', in A. I. Macinnes and A. H. Williamson (eds), *Shaping the Stuart World, 1603–1714: The Atlantic Connection* (Leiden and Boston, MA: Brill Academic Publishers, 2006), pp. 1–30, on pp. 1–2.

9. Kupperman, *The Jamestown Project*, pp. 1–11.

10. J. R. Seeley, *The Expansion of England: Two Courses of Lectures* (1895; Chicago, IL: University of Chicago Press, 1971), p. 8. Perhaps significantly, for all of the impact they generated respectively, neither Seeley's nor Turner's 'thesis' ever developed into a monograph.

11. See e.g., T. Cogswell, R. Cust and P. Lake (eds), *Politics, Religion, and Popularity in Early Stuart Britain: Essays in Honour of Conrad Russell* (Cambridge: Cambridge University Press, 2002); M. Kishlansky, *A Monarchy Transformed: Britain, 1603–1714* (London: Penguin, 1996); R. Cust and A. Hughes (eds), *Conflict in Stuart England: Studies in Religion and Politics, 1603–1642* (London: Longman, 1989); T. Harris, *London Crowds in the Reign of Charles II: Propaganda and Politics from the Restoration until the Exclusion Crisis* (Cambridge: Cambridge University Press, 1987); T. Harris, *Politics under the Later Stuarts: Party Conflict in a Divided Society, 1660–1715* (London: Longman, 1993); J. Scott, *England's Troubles: Seventeenth-Century English Political Instability in European Context* (Cambridge: Cambridge University Press, 2000); J. C. D. Clark, *English Society, 1688–1832: Ideology, Social Structure, and Political Practice during the Ancien Regime*, 2nd edn (Cambridge: Cambridge University Press, 2000); J. C. D. Clark, *The Language of Liberty, 1660–1832: Political Discourse and Social Dynamics in the Anglo-American World* (Cambridge: Cambridge University Press, 1994). In addition to the latter title and those cited in notes 8 and 12, other works which have incorporated England's colonies include D. Cressy, *Coming Over: Migration and Communication between England and New England in the Seventeenth Century* (Cambridge: Cambridge University Press, 1987); D. Cressy, *Bonfires and Bells: National Memory and the Protestant Calendar in Elizabethan and Stuart England* (London: Weidenfeld and Nicolson, 1989).

12. M. Braddick, *State Formation in Early Modern England, c. 1550–1700* (Cambridge: Cambridge University Press, 2000), pp. 397–8, and see also pp. 16–20, 96–100; D. Armitage, 'Greater Britain: A Useful Category of Analysis?', *American Historical Review*, 104:2 (1999), pp. 427–45.

13. Braddick, *State Formation in Early Modern England*, pp. 398–404.

14. Ibid., pp. 404–19.

15. D. Armitage, *The Ideological Origins of the British Empire* (Cambridge: Cambridge University Press, 2001), esp. pp. 16–23, 197–98. D. H. Sacks argues more forcefully for a characterization of the younger Richard Hakluyt as an imperialist with an avowedly Protestant ideology in 'Discourses of Western Planting: Richard Hakluyt and the Making of the Atlantic World', in Mancall (ed.), *The Atlantic World and Virginia*, pp. 410–53.
16. Horn, *Adapting to a New World*.
17. Bailyn, 'Politics and Social Structure in Virginia'; Morgan, 'The First American Boom'.
18. L. H. Roper, 'Big Fish in a Bigger Transatlantic Pond: The Social and Political Leadership of Early Modern Anglo-American Colonies', in C. Laux, F.-J. Ruggiu and P. Singaravelou (eds), *Les élites européennes dans les colonies du début du XVI siècle au milieu du XXe siècle* (Bern: Peter Lang, forthcoming).
19. The standard account remains W. F. Craven, *Dissolution of the Virginia Company: The Failure of a Colonial Experiment* (1932; Gloucester, MA: Peter Smith, 1964).
20. See e.g., Mancall (ed.), *Virginia and the Atlantic World*.
21. C. Dyer, *An Age of Transition? Economy and Society in England in the Late Middle Ages* (Oxford: Clarendon Press, 2001); M. Zell (ed.), *Early Modern Kent, 1540–1640* (Woodbridge, Suffolk: Boydell Press, 2000).
22. A. Macfarlane, *The Origins of English Individualism: The Family, Property, and Social Transition* (Cambridge: Cambridge University Press, 1978); Greene, *Pursuits of Happiness*.
23. Despite the exhaustive efforts of Joyce Hoad. I am grateful to Mrs Hoad for a series of discussions about Rolfe and his world.
24. J. Rolfe, *A True Relation of the State of Virginia lefte by Sir Thomas Dale Knight in May last 1616* (1617), in Smith, *Writings*, pp. 1174–85.
25. See e.g., R. Johnson, *Nova Britannia Offering Most Excellent Fruits by Planting in Virginia* (1609), in *American Colonial Tracts Monthly*, 1:6 (1897–8); R. Johnson, *The New Life of Virginia Declaring the Former Success and Present Estate of the Plantation, being the Second Part of Nova Britannia* (1612), in *American Colonial Tracts Monthly*, 1:7 (April–May 1897); cf. M. Braddick, 'Civility and Authority', in Armitage and Braddick (eds), *The British Atlantic World*, pp. 93–112.
26. This pattern continued throughout the colonial period of North American history, see e.g., L. H. Roper, *Conceiving Carolina: Proprietors, Planters, and Plots, 1662–1729* (New York and Houndmills, Hampshire: Palgrave Macmillan, 2004).
27. For England's medieval empire, see J. Gillingham, 'Images of Ireland 1170–1600: The Origins of English Imperialism', *History Today*, 37:2 (1987), pp. 16–22; J. Gillingham, 'The Beginnings of English Imperialism', *Journal of Historical Sociology*, 5:4 (1992), pp. 392–409; J. Gillingham, *The English in the Twelfth Century: Imperialism, National Identity, and Political Values* (Woodbridge, Suffolk, and Rochester, NY: Boydell Press, 2000). For migration, see Z. Ravi, 'The Myth of the Immutable English Family', *Past and Present*, 140 (1993), pp. 3–44; P. McClure, 'Patterns of Migration in the Late Middle Ages: The Evidence of English Place-Name Surnames', *Economic History Review*, 2nd series, 32:2 (1979), pp. 167–82.
28. P. Sidney, *The Countesse of Pembrokes Arcadia* (London, 1590); M. Wroth, *The Countesse of Mountgomeries Urania* (London, 1621).
29. P. E. J. Hammer, *The Polarization of English Politics: The Political Career of Robert Devereux, 2nd Earl of Essex, 1585–1597* (Cambridge: Cambridge University Press, 1999).

30. Cf. D. B. Quinn, *Raleigh and the British Empire* (London: English Universities Press, 1962); B. Schmidt, 'Reading Ralegh's America: Texts, Books, and Readers in the Early Modern Atlantic World', in Mancall (ed.), *The Atlantic World and Virginia*, pp. 454–88.
31. By assassination, apparently, in Marlowe's case; C. Nicholl, *The Reckoning: The Murder of Christopher Marlowe* (Chicago, IL: University of Chicago Press, 1992) offers a painstaking recreation of the playwright's world.
32. L. H. Roper, 'Unmasquing the Connections between Jacobean Politics and Colonization: The Circle of Anna of Denmark and the Beginning of the English Empire, 1614–1618', in C. Levin, J. E. Carney and D. Barrett-Graves (eds), *High and Mighty Queens of Early Modern England* (New York: Palgrave Macmillan, 2003), pp. 45–59.
33. J. L. Barroll, *Anna of Denmark, Queen of England: A Cultural Biography* (Philadelphia, PA: University of Pennsylvania Press, 2001).
34. The view of another redoubtable Victorian, S. R. Gardiner, *History of England from the Accession of James I to the Outbreak of the Civil War*, 10 vols (London: Longman, Green, and Co., 1883–4), vol. 3, p. 294, has remained current.
35. W. M. Billings, *A Little Parliament: The Virginia General Assembly in the Seventeenth Century* (Richmond, VA: Library of Virginia, 2007).
36. L. H. Roper, 'Charles I, Virginia, and the Idea of Atlantic History', *Itinerario*, 30:2 (2006), pp. 33–53. Claiborne and Clobery had a falling out and their dispute reached the High Court of Admiralty, see 'Claiborne v Clobery in the High Court of Admiralty', *MHM*, 23 (1932), pp. 21–3, 193–8, 208–11.
37. 'Proceedings of the Council of Maryland, 1667–1687/8', *Archives of Maryland Online*, at http://www.aomol.net/html/index.html, 5:156–239.
38. W. M. Billings, *Sir William Berkeley and the Forging of Colonial Virginia* (Baton Rouge, LA: Louisiana State University Press, 2004); L. H. Roper and B. Van Ruymbeke (eds), *Constructing Early Modern Empires: Proprietary Ventures in the Atlantic World, 1500–1750* (Leiden and Boston, MA: Brill Academic Publishers, 2007); cf. Elizabeth Mancke, 'Empire and State' in Armitage and Braddick (eds), *The British Atlantic World*, pp. 175–95.

1 Deep Background

1. R. Hakluyt, 'Discourse of Western Planting' (1584), in *The Original Writings and Correspondence of the Two Richard Hakluyts*, E. G. R. Taylor, 2 vols (London: Hakluyt Society, 1935), vol. 2, pp. 211–326, on p. 211.
2. P. C. Mancall, *Hakluyt's Promise: An Elizabethan's Obsession for an English America* (New Haven, CT: Yale University Press, 2007); D. H. Sacks, 'Discourses of Western Planting: Richard Hakluyt and the Making of the Atlantic World' in Mancall (ed.), *The Atlantic World and Virginia*, pp. 410–53.
3. See e.g., P. Banerjee, 'The White Othello: Turkey and Virginia in John Smith's *True Travels*', and S. Iwanisziw, 'England, Morocco, and Global Geopolitical Upheaval', in Appelbaum and Sweet (eds), *Envisioning an English Empire*, pp. 135–51, 152–71; E. A. McDougall, 'The Caravel and the Caravan: Reconsidering Received Wisdom in the Sixteenth-Century Sahara', and J. H. Sweet, 'African Identity and Slave Resistance in the Portuguese Atlantic', in Mancall (ed.), *The Atlantic World and Virginia*, pp. 143–69, 225–49.

4. B. Bailyn, *The Peopling of British North America: An Introduction* (New York: Alfred A. Knopf, 1986); Greene, *Pursuits of Happiness*; A. Games, *Migration and the Origins of the English Atlantic World* (Cambridge, MA: Harvard University Press, 1999).
5. M. Aston, 'English Ruins and English History: the Dissolution and the Sense of the Past', *Journal of the Warburg and Courtauld Institutes*, 36 (1973), pp. 231–55.
6. M. Bailey, 'The Commercialisation of the English Economy, 1086–1500', *Journal of Medieval History*, 24:3 (1998), pp. 297–311, on p. 298.
7. Ibid., p. 299.
8. R. Britnell, 'Town Life', in R. Horrox and W. M. Ormrod (eds), *A Social History of England, 1200–1500* (Cambridge: Cambridge University Press, 2006), pp. 134–78; C. Dyer, 'Small Places with Large Consequences: The Importance of Small Towns in England, 1000–1540', *Historical Research*, 75:187 (2002), pp. 1–24; J. Russell, 'Medieval Midland and Northern Migration to London, 1100–1365', *Speculum*, 34:4 (1959), pp. 641–5.
9. T. More, *Utopia* (1516), ed. G. M. Logan and R. M. Adams (Cambridge: Cambridge University Press, 1989), pp. 18–20; J. Winthrop, 'A Modell of Christian Charity' (1630), in E. S. Morgan (ed.), *The Founding of Massachusetts: Historians and the Sources* (Indianapolis, IN: Bobbs-Merrill Co., 1964), pp. 190–204. By 1500, only a third of English land, according to a recent estimate, remained common, of which only 4 per cent ('waste') offered open access, see G. Clark and A. Clark, 'Common Rights to Land in England, 1475–1839', *Journal of Economic History*, 61:4 (2001), pp. 1009–36. For medieval social mobility, see P. C. Madden, 'Social Mobility', in Horrox and Ormrod (eds), *A Social History of England*, pp. 113–33. For English overseas trade, see M. Rorke, 'English and Scottish Overseas Trade, 1300–1600', *Economic History Review*, 59:2 (2006), pp. 265–88.
10. E. A. Wrigley and R. S. Schofield, *The Population of England, 1541–1871* (Cambridge, MA: Harvard University Press, 1981), pp. 81–2 (years of London plague), 167 (baptism and burial figures), 208–9 (population of England), 234 (life expectancy); R. Tittler, *Townspeople and Nation: English Urban Experiences, 1540–1640* (Stanford, CA: Stanford University Press, 2001), p. 32 (London population figure).
11. Tittler, *Townspeople and Nation*, p. 7; J. Guy, 'The 1590s: The Second Reign of Elizabeth I?', in J. Guy (ed.), *The Reign of Elizabeth I: Court and Culture in the Last Decade* (Cambridge: Cambridge University Press, 1995), pp. 1–19, on p. 10.
12. The best estimates place the population of England at approximately 2.8 million in the 1370s, extrapolated from the poll tax of 1377, and 2.3 million in the 1520s, see M. Bailey, 'Demographic Decline in Late Medieval England: Some Thoughts on Recent Research', *The Economic History Review*, n.s., 49:1 (1996), pp. 1–19, on p. 1. On the other hand, even in the 1530s, a variety of observers remarked upon the apparent underpopulation of England, see J. Hammer, *Plague, Population, and the English Economy, 1348–1550* (London: Macmillan, 1977), pp. 63–7. Conceivably, the population could have reached between 4.5 and 6 million inhabitants at the onset of the Black Death and the Hundred Years War (p. 68).
13. W. Harrison, *The Description of England: The Classic Contemporary Account of Tudor Social Life* (1587), ed. G. Edelen (New York: Dover Publications, Inc., 1994), pp. 257–8; P. Clark, 'The Migrant in Kentish Towns 1580–1640', in P. Clark and P. Slack (eds), *Crisis and Order in English Towns 1500–1700: Essays in Urban History* (Toronto and Buffalo, NY: University of Toronto Press, 1972), pp. 117–63.

14. Tittler, *Townspeople and Nation*, pp. 11–18. The question remains open for scholars of early modern English religion as well, see J. Craig, 'Reformers, Conflict, and Revisionism', *Historical Journal*, 42:1 (1999), pp. 1–23. For the role of conscience in the confessional polemics of the sixteenth and seventeenth centuries, see J. Wright, 'The World's Worst Worm: Conscience and Conformity during the English Reformation', *Sixteenth Century Journal*, 30:1 (1999), pp. 113–33.
15. S. Brigden, 'Religion and Social Obligation in Early Sixteenth-Century London', *Past and Present*, 103 (May 1984), pp. 67–112; C. W. D'Alton, 'Cuthbert Tunstall and Heresy in Essex and London, 1528', *Albion*, 35:2 (2003), pp. 210–28; J. W. Martin, 'Elizabethan Familists and English Separatism', *Journal of British Studies*, 20:1 (1980), pp. 53–73.
16. See e.g., Anon., *Some Reasons Humbly Offered to the Consideration of the Parliament for the Continuance of the Writs of Capias, and Process of Arrest, in Actions of Debt, &c.* (London, 1671); K. Wrightson, *English Society, 1580–1680* (New Brunswick, NJ: Rutgers University Press, 1982), pp. 121–82.
17. *A Relation of Maryland* (1635), in Hall, *Narratives*, pp. 70–112, on p. 92. Important vestiges of this landed system, such as the property tax and escheat, remain evident in the United States even today. For Cranfield, see M. Prestwich, *Cranfield: Politics and Profits under the Early Stuarts* (Oxford: Clarendon Press, 1966).
18. For the career of Essex, see Hammer, *The Polarization of English Politics*; for Buckingham, see R. Lockyer, *Buckingham: The Life and Political Career of George Villiers, First Duke of Buckingham, 1592–1628* (London: Longman, 1981).
19. S. Hindle, *The State and Social Change in Early Modern England, c. 1550–1640* (New York: St Martin's Press, 2000), pp. 1–36 (quotation on p. 7); G. E. Aylmer, 'Buckingham as an Administrative Reformer?', *English Historical Review*, 105:415 (1990), pp. 355–62; M. B. Young, 'Illusions of Grandeur and Reform at the Jacobean Court: Cranfield and the Ordnance', *Historical Journal*, 22:1 (1979), pp. 53–73.
20. A. Wall, 'Faction in Local Politics, 1580–1620: Struggles for Supremacy in Wiltshire', *Wiltshire Archaeological Magazine*, 72/3 (1980), pp. 119–33, on pp. 123–4.
21. P. Hyde and M. Zell, 'Governing the County', M. Zell, 'Landholding and the Land Market in Early Modern Kent', J. Thirsk, 'Agriculture in Kent, 1540–1640', and J. Eales, 'The Rise of Ideological Politics in Kent, 1558–1640', all in Zell (ed.), *Early Modern Kent*, pp. 7–38, 39–74, 75–103, 279–313.
22. N. Cuddy, 'The Conflicting Loyalties of a "Vulgar Counselor": The Third Earl of Southampton, 1597–1624', in A. Fletcher and P. Roberts (eds), *Religion, Culture, and Society in Early Modern Britain: Essays in Honour of Patrick Collinson* (Cambridge: Cambridge University Press, 1994), pp. 121–50.
23. Sir William Berkeley to Edward Hyde, Earl of Clarendon, 30 March 1663, in W. M. Billings (ed.), *The Papers of Sir William Berkeley* (Richmond, VA: Library of Virginia, 2007), pp. 189–91, on p. 191. All dates from the sources are rendered Old Style.
24. M. Zell, 'Walter Morrell and the New Draperies Project, c. 1603–1631', *Historical Journal*, 44:3 (2001), pp. 651–75; T. Cogswell, '"In the Power of the State": Mr Anys's Project and the Tobacco Colonies, 1616–1628', *English Historical Review*, 123:500 (2008), pp. 35–64; A. Friis, *Alderman Cockayne's Project and the Cloth Trade: The Commercial Policy of England in its Main Aspects, 1603–1625* (London, 1927).
25. There has been a debate over whether the collapse of the Antwerp entrepôt compelled English traders to pursue new markets or whether a group of new merchants, keen on supplanting their predecessors, went after new opportunities on their own initiative as

part of an attempt to supplant the old order (socio-political, in the end, as well as commercial), see e.g., R. Brenner, 'The Civil War Politics of London's Merchant Community', *Past and Present*, 58 (1973), pp. 53–107, and R. Brenner, *Merchants and Revolution: Commercial Change, Political Conflict, and London's Overseas Traders, 1550–1653* (1993; London: Verso, 2003), esp. pp. 199–315. Such a proposition appears impossible to test.

26. Cf. e.g., A. Fitzmaurice, *Humanism and America: An Intellectual History of English Colonisation, 1500–1625* (Cambridge: Cambridge University Press, 2003); A. B. Haskell, 'The Affections of the People: Ideology and the Politics of State Building in Colonial Virginia' (PhD dissertation, Johns Hopkins University, 2004); E. Rose, 'The Politics of Pathos: Richard Frethorne's Letters Home', in Appelbaum and Sweet (eds), *Envisioning an English Empire*, pp. 92–108.

2 Genesis

1. Johnson, *The New Life of Virginia*, p. 3.
2. J. Brereton, *A Briefe and True Relation of the Discouerie of the North Part of Virginia* (London, 1602); D. B. Quinn, 'James I and the Beginnings of Empire in America', *Journal of Imperial and Commonwealth History*, 2 (1974), pp. 135–52; J. Lorimer, 'The Failure of the English Guiana Ventures 1595–1667 and James I's Foreign Policy', *Journal of Imperial and Commonwealth History*, 21 (1993), pp. 1–30; J. Lorimer (ed.), *English and Irish Settlement on the River Amazon, 1550–1646* (London: Hakluyt Society, 1989), *passim* and pp. 69–72 (for the Amazon Company). The English founded their colonies on St Christopher and Barbados at the time of the breakdown of the 'Spanish Match' between Prince Charles and the Infanta followed by war with Spain. On the imperial claims and activities of James VI and I within the British Isles, see D. Armitage, 'Making the Empire British: Scotland in the Atlantic World, 1542–1707', *Past and Present*, 155 (May 1997), pp. 34–63, on pp. 42–54.
3. D. B. Quinn, 'Thomas Hariot and the Virginia Voyages of 1602', *WMQ*, 3rd series, 27:2 (1970), pp. 268–81; W. F. Gookin, 'Who Was Bartholomew Gosnold?', *WMQ*, 3rd series, 6:3 (1949), pp. 398–415. Southampton may have been a backer of these voyages, see D. B. Quinn, *England and the Discovery of America, 1481–1620* (New York: Alfred A. Knopf, 1974), pp. 382–3.
4. D. Armitage, 'Literatures and Empire', in N. P. Canny (ed.), *The Origins of Empire*, vol. 1 in W. R. Louis (ed.), *The Oxford History of the British Empire*, 5 vols (Oxford: Oxford University Press, 1998–2000), pp. 99–123, on pp. 99 (quoting Blake), 122.
5. According to Fitzmaurice, the 'humanism' of Virginia's backers, as opposed to the pursuit of opportunity, constituted the primary impulse of early English colonization, see *Humanism and America*.
6. Cuddy, 'The Conflicting Loyalties of a "Vulgar Counselor"'; M. James, 'At a Crossroads of the Political Culture: the Essex Revolt', in M. James (ed.), *Society, Politics and Culture: Studies in Early Modern England* (Cambridge: Cambridge University Press, 1988), pp. 416–65; P. E. J. Hammer, 'Patronage at Court, Faction and the Earl of Essex', in Guy (ed.), *The Reign of Elizabeth I*, pp. 65–86; L. L. Peck, *Northampton: Patronage and Policy at the Court of James I* (London and Boston, MA: Allen & Unwin, 1982), pp. 40, 70–4.
7. Coincidentally, at the accession of James, when Southampton and his friends were rehabilitated, Ralegh and several others who had battled with the Essex faction were charged

with treason. For an episode from the stormy history of Essex and Ralegh, see 'The Journey of Cadiz by Sir Francis Vere', [1597], Osborn Shelves fb 21/8v, James Marshall and Marie-Louise Osborn Collection, Beinecke Rare Book and Manuscript Library, Yale University.

8. J. L. Barroll, 'The Court of the First Stuart Queen', in L. L. Peck (ed.), *The Mental World of the Jacobean Court* (Cambridge: Cambridge University Press, 1992), pp. 191–208; J. L. Barroll, 'The Arts at the English Court of Anna of Denmark', in S. P. Cerasano and M. Wynne-Davies (eds), *Readings in Renaissance Women's Drama: Criticism, History, and Performance, 1594–1998* (London and New York: Routledge, 1998), pp. 47–59.

9. Cf. H. M. Jones, 'The Colonial Impulse: An Analysis of the "Promotion" Literature of Colonization', *Proceedings of the American Philosophical Society*, 90 (1946), pp. 131–61. Subsequent generations of writers, while jettisoning Jones's favourable interpretation, have retained his focus on the purported links between English colonization and literature, both promotional and theatrical, see G. Will, 'Literary Politics', S. Greenblatt, 'The Best Way to Kill Our Literary Inheritance is to Turn it into a Decorous Celebration of the New World Order', P. Brown, '"This Thing of Darkness I Acknowledge Mine": *The Tempest* and the Discourse of Colonialism', and F. Barker and P. Hulme, 'Nymphs and Reapers Heavily Vanish: The Discursive Contexts of *The Tempest*', all in G. Graff and J. Phelan (eds), *The Tempest: A Case Study in Critical Controversy* (Boston, MA: Bedford/ St Martin's, 2000), pp. 110–13, 113–15, 205–29, and 229–46.

10. Marston fled to France, but Chapman and Jonson appealed successfully to their patron, the Countess of Bedford, for her help in securing their release from prison. The offending passages were removed for the second edition. The play's lampooning of colonization arises from its general critique of early Jacobean behaviour – female as well as male, cf. Brown, *Good Wives, Nasty Wenches and Anxious Patriarchs*, pp. 53–4.

11. *Eastward Hoe!*, II.ii.146–9, 162–9; references to the play come from C. H. Herford and Percy Simpson (eds), *Works of Ben Jonson*, 10 vols (Oxford: Clarendon Press, 1932), vol. 4, pp. 489–619.

12. *Eastward Hoe!*, III.iii.14–20.

13. *Eastward Hoe!*, III.iii.25–54.

14. *Eastward Hoe!*, IV.i.179. The reference to 'thirty pound knights' comes from the budgetary expedient devised by James I to sell baronetcies at that price to those with the ready cash. For Utopian attitudes, see More, *Utopia*, pp. 61–5.

15. *Eastward Hoe!*, IV.ii.62–4, 214–20.

16. *Eastward Hoe!*, V.v.205–10.

17. The comic context of this quasi-subversive attempt to skip up the social ladder has an echo in the drunken plot of Caliban, Stephano and Trinculo to overthrow established authority in *The Tempest* discussed below. Tristan Marshall includes *Eastward Hoe!* in his excellent discussion of the context in which Shakespeare wrote his play, as one of the attacks of 'players' on plantations, but does not provide a further analysis of the work, nor does he assess the musings of Gonzalo and company in terms of the promotional literature in the way it is discussed here, see Marshall, '*The Tempest* and the British Imperium in 1611', *Historical Journal*, 41:2 (1998), pp. 375–400, on pp. 388–90, 397–9. Jean Howard argues that the play actually celebrates this subversion and the individualistic, acquisitive behaviour which drove it, as manifestations of an increasingly self-confident City. Accordingly, she suggests, Quicksilver duped the earnest new magistrate and the stolid Touchstone into accepting his reformation, see *Theater of a City: The Places of London Comedy, 1598–1642* (Philadelphia, PA: University of Pennsylvania Press, 2007),

pp. 98–105. Unfortunately, the play provides no evidence of this; moreover, it offers no prospect of reformation for Sir Petronel Flash and the rest of his company.
18. For Newport, see K. R. Andrews, *Elizabethan Privateering: English Privateering during the Spanish War, 1585–1603* (Cambridge: Cambridge University Press, 1964), p. 86; for Gosnold, see Gookin, 'Who was Bartholomew Gosnold?', pp. 399–400.
19. Morgan, *American Slavery, American Freedom*, pp. 44–130.
20. Johnson, *Nova Britannia*, pp. 10, 21–2.
21. W. Barret, *A True Declaration of the Estate of the Colonie in Virginia* (1610), in P. Force (ed.), *Tracts and Other Papers Related to the Settlement of the United States*, 4 vols (Washington, DC, 1838–46), vol. 3, pp. 8–12, 15–17, 20–1. As noted in Chapter 1, Fitzmaurice, in *Humanism and America*, believes that we should take the civic characterizations that the company made of its undertaking at face value.
22. The vast Jamestown literature dates practically from the moment the colonists took their first steps on American shores. In addition to the works discussed herein, e.g., Rolfe, *A True Relation of the State of Virginia*; J. Smith, *The Generall Historie of Virginia, New-England, and the Summer Isles* (1624), in Smith, *Writings*, pp. 199–670, subsequent accounts include, but are by no means limited to, R. Beverly, *The History and Present State of Virginia* (London, 1705); A. M. Brown (ed.), *The Genesis of the United States*, 2 vols (New York, 1899–1901); Craven, *The Dissolution of the Virginia Company*; B. Bailyn, 'Politics and Social Structure in Virginia'; K. O. Kupperman, 'The Puzzle of the American Climate in the Early Colonial Period', *American Historical Review*, 87:5 (1982), pp. 1262–89; Morgan, *American Slavery, American Freedom*; J. Horn, *A Land As God Made It* (New York: Basic Books, 2005).
23. K. O. Kupperman, *Indians and English: Facing Off in Early America* (Ithaca, NY: Cornell University Press, 2000); in a more 'popular' vein, see D. A. Price, *Love and Hate in Jamestown: John Smith, Pocahontas, and the Heart of a New Nation* (New York: Alfred A. Knopf, 2003). Shakespeare's status as the golden boy of the golden age of English theatre has inevitably given 'the Bard' the most prominent role in efforts, most recently from a dismayed perspective, that seek to link 'English literature' with 'English colonialism', see e.g., B. Fuchs, 'Conquering Islands: Contextualizing *The Tempest*', *Shakespeare Quarterly*, 48:1 (1997), pp. 45–62; 'Introduction', and P. Hulme, 'Postcolonial Theory and Early America: An Approach from the Caribbean', in R. B. St George (ed.), *Possible Pasts: Becoming Colonial in Early America* (Ithaca, NY: Cornell University Press, 2000), pp. 1–29, on p. 22, and pp. 33–48, on pp. 42–5; R. Takaki, 'The "Tempest" in the Wilderness', in Graff and Phelan (eds), *The Tempest*, pp. 140–72.
24. Marshall, '*The Tempest* and the British Imperium in 1611'; R. Wilson, 'Voyage to Tunis: New History and the Old World of *The Tempest*', *ELH*, 64:2 (1997), pp. 333–57; cf. V. M. Vaughan and A. T. Vaughan (eds), *The Tempest* (London, 1999, the Arden Shakespeare Edition), pp. 39–54 (all references to the play itself come from this edition).
25. The 'Bermudas' reference does not, of course, mean that the play was supposed to take place in the Americas; rather, Prospero had ordered Ariel 'to fetch dew' from there (I.ii.228–9). For a discussion of *The Tempest* and the 'New World', see B. J. Sokol, 'Text-in-History: *The Tempest* and New World Cultural Encounter', in E. D. Hill and W. Kerrigan (eds), *The Wit to Know: Essays on English Renaissance Literature for Edward Taylor* (Fairfield, CO: George Herbert Journal Special Studies and Monographs, 2000), pp. 21–40. For the classic account of the relationship between Southampton and Shakespeare, see A. L. Rowse, *Shakespeare's Southampton, Patron of Virginia* (New York: Harper & Row, 1965).

26. *The Tempest*, I.i.10–25. D. Norbrook, "'What Cares these Roarers for the Name of King?'": Language and Utopia in *The Tempest*', in G. McMullan and J. Hope (eds), *The Politics of Tragicomedy: Shakespeare and After* (London and New York: Routledge, 1992), pp. 21–54.
27. Even Caliban, lifelong resident, famously remarks on the mysterious 'sounds and sweet airs' of the place (III.ii.135–43).
28. *The Tempest*, II.i.37, 40, 44–5.
29. *The Tempest*, II.i.46–62.
30. *The Tempest*, II.i.144, 148–65.
31. *The Tempest*, IV.i.188–92, II.ii.347–9, 364–6.
32. This famous speech has provided the foundation for myriad conceptions of the play as proto-colonialist, *viz.* that Prospero, representing some sort of English (or, more generically, European) colonial presence, seized the island from its 'rightful owner', Caliban (a purported representation of an 'Indian'), and then enslaved him. Unfortunately, this reading, as Dr Marshall has pointed out (almost 400 years after the play was first performed), regarding the fictional island as America, neglects to take into account actual English views of indigenous Americans prior to 1622, while Caliban himself was the offspring of the witch Sycorax, an interloper and enslaver (of Ariel) herself, see '*The Tempest* and British Imperium in 1611', pp. 379–87. It also neglects the important realities that, first, Prospero was not a 'colonist', but an exile and, second, the leading 'Europeans' leave the island at the end of the play.
33. *The Tempest*, I.ii.352, e.g., II.ii.1–17. Cf. A. Gurr, 'Industrious Ariel and Idle Caliban', in J.-P. Maquerlot and M. Willems (eds), *Travel and Drama in Shakespeare's Time* (Cambridge: Cambridge University Press, 1996), pp. 193–208.
34. *The Tempest*, II.i.113–15, III.ii.1–150, IV.i.195–257.
35. *The Tempest*, V.i.274–5, 295–8. Prospero implies that Stephano, 'who would be king' of the island, Trinculo and Caliban would stay behind when the other Europeans departed for Italy (V.i.287).
36. *The Tempest*, IV.i.36, II.i.198–309, III.iii.13–18.
37. *The Tempest*, Epilogue 3, III.iii.53, V.i.124–8.
38. See e.g., *A True and Sincere Declaration of the Purpose and Ends of the Plantation begun in Virginia* (London, 1610), p. 2; William Crashaw, *A New-Yeeres Gift to Virginiea, a Sermon Preached in London before the Right Honourable the Lord Lawarre, Lord Gouernour and Captaine Generall of Virginea, and others of his Maiesties Counsell for that Kingdome, and the Rest of the Aduenturers in that Plantation* (London, 1610), f. C3r. According to Fitzmaurice, a leading non-clerical advocate of the Virginia enterprise, Alderman Robert Johnson (quoted at the beginning of this chapter), drew on the idea of *grandezza*, applauding a commitment to the 'virtuous' pursuit of commercial wealth as the best method of combating Spanish pretensions to universal monarchy and promoting English interests – articulated by Giovanni Botero. Given Alderman Johnson's role in the dispute which fatally wracked the Virginia Company in the early 1620s (for which see Chapter 4), it remains unclear to what degree contemporaries (at least his opponents) regarded his career as 'virtuous' and, correspondingly, how attractive they found his views (although Johnson's translations of Botero had four editions), which were somewhat at odds with prevailing English sensibilities of political and social virtue (for which see Chapter 1). Cf. A. Fitzmaurice, 'The Commercial Ideology of Colonization in Jacobean England: Robert Johnson, Giovanni Botero, and the Pursuit of Greatness', *WMQ*, 3rd series, 64:4 (2007), pp. 791–820.

39. The point, seemingly obvious, requires making in light of the claims for the Caribbean, notwithstanding a lack of permanent settlement there until 1624, as a 'prototype' for Virginia made by P. D. Morgan, 'Virginia's Other Prototype: The Caribbean', in Mancall (ed.) *The Atlantic World and Virginia*, pp. 342–80. Of course, those involved in settling Virginia utilized relevant experiences in the Amazon and in the Caribbean, as well as Ireland and elsewhere, see Chapter 3. For the first Virginia charter, see 'Letters Patent to Sir Thomas Gates, Sir George Somers and others, for two several Colonies and Plantations, to be made in Virginia, and other parts and Territories of America. Dated April 10, 1606', in Brown (ed.), *Genesis*, vol. 1, pp. 52–63; for the second charter, see ibid., vol. 1, pp. 206–37; for the third, see ibid., vol. 2, pp. 540–53. The Virginia Company of Plymouth, counterpart of the Virginia Company of London and recipient of similar powers, founded a colony at Saghedoc in present-day Maine which failed.
40. The Virginia Company sent some 6,000 people to Jamestown between 1607 and 1624, but the European population of the colony has been estimated at 1,200 at the end of its time in control, see D. W. Meinig, *The Shaping of America: A Geographical Perspective on 500 Years of History, Volume 1, Atlantic America, 1492–1800* (New Haven, CT: Yale University Press, 1986), p. 146, and p. 80 below.
41. G. S. Wood, 'The Creative Imagination of Bernard Bailyn', in J. A. Henretta, M. Kammen, and S. N. Katz (eds), *The Transformation of Early American History: Society, Authority, and Ideology: How the Writings and Influence of Bernard Bailyn have Changed our Understanding of the American Past* (New York: Alfred A. Knopf, 1991), pp. 16–50, on pp. 47–8.

3 Birth Pangs

1. 'Discourse of the Old Company', April [?] 1625, in *RVC*, vol. 4, pp. 519–51, on p. 520.
2. Rolfe, *A True Relation of the State of Virginia*, p. 1174.
3. 'Articles of Agreement', 30 October 1605, in Brown, *Genesis*, vol. 1, pp. 33–5.
4. Smith, *The Generall Historie of Virginia*, p. 307. Captains Bartholomew Gosnold and John Smith and the Revd Robert Hunt, although not patentees, also undertook, through 'their great charge and industrie', to 'move' the plantation, ibid., p. 306.
5. J. Smith, *The Proceedings of the English Colonie in Virginia* (1612), in Smith, *Writings*, pp. 35–118, on pp. 42–3.
6. For Spanish hostility – never pursued because of diplomatic and economic concerns related to the negotiation of a truce with the United Provinces – see e.g., 'Report of the Council of State', 10 November 1607 (NS), in Brown, *Genesis*, vol. 1, pp. 125–7; I. A. Wright, 'Spanish Policy Toward Virginia, 1606–1612: Jamestown, Ecija, and John Clark of the Mayflower', *American Historical Review*, 25:3 (1920), pp. 448–79. For contemporary French interest in North America, see 'New France', 12 June 1609, in Brown, *Genesis*, vol. 1, pp. 321–4. Québec was founded, of course, in 1608.
7. *The Proceedings of the English Colonie in Virginia*, pp. 42–6.
8. Ibid., p. 43. For the effects of the Spanish example on the English, see J. Cañizeras-Esguerra, *Puritan Conquistadors: Iberianizing the Atlantic* (Stanford, CA: Stanford University Press, 2006).
9. J. F. Fausz, 'The Invasion of Virginia: Indians, Colonialism, and the Conquest of Cant: A Review Essay on Anglo-Indian Relations in the Chesapeake', *VMHB*, 95:2 (1987), pp. 133–56; J. F. Fausz, 'An Abundance of Blood Shed on Both Sides: England's First Indian War, 1609–1614', *VMHB*, 98:1 (1990), pp. 3–56. For Argall's expedition, see Fr

Pierre Biard to Fr Claude Acquaviva, General of the Society of Jesus, 16/26 May 1614, in Brown, *Genesis*, vol. 2, pp. 698–708.
10. Sir Samuel Argall to Nicholas Hawes, June 1613, in Brown, *Genesis*, vol. 2, pp. 640–4, on pp. 642–4.
11. Kupperman, *Indians and English*.
12. D. Green, 'Lordship and Principality: Colonial Policy in Ireland and Aquitaine in the 1360s', *Journal of British Studies*, 47:1 (2008), pp. 3–29.
13. N. P. Canny, 'The Ideology of English Colonization from Ireland to America', *WMQ*, 3rd series, 30:4 (1973), pp. 573–98; D. B. Quinn, 'Sir Thomas Smith (1513–1577) and the Beginnings of English Colonial Theory', *Proceedings of the American Philosophical Society*, 89 (1945), pp. 543–60.
14. M. H. Fernald, 'Members of the Essex Rebellion of 1601' (PhD dissertation, Brown University, 1976), provides a helpful synopsis of the careers of the Essex rebels, pp. 205–331. For Wynn, see A. H. Dodd, 'North Wales in the Essex Revolt of 1601', *English Historical Review*, 59:235 (1944), pp. 348–70.
15. Confronted with an unmarried childless queen, whose successor for much of her reign was the Catholic Mary Stuart, Elizabeth's ministers went to great lengths to preserve their queen and themselves. They kept close tabs on the deposed Scottish queen and her circle, ultimately collecting evidence sufficient for Elizabeth to accept finally the need to execute Mary and, when Elizabeth became deathly ill, they went so far as to form a 'Bond of Association'. In both instances, they risked the wrath of their sovereign, see P. Collinson, 'The Monarchical Republic of Queen Elizabeth I', in P. Collinson (ed.), *Elizabethan Essays* (London: Hambledon Press, 1994), pp. 31–56
16. As painstakingly recreated by Charles Nicholl in *The Reckoning*. Nicholl's careful research suggests that the playwright became enmeshed in the English government's efforts to monitor English Jesuits at Douai, Flanders, and the relationship with other renegades with the government of the Spanish Netherlands.
17. P. E. J. Hammer, 'A Welshman Abroad: Captain Peter Wynn of Jamestown', *Parergon*, n.s., 16 (1998), pp. 59–92. Interestingly, Wynn, like Captain John Smith, also served the Holy Roman Emperor in the Hungarian wars against the Ottoman Turks.
18. In addition to the 'Discourse' cited in note 1, the batteries of printed and manuscript works trained at each other between 1607 and 1651 include E. M. Wingfield, 'A Discourse of Virginia' (1608), in Smith, *Writings*, pp. 950–66; Smith, *A True Relation of such Occurrences and Accidents of Noate*; M. Nicholls (ed.), 'George Percy's "Trewe Relaycion" [1625]: A Primary Source for the Jamestown Settlement', *VMHB*, 113:3 (2005), pp. 212–75; N. Ferrar, *Sir Thomas Smith's Misgovernment of the Virginia Company* (1625), ed. D. R. Ransome (Cambridge: Roxburghe Club, 1990); A. W[odenoth], *A Short Collection of the Most Remarkable Passages from the Original to the Dissolution of the Virginia Company* (London, 1651).
19. Smith, *The Generall Historie*, p. 309.
20. Smith, *A True Relation of such Occurrences and Accidents of Noate*, p. 8; Smith, *The Proceedings of the English Colonie*, pp. 47–8; Smith, *The Generall Historie*, pp. 312–3; Wingfield, 'A Discourse on Virginia', pp. 954–61.
21. Wingfield, 'A Discourse of Virginia', pp. 951–2, 954–62; George Percy, 'Observations Gathered out of a Discourse of the Plantation of the Southerne Colonie in Virginia' (London, 1606/7), in Smith, *Writings*, pp. 920–34, on p. 933.
22. Wingfield, 'A Discourse of Virginia', pp. 959–60.

23. P. L. Barbour, 'Captain George Kendall: Mutineer or Intelligencer?', *VMHB*, 70:3 (1962), pp. 297–313. Wingfield's account, the most comprehensive (perhaps naturally, since Kendall's arrest and execution cast the author's enemies in a poor light) of this incident, remained in manuscript until the nineteenth century. Peter Wynn, noted above, had a career remarkably similar to Kendall's – and John Smith's, including Hungarian service against the Turk. He pitched up at Jamestown, through the good offices of Sir Thomas Gates, in the autumn of 1608 and in the autumn of his life, see Hammer, 'A Welshman Abroad', p. 60.
24. See Smith, *Writings*, pp. 49 (1612 version), 314–15 (*Generall Historie* version) for accounts of Kendall's death.
25. Wingfield, 'A Discourse of Virginia', p. 958.
26. L. P. Striker and B. Smith, 'The Rehabilitation of Captain John Smith', *Journal of Southern History*, 28:4 (1962), pp. 474–81.
27. Wingfield, 'A Discourse of Virginia', p. 952.
28. G. Percy, 'A Trewe Relaycion of the Proceedings and Ocurrentes of Momente which have Hapned in Virginia', in Smith, *Writings*, pp. 1093–114, on pp. 1096–9.
29. Smith, *The Generall Historie*, pp. 328–9.
30. Ibid., pp. 353–4.
31. Ibid., pp. 355–6.
32. Ibid., p. 364. However, Ratcliffe remained in the colony to die miserably, after Smith's departure, at the hands of the Indians, see Percy, 'A Trewe Relacyon', p. 1099. Archer seems to have stayed as well, according to Smith's own account, see *The Generall Historie*, p. 400.
33. Smith, *The Generall Historie*, pp. 385–9.
34. Ibid., pp. 389–402 (quotations on pp. 395, 398, 402). For Smith as 'cheerleader', see *A Description of New England* (1616), in Smith, *Writings*, pp. 119–71, and Smith, *Advertisements for the Unexperienced Planters of New-England or any where* (1631), in Smith, *Writings*, pp. 771–816. For Hakluyt's employment by the East India Company in the preparation of a Malay dictionary, see Mancall, *Hakluyt's Promise*, pp. 282–7.
35. Percy, 'A Trewe Relaycion', pp. 1095–7; Wingfield, 'A Discourse of Virginia', pp. 964–5.
36. Kupperman, *The Jamestown Project*, pp. 9–10.
37. It is customarily forgotten that Smith, despite his self-characterization as an outsider, went to the colony as an agent of the company, a designated member of the council, like Wingfield and Gosnold (once he sorted out his difficulties with Wingfield and others on the voyage over).
38. As chronicled by William Strachey, the colony's new secretary and fellow shipwreck of Gates, in *A True Reportory of the Wracke, and Redemption of Sir Thomas Gates Knight* (1612), in Smith, *Writings*, pp. 979–1037.
39. Percy, 'A Trewe Relacyon', pp. 1097–102.
40. Ibid., pp. 1102–8. Pursuant to martial law, de la Ware had executed several men who had plotted to take one of the colony's barks and return to England.
41. Ibid., pp. 1108–13.
42. *Relation of the Lord De-La-Warre* (1611), in Tyler, *Narratives*, pp. 209–14, on p. 209.
43. Ibid., p. 214.
44. R. Hamor, *A True Discourse of the Present Estate of Virginia, and the Successe of the Affaires there till the 18 of June 1614* (1615), in Smith, *Writings*, pp. 1115–68, on pp. 1142–5.
45. Ibid., p. 1168.

46. See *The Complete Works of Captain John Smith (1580–1631)*, ed. P. L. Barbour, 3 vols (Chapel Hill, NC: University of North Carolina Press, 1986).
47. B. McConville, *The King's Three Faces: The Rise and Fall of Royal America, 1688–1776* (Chapel Hill, NC: University of North Carolina Press, 2006).
48. Smith, *The Generall Historie*, at pp. 321–4. This episode, which may have been a ceremony by which the Powhatans initiated Smith into their community (although its significance entirely escaped Smith just as it remains frustratingly elusive to modern historians), does not appear in either the 1608 or 1612 versions of Smith's histories, see M. LeMaster, 'Pocahontas: (De)Constructing an American Myth', *WMQ*, 3rd series, 62:4 (2005), pp. 774–81. To the chagrin of historians, the popular vision of Smith received a considerable boost – and incorporated further error (notably a love story between the captain and Pocahontas, a child of eleven or twelve when John Smith resided in America) – from the portrayal of his character in the wildly popular Walt Disney Studio's film, *Pocahontas* (1995).
49. P. C. Mancall, 'Review Essay: Savagery in Jamestown', *Huntington Library Quarterly*, 70:4 (2007), pp. 661–70, on p. 663; Smith, *The Generall Historie*, p. 402.
50. Smith, *A Description of New England*, p. 123; Smith, *New England's Trials* (London, 1622) in Smith, *Writings*, pp. 175–97, on p. 177 (dedications to Prince Charles); Smith, *The Generall Historie*, p. 203 (dedication to the Duchess of Lennox).
51. For Wynn, see Hammer, 'A Welshman Abroad'.
52. Bailyn, 'Politics and Social Structure in Virginia'.
53. M. Nicholls, '"As Happy a Fortune as I Desire": The Pursuit of Financial Security by the Younger Brothers of Henry Percy, 9th Earl of Northumberland', *Historical Research*, 65 (1992), pp. 296–314. The earl's steward and kinsman Thomas Percy had been one of the ringleaders of the plot. Unfortunately, his death under pursuit in the aftermath of its failure left evidence of Northumberland's non-complicity open and he remained in the Tower from the end of 1605 until 1621, see M. Nicholls, 'The "Wizard Earl" in Star Chamber: The Trial of the Earl of Northumberland, June 1606', *Historical Journal*, 30:1 (1987), pp. 173–89.
54. Rolfe composed an elaborate justification addressed to Sir Thomas Dale for this marriage, published with Hamor's narrative, in Smith, *Writings*, pp. 1163–7; Hamor, *A True Discourse of the Present Estate of Virginia*, p. 1137 (Rolfe's tobacco 'triall'); Strachey, *A True Reportory*, pp. 1008–9 (for Rolfe and Gates).
55. Rolfe, *A True Relation of the State of Virginia*, pp. 1175–6.
56. Ibid., pp. 1177–80.

4 Fatal and Near-Fatal Attractions

1. *The Letters of John Chamberlain*, ed. N. E. McClure, 2 vols (Philadelphia, PA: Memoirs of the American Philosophical Society, 1939), vol. 2, pp. 50, 56.
2. For the attendance of the de la Wares at the masque, see Smith, *The Generall Historie*, p. 443.
3. Barroll, *Anna of Denmark*, pp. 14–35.
4. Penelope Devereux, the sister of Essex (and mother of the future overseas adventurers, Henry Rich, Earl of Holland, and Robert Rich, Earl of Warwick), provided much of the prompting of her brother's failed revolt, including convincing him that Sir Thomas Smythe, then sheriff of London, would join the rebellion, see James, 'At a Crossroads of the Political Culture', p. 451. For Anna of Denmark's career, see Barroll, *Anna of Den-*

mark, pp. 36–73; Barroll, 'The Court of the First Stuart Queen', pp. 191–208; B. K. Lewalski, 'Lucy, Countess of Bedford: Images of a Jacobean Courtier and Patroness', in K. Sharpe and S. N. Zwicker (eds), *Politics of Discourse: The Literature and History of Seventeenth-Century England* (Berkeley and Los Angeles, CA: University of California Press, 1987), pp. 52–77; B. K. Lewalski, *Writing Women in Jacobean England* (Cambridge, MA: Harvard University Press, 1993), 'Enacting Opposition: Queen Anne and the Subversions of Masquing' and 'Exercising Power: The Countess of Bedford as Courtier, Patron, and Coterie Poet', pp. 15–43, 95–123.

5. The observation of Edward Somerset, Earl of Worcester, quoted in M. Brennan, *Literary Patronage in the English Renaissance: The Pembroke Family* (London and New York: Routledge, Chapman & Hall, Inc., 1988), p. 104.

6. Lewalski, *Writing Women in Jacobean England*, pp. 24, 107.

7. P. Croft, 'Robert Cecil and the Early Jacobean Court', in Peck (ed.), *The Mental World of the Jacobean Court*, pp. 134–47, on 142–3.

8. Barroll, *Anna of Denmark*, pp. 56–62; Brennan, *Literary Patronage in the English Renaissance*, pp. 104–5. Of course, who was directing whom (and indeed whether 'direction' is an accurate assessment of this 'opposition') remains unknown since early seventeenth-century English people engaging in politics outside the recognized organs of government did not take minutes of their meetings, although we do know that unofficial political gatherings took place both privately and at court.

9. Barroll, *Anna of Denmark*, p. 34; L. L. Peck, *Court Patronage and Corruption in Early Stuart England* (London: Allen & Unwin, 1990), p. 223n., lists the members of Anna's council.

10. The sentence of death was stayed by the king, however, and the couple remained in the Tower themselves until 1622, see A. Bellany, *The Politics of Court Scandal in Early Modern England: News Culture and the Overbury Affair, 1603–1660* (Cambridge: Cambridge University Press, 2002).

11. For Anna and Northampton's tiff, see Peck, *Northampton*, pp. 40, 74. It was the view of the redoubtable Victorian S. R. Gardiner (who regarded the queen as a staunch papist) that Anna, under the alleged influence of her Scottish lady-in-waiting, the Catholic Jean Drummond, Countess of Roxborough, accepted a Spanish pension and worked hand-in-glove with the Spanish ambassador, Count Gondomar, to wield her weak influence on her husband, see Gardiner, *History of England*, vol. 2, p. 224. In light of Barroll's research, this verdict cannot be sustained: indeed, the queen dismissed this 'influential' lady, curiously, at the beginning of 1617, *Anna of Denmark*, pp. 117–21, 155–9, 162–72.

12. Brennan, *Literary Patronage in the English Renaissance*, pp. 123–4; Peck, *Northampton*, pp. 70–1; Barroll, *Anna of Denmark*, pp. 36–73.

13. J. D. Alsop, 'William Welwood, Anne of Denmark and the Sovereignty of the Sea', *Scottish Historical Review*, 59 (1980), pp. 171–4. The discoverer of this patronage relationship put it down to the queen's desire to preserve her monopoly to license foreign fishing expeditions in British waters, obtained in 1614 – a 21-year patent she purportedly obtained so that she could 'maintain her elegant life style without the necessity of a further increase in her allowances from the state'. This is possible, but why did Anna pursue this particular monopoly and how did she know to encourage Welwood?

14. Ralegh to Secretary Sir Ralph Winwood, [January 1615/16?] and Ralegh to Queen Anne of Denmark, [1611], in E. Edwards, *The Life of Sir Walter Ralegh ... together with his Letters* (London, 1868), pp. 339–41, on pp. 340 (quotation), 334–5.

15. Smith's letter to Queen Anna appears in his *Generall Historie*, pp. 440–3 (quotations on pp. 441–2).
16. Although, to their embitterment, he soon forgot his backers as he engrossed most of the patronage for himself during his meteoric career. For Villiers, see Lockyer, *Buckingham*, pp. 19–20, for the creation of the Earl of Buckingham.
17. The Venetian ambassador, for one, had little doubt that the political centre of England shifted to Anna's palace at Greenwich. The council to rule the realm in the king's absence had been created by 19 January and James finally crossed into Scotland on 13 May, remaining until November, see Gardiner, *History of England*, vol. 1, p. 215, vol. 3, pp. 224, 228; Brennan, *Literary Patronage in the English Renaissance*, pp. 129–46; Barroll, *Anna of Denmark*, pp. 130–53, for this council; Barroll, *Anna of Denmark*, pp. 51–4, for the relationship between the queen and the two countesses.
18. Smith, *The Generall Historie*, p. 443.
19. 'A Complete List in Alphabetical Order of the "Adventurers to Virginia", with the Several Amounts of their Holdings', [1618?], in *RVC*, vol. 3, pp. 79–90.
20. Hamor, *A True Discourse of the Present State of Virginia*, pp. 1131–2; [W. Strachey], *For the Colony in Virginea Britannia. Laws Divine, Morall and Martiall* (London, 1612).
21. As with all patron–client relations of the day, it can be difficult to ascertain precisely who undertook responsibility for what matters. However, it does seem clear that, while Sandys and the Ferrars managed the company's affairs, including the provisioning of ships and colonists and the receipt of tobacco, they consulted with and sought the approval of Southampton on such issues as they regarded appropriate for consideration by higher authority, see e.g., Sir Edwin Sandys to the Earl of Southampton, 29 September 1619, in *RVC*, vol. 3, pp. 216–19. The colonists certainly regarded Southampton as the member of the council for Virginia with the best 'clout' for securing, for instance, a revocation of a royal proclamation against the importation of tobacco, see Sir George Yeardley and the Council in Virginia to the Earl of Southampton and the Council and Company for Virginia, 21 January 1620/1, in *RVC*, vol. 3, pp. 424–5; cf. Sandys's champion, T. K. Rabb, *Jacobean Gentleman: Sir Edwin Sandys, 1561–1629* (Princeton, NJ: Princeton University Press, 1998), pp. 321–2.
22. 'Instructions to Governor Yeardley', in *RVC*, vol. 3, pp. 98–109, on pp. 100–1.
23. 'An Ordinance and Constitution for Council and Assembly in Virginia', 24 July 1621, in *RVC*, vol. 3, pp. 482–4, on p. 483. For the House of Burgesses and its subsequent veneration, see 'Proceedings of the Virginia Assembly, 1616', in Tyler (ed.), *Narratives*, pp. 247–78.
24. S. Purchas, *Hakluytus Posthumus or Purchas His Pilgrimes: Contayning a History of the World in Sea Voyages and Lande Travells by Englishmen and others*, 20 vols (New York: AMS Press, 1965), vol. 19, p. 122.
25. Sir Edwin Sandys to the Marquis of Buckingham, 7 June 1620, in *RVC*, vol. 3, pp. 294–6, on p. 295.
26. 'Mr. Wroth. Notes from Lists showing Total Number of Emigrants to Virginia', 1622, in *RVC*, vol. 3, pp. 536–7; 'A Court held for Virginia and ye Sumer Ilande on Wednesday in ye Afternoone the 7th of May 1623', in *RVC*, vol. 2, pp. 390–412, on pp. 398–9; I. W. D. Hecht, 'The Virginia Muster of 1624/5 as a Source for Demographic History', *WMQ*, 3rd series, 30:1 (1973), pp. 65–92, on pp. 70–1. The 'List of the Men nowe sent for Plantacon under Captayne Woodleefe Governor', September 1619, makes grim reading, in *RVC*, vol. 3, pp. 197–9.

27. D. R. Ransome, 'Village Tensions in Early Virginia: Sex, Land, and Status at the Neck of Land in the 1620s', *Historical Journal*, 43:2 (2000), pp. 365–81.
28. W. Thorndale, 'The Virginia Census of 1619', *Magazine of Virginia Genealogy*, 33:3 (1996), pp. 155–70.
29. John Rolfe to Sir Edwin Sandys, January 1619/20, in *RVC*, vol. 3, pp. 241–8, on p. 243; E. Sluiter, 'New Light on the "20. and Odd Negroes" Arriving in Virginia, August 1619', *WMQ*, 3rd series, 54:2 (1997), pp. 395–8. For Bermuda, see V. Bernhard, 'Beyond the Chesapeake: The Contrasting Status of Blacks in Bermuda, 1616–1663', *Journal of Southern History*, 54:4 (1988), pp. 545–64.
30. See e.g., the classic accounts of W. D. Jordan, *White over Black: American Attitudes toward the Negro, 1550–1812* (Chapel Hill, NC: University of North Carolina Press, 1968); Morgan, *American Slavery, American Freedom*. These debates date back at least to the appearance of O. Handlin and M. F. Handlin, 'The Origins of the Southern Labor System', *WMQ*, 3rd series, 7:2 (1950), pp. 199–222. As with most discussions of 'origins', the issues which concern historians did not concern contemporaries, making the exercise a tricky one.
31. Interestingly, they relocated to the peripheral eastern shore of Chesapeake Bay after receiving their freedom, see D. Deal, 'A Constricted World: Free Blacks on Virginia's Eastern Shore, 1680–1750', in Carr et al. (eds), *Colonial Chesapeake Society*, pp. 275–305.
32. 'A Court held for Virginia and ye Sumer Ilande on Wednesday in ye Afternoone the 7th of May 1623', in *RVC*, vol. 2, pp. 390–412, on p. 407.
33. 'Answer to the Request of the Walloons and French to Plant in Virginia', 11 August 1621, in *RVC*, vol. 3, pp. 491–2. The company lacked the means to support the migration of sixty Walloon and French families and regarded their settling as one group as 'not expedient'. Denization was an important issue for Huguenots, for instance, throughout the English-speaking world, see B. Van Ruymbeke, 'Refuge or Diaspora? Historiographical Reflections on the Huguenot Dispersion in the Atlantic World', in C. Schnurmann and S. Lachenicht (eds), *Religious Refugees in Europe, Asia, and the Americas (6th–20th Centuries)* (Münster: Lit Verlag, 2007), pp. 167–82; D. Statt, 'The City of London and the Controversy over Immigration, 1660–1722', *Historical Journal*, 33:1 (1990), pp. 45–61.
34. J. Thornton, 'The African Experience of the "20. and Odd Negroes" Arriving in Virginia in 1619', *WMQ*, 3rd series, 55:3 (1998), pp. 421–34. Portugal was under the sovereignty of the Spanish monarchy in 1619.
35. A. Kussmaul, *Servants in Husbandry in Early Modern England* (Cambridge: Cambridge University Press, 1981).
36. See e.g., S. Hadden, *Slave Patrols: Law and Violence in Virginia and the Carolinas* (Cambridge, MA: Harvard University Press, 2001); P. J. Schwarz, *Slave Laws in Virginia* (Athens, GA: University of Georgia Press, 1996).
37. For a reminder of the wide transmission of knowledge of Atlantic slavery, as with other things, see Hatfield, *Atlantic Virginia*, pp. 137–8, for slave responses to enslavement, pp. 159–63. By the 1670s, the African population of Virginia numbered about one-tenth of the total, see ibid., pp. 111, 144.
38. Ibid., pp. 48–51, 99–102. Dutch interest in finding a route through America, as manifested by the 1609 voyage by the Englishman Henry Hudson, had gone into abeyance with the truce. The States-General chartered the Dutch West India Company on 3 June 1621, which was founded to fight the renewed conflict in the Americas, but blood was

in the water by 1619: Johan van Oldenbarneveldt, *lansavocaat* for the State of Holland and leader of the peace party, was executed on trumped-up treason charges on 13 May of that year.

39. News of 'the great Massacre' did not reach London, though, until the summer, see Treasurer and Council for Virginia to Governor and Council in Virginia, 1 August 1622, in *RVC*, vol. 3, pp. 666–73, on p. 670; Hecht, 'The Virginia Muster of 1624/5'. For the purposes of the college, see 'Instructions to Governor Yeardley', 18 November 1618, in *RVC*, vol. 3, pp. 98–109, on p. 102. For the Virginia response in 1622 and its consequences, see A. T. Vaughan, '"Expulsion of the Savages": English Policy and the Virginia Massacre of 1622', *WMQ*, 3rd series, 35:1 (1978), pp. 57–84. It is not beyond the realm of possibility to suggest that Opechancanough, who replaced Wahunsonacock as leader of the Powhatans after his brother's death in 1618 and who seems to have maintained a healthy hatred for the English throughout his long life, would have attacked the settlements anyway. He led another attack, at the age of approximately 90 years, in 1644, which, of course, also failed; he was captured and murdered, see P. C. Mancall, 'Native Americans and Europeans in English America, 1500–1700', in Canny (ed.), *The Origins of Empire*, pp. 328–50, on pp. 337–8. It is another remarkable recurrence of early Indian–English relations that those colonists who professed themselves the keenest friends to indigenous people often, like Thorpe, numbered among the first victims of these attacks, see Edward Waterhouse, *A Declaration of the State of the Colony and ... a Relation of the Barbarous Massacre* (1622), in *RVC*, vol. 3, pp. 541–71, on pp. 552–5.

40. W. F. Craven, 'The Earl of Warwick, a Speculator in Piracy', *Hispanic American Historical Review*, 10:4 (1930), pp. 457–79; Craven, *Dissolution of the Virginia Company*, pp. 83–8.

41. Committee of the Council of Virginia, 'Copy of Minutes relating to the Censure passed on Alderman Johnson', 8 July 1619, in *RVC*, vol. 3, pp. 149–50, on p. 149. Warwick had contributed £75 to the capital campaign of 1617, see *RVC*, vol. 3, p. 332; he makes his first appearance, as co-leader with Southampton of a company quarter court, in the company's records on 9 June 1619, in *RVC*, vol. 1, p. 224. We can only speculate what, if any, influence the history between the Earl of Southampton and Sir Thomas Smythe played in this hostility, for Smythe, as sheriff of London, had denied the Earl of Essex access to the Tower arsenal and the London trained bands, thereby dooming his 1601 revolt; Essex having received (erroneous) information that Smythe would support him. In addition, Alderman Johnson, Smythe's son-in-law, published an essay following the rebellion which characterized its suppression as a Tacitean necessity, the saving of the state from the dangerous grasping of an over-mighty subject, see Fitzmaurice, 'The Commercial Ideology of Colonization in Jacobean England', pp. 808–11. This was the opposite of the view taken by the Essexians that they were engaged in a selfless, Ciceronian, campaign to save the state from the queen's corrupt advisors. Southampton, as noted above, went to the Tower and narrowly escaped the block for his role in the rebellion. One contemporary Southampton partisan, after the facts, did note this history, see W[odenoth], *A Short Collection*.

42. Sir N. Rich, 'Rough Notes for his Defense before the Council of the Virginia Company on the Charge of having altered an Order of the Council', in *RVC*, vol. 3, pp. 232–5; Craven, *Dissolution of the Virginia Company*, pp. 126–33.

43. 'The Virginia Planters Answer to Captain Butler, 1623', which incorporates Butler's 'unmasking', in Tyler (ed.), *Narratives*, pp. 412–18.

44. Minutes of a 'Court held for Virginia and ye Sumer Ilande in ye Afternoon of the 7th of May 1623', in *RVC*, vol. 2, pp. 390–412, on pp. 393, 395, 396.
45. 'At a Court held for Virginia', 4 December 1622, in *RVC*, vol. 3, pp. 161–78. The crown, suspicious of the 'inconueniences and evils thereby arising', suspended these lotteries, which had helped keep the company afloat since 1612, in 1621, see 'Proclamation to Virginia Company prohibiting Lottery', 8 March 1620/1, in *RVC*, vol. 3, pp. 434–5; R. C. Johnson, 'The Lotteries of the Virginia Company, 1612–1621', *VMHB*, 74:3 (1966), pp. 259–92.
46. 'At a Court held for Virginia', 29 January 1622/3, in *RVC*, vol. 3, pp. 178–87. The company, with some grumbling, awarded Sandys a salary of £500 per annum and Nicholas Ferrar one of £400 at its meeting of 27 November 1622, see *RVC*, vol. 3, pp. 146–57, on p. 151. The money was supposed to come from the promised 'tobacco contract', by which the company was to have a monopoly over all tobacco imported into England (for the failure of which see Chapter 5). As it happens, none of the Smythe-Warwick group attended this court (see pp. 146–7).
47. Virginia Company, 'A Note of the Shipping, Men, and Prouisions Sent and Provided for Virginia ... in the Yeere 1621', [end of May 1622], in *RVC*, vol. 3, pp. 639–43, but see note 39 above. News of 'the great Massacre' did not reach London, though, until the summer, see Treasurer and Council for Virginia to Governor and Council in Virginia, 1 August 1622, in *RVC*, vol. 3, pp. 666–73. Ferrar also prepared a screed against Sir Thomas Smythe's administration of the company for Cavendish, see Ransome (ed.), *Sir Thomas Smith's Misgovernment of the Virginia Company*.
48. Sandys to John Ferrar, 22 April 1622, in *RVC*, vol. 3, pp. 615–16.
49. Captain John Bargrave, 'Disclaimer of Opposition to the Present Management', 30 May 1622, in *RVC*, vol. 3, pp. 637–8. Bargrave reiterated his position in a petition to the Privy Council, [June? 1622], in *RVC*, vol. 3, pp. 644–5, as recommended by company treasurer Sandys and his fellow officers, in *RVC*, vol. 3, pp. 645–6. For the vehement denials of Smythe and Johnson of Bargrave's charges against them, including counter-charges of piracy and lying, see 'Reply to the Petition of Captain Bargrave', November 1621, in *RVC*, vol. 3, pp. 521–4.
50. [Sir Nathaniel Rich], 'Note which I presently took of Captain John Bargrave' Discourse to Me concerning Sir Edwin Sandys', 16 May 1623, in *RVC*, vol. 4, pp. 194–5. Rich took the precaution of making a note of Bargrave's complaint against Sir Thomas Smythe, see 'Charges against Sir Thomas Smyth, with Answers in Rough Draft', in *RVC*, vol. 4, pp. 81–4. Sandys, of course, facilitated the migration of the Brownist group of Scrooby, Nottinghmashire (also kown as 'the Pilgrim Fathers'), in exile in Leiden, to North America, where they founded a third English colony, see Rabb, *Jacobean Gentleman*, p. 330. For Sandys and the 1621 parliament, see ibid., pp. 209–69, and p. 264 for governmental suspicions of Brownism. Sandys, as we know (and, undoubtedly, Bargrave knew), had been a nuisance in parliament to James I since 1604. He had fallen under suspicion of anti-monarchical sentiment, see e.g., ibid., pp. 192–5, and thus made an easy target as a seditious person. Despite these charges – and the enduring historiographical view of Sandys as the personification of an independent English gentry standing up to resist, in the name of the liberties of the subject, the encroaching tendencies of the early Stuart monarchs – the reality remains that Sir Edwin remained orthodox, at least officially, in matters of state and religion throughout his life and died in his bed, see e.g., Sir Edwin Sandys to the Marquis of Buckingham, 7 June 1620, in *RVC*, vol. 3, pp. 294–7, with its due references to respect for royal authority and its solicitation of the protection of

the favourite; cf. Rabb, *Jacobean Gentleman*. Regardless, Rich did not use Bargrave's allegations publicly against Sandys, see Craven, *Dissolution of the Virginia Company*, p. 278. On the other hand, Bargrave's shift of sides, and the apparently personal basis upon which he made it, makes it unclear, at best, the degree to which we can accept his analysis of the Virginia government as a disinterested one, cf. Haskell, 'The Affections of the People', pp. 38–53.

51. For the king's involvement here, see King to Privy Council, 17 June 1622, in *RVC*, vol. 3, pp. 653–4.
52. Richard Frethorne to Mr Bateman, 5 March 1622/3, in *RVC*, vol. 4, pp. 41–2, on p. 41; Frethorne to his Father and Mother, 20 March, 2 and 3 April 1623, in *RVC*, vol. 4, pp. 58–62. Cf. Rose, 'The Politics of Pathos'.
53. 'Commission to Sir William Jones and Others', 9 May 1623, in *RVC*, vol. 4, pp. 575–80.
54. Rabb, *Jacobean Gentleman*, p. 374n. Sandys's biographer suggests in a footnote that the membership of this commission was necessarily hostile to Sandys, but much of the rationale offered amounts to little more than guilt by association. Notwithstanding, its members would not have been sympathetic to Sir Edwin. Sir Nathaniel Rich did take the trouble of drafting a set of instructions for the commissioners even before the king had named them, 14 April 1623, in *RVC*, vol. 4, pp. 116–18.
55. 'Commission to certain Lords of the Privy Council and Others for settling a Government in Virginia', 15 July 1624, in *RVC*, vol. 4, pp. 490–7, on p. 493. Southampton had already departed for military service in the Low Countries, in Essexian style, where he became very ill almost immediately and died in November. The judgement of the court of King's Bench against the company ('Nicholas Ferrar *et al.*') appears in *RVC*, vol. 4, pp. 295–398.
56. 'Commission to certain Lords of the Privy Council and Others for Settling a Government in Virginia', 15 July 1624, in *RVC*, vol. 4, pp. 490–7.
57. Commissioners for Virginia, 'Orders set down at a Meeting', 16 July 1624, in *RVC*, vol. 4, pp. 497–500; 'Commission to Sir Francis Wyatt as Governor and to the Council of Virginia', 26 August 1624, in *RVC*, vol. 4, pp. 501–4. Mathews, Harvey, Peircey and John Pory had served as the agents of the Jones Commission in Virginia, see Commissioners in Virginia, 'Declaration to the Assembly', 2 March 1623/4, in *RVC*, vol. 4, pp. 464–5.
58. 'The Humble Representation and Petition of your Majesty's Commissioners for your Plantation of Virginia' [to Charles I], including Dorset, Danvers, Sandys, Wolstenholme, Wrote and Wyatt, [1641], MS Bankes, 8/2, Bodleian; 'Declaration against the Virginia Company', 1 April 1642, in Billings (ed.), *Berkeley Papers*, pp. 40–4, on pp. 41–2. Sir Francis Wyatt seems to have signed this declaration as well, having returned to the colony.
59. Sir Francis Wyatt to [Sir Francis Windebanke, secretary of state], 25 March 1640, CO 1/10, f. 162.
60. The Treasurer Covncell and Company of Virginia to the Gouernour and Councell of State in Virginia Residing, 9 July 1622, in *RVC*, vol. 3, pp. 663–4. For allegedly positive prospects and reception of silk in Virginia, see e.g., John Pory to Sir Edwin Sandys, 12 June 1620, in *RVC*, vol. 3, pp. 300–5, on p. 303–4; Council in Virginia to Virginia Company of London, January 1621/2, in *RVC*, vol. 3, pp. 581–8, on p. 582. James I approved of these efforts, see *His Maiesties Gracious Letter to the Earle of Southampton, Treasurer, and to the Councell and Company of Virginia here: Commending the present setting up of Silke Works, and Planting of Vines in Virginia* (London, 1622).

61. See e.g., John Stirrup to John Ferrar, 26 January 1649/50, in D. R. Ransome (ed.), *The Ferrar Papers, 1590–1790 in Magdalene College, Cambridge* (East Ardsley, Yorkshire: Microform Academic Publishers, 1992), reel 6, #1152.
62. R. Wodenoth, *A New Description of Virginia* (London, 1649), pp. 9–10; R. Wodenoth, *A Rare and New Discovery* (London, 1652), which celebrates the 'speedy' way to feed silkworms discovered by John Ferrar's daughter, Virginia, who maintained the family tradition of strong interest in and contact with the colony. See, e.g., Virginia Ferrar to [Lady Frances Berkeley], 20 August 1650, in Ransome (ed.), *The Ferrar Papers*, reel 6, #1176 and [Sir W. Berkeley], *A Discourse and View of Virginia* (London, 1661/2), in Billings (ed.), *Berkeley Papers*, pp 161–8, esp. pp. 162–5. See also John Ferrar's marginalia in his copy of William Bullock's *Virginia Impartially Examined*, in P. Thompson, 'William Bullock's "Strange Adventure": A Plan to Transform Seventeenth-Century Virginia', *WMQ*, 3rd series, 61:1 (2004), pp. 107–28, and supplemental material accessible at http://oieahc.wm.edu/wmq/Jan04/ThompsonWeb.pdf. For Nicholas Ferrar's career, see A. Maycock, *Chronicles of Little Gidding* (London: Society for the Propagation of Christian Knowledge, 1954).
63. See e.g., W[odenoth], *A Short Collection*, p. 8.
64. For Gondomar's activities, see A. J. Loomie, 'Gondomar's Selection of English Officers in 1622', *English Historical Review*, 88:348 (1973), pp. 574–81; B. C. Pursell, 'James I, Gondomar and the Dissolution of the Parliament of 1621', *History*, 85:3 (2000), pp. 428–45. For the history of the 'Spanish Match', see T. Cogswell, *The Blessed Revolution: English Politics and the Coming of War, 1621–1624* (Cambridge: Cambridge University Press, 1989).

5 An Empire of 'Smoak'

1. [W. Berkeley], *A Discourse and View of Virginia* (London, 1663), p. 5.
2. *Winthrop's Journal: 'History of New England'*, ed. J. K. Hosmer, 2 vols (New York: Charles Scribner's Sons, 1908), entry of 4 June 1648, vol. 2, p. 343.
3. The literature on the causes of the 'British Civil Wars', which began in Scotland with a revolt against the 1637 attempt to introduce a new prayer book for the Kirk and which ended with the defeat of the Scottish army of Charles II at the battle of Dunbar (1651), is too vast to summarize satisfactorily here. It has also, like its subject, endured a series of phases and has involved various historiographical schools of thought whose behaviour has, on occasion, proved the academic equivalent of that displayed by the historical actors. The present state of play entails 'post-revisionism': the attempt to reconcile the twin realities that while few contemporaries applauded let alone desired it, civil war (one, two or three, depending on how one counts them) and, perhaps albeit briefly, 'revolution' took place. For representative earlier treatments, see e.g., C. Russell, *The Fall of the British Monarchies, 1637–1642* (Oxford: Clarendon Press, 1991; C. Hill, *Intellectual Origins of the English Revolution Revisited* (Oxford: Clarendon Press, 1997). On the other hand, Gardiner, *History of England*, remains the standard narrative notwithstanding the massive volume of ink spilled on these issues since General Gordon was killed at Khartoum.
4. For the recruitment of the 'Pilgrims' and their decision 'to live as a distincte body by them selves, under ye generall Government of Virginia', which plans were delayed by 'factions and quarrels' within the Virginia Company, see [W. Bradford], *Bradford's History 'Of Plimoth Plantation'* (Boston, MA, 1928), pp. 36–50, including Sir Edwin Sandys to John Robinson and William Brewster, 12 November 1617, Robinson and Brewster to

Sandys, 15 December 1617, and Robinson and Brewster to Sir John Wolstenholme, 27 January 1617/18, on pp. 40–4. In addition, the important fishery which then existed off the Atlantic coast of Canada, which had attracted English fishing folk (and others) since at least the 1480s, had been the target of Jacobean colonizing interest although no permanent settlement took root, see G. T. Cell, *Newfoundland Discovered: English Attempts at Colonisation, 1610–1630* (London: Hakluyt Society, 1982). For the earliest English probing of this area, which came out of Bristol during the reign of Edward IV, see Quinn, *England and the Discovery of America*, pp. 5–23.

5. [Bradford], *'Of Plimoth Plantation'*, p. 32. 'Brownist' was a common epithet directed at supporters of separation of church and state who were, consequently, deemed to be followers of the early and rabid opponent of episcopacy, Robert Browne (*c.* 1550–1633). Since, at least, the time of William Tyndall (*c.* 1494–1536), dissenters from the established church in England, like the Scrooby congregation, had made their way to the Netherlands to avoid the penalties prescribed for their beliefs and the scorn and loathing of their neighbours, see K. L. Sprunger, *Dutch Puritanism: A History of English and Scottish Churches of the Netherlands in the Sixteenth and Seventeenth Centuries* (Leiden: Brill, 1982); H. C. Porter, *Reform and Reaction at Tudor Cambridge* (Cambridge: Cambridge University Press, 1958).

6. This group, led by Elder William Bradford, William Brewster and the minister John Robinson, whether by divine providence (e.g., *'Of Plimoth Plantation'*, pp. 90–107), design or accident, wound up well north of Virginia, intending originally 'to finde some place aboute Hudsons river' (*'Of Plimoth Plantation'*, p. 93; see also Edward Winslow's relation in Smith, *A Generall Historie of Virginia*, pp. 637–60). Since they had no charter or licence to settle there, the leadership had to establish *de novo* their authority to establish a colony, which they did in the form of the celebrated compact. This document, which – as with so much else surrounding the 'Pilgrims' has been steeped in misleading lore by generations of Americans who identify them as the progenitors of the United States – simply declared their 'covenant' to 'combine ourselves into a civil Body Politick' with the power to enact laws and select officers 'for the general Good of the Colony', Mayflower Compact, 11 November 1620, see the Avalon Project at Yale Law School, at http://www.yale.edu/lawweb/avalon/amerdoc/mayflower.htm [accessed 23 August 2008]. 'Brownists' of the Plymouth sort were uninterested in 'religious freedom', except for themselves. For contemporary views of Brownism, see e.g., C. Lawne, *Brownisme Turned the In-Side Out-Ward* (London, 1613). For their own views, see e.g., J. Robinson, *A Iustification of Separation from the Church of England* ([Amsterdam], 1610).

7. For the settlement of St Christopher (today known as St Kitts), see J. Smith, *The True Travels, Adventures, and Obsevations of Captaine John Smith* (1630), in Smith, *Writings*, pp. 671–770, on pp. 755–64. For Providence Island (today the island of Santa Catalina off of the coast of Colombia), see K. O. Kupperman, *Providence Island: The Other Puritan Colony, 1630–1641* (Cambridge: Cambridge University Press, 1993). For the unsuccessful attempt to colonize Madagascar, see W. Foster, 'An English Settlement in Madagascar in 1645–6', *English Historical Review*, 27:106 (1912), pp. 239–50. Sir William Alexander, later Earl of Stirling, planned a Scottish colony for Nova Scotia from 1624, *An Encouragement to Colonies* (London, 1624).

8. Cf. D. Armitage, *Ideological Origins of the British Empire*, pp. 61–99; Hakluyt, 'Discourse of Western Planting'.

9. D. Cressy, *Coming Over*, p. 70. Enough 'Puritans' moved to Long Island to cause trouble for the government of New Netherland (founded in 1624) and to support a bid

by Connecticut to annex the island, see R. S. Dunn, 'John Winthrop, Jr., Connecticut Expansionist: The Failure of His Designs on Long Island, 1663–1675', *WMQ*, 3rd series, 29:1 (1956), pp. 3–26.
10. J. Winthrop, 'A Modell of Christian Charity', in Morgan (ed.), *The Founding of Massachusetts*, pp. 190–204.
11. Russell, *Parliaments and English Politics*.
12. Kupperman, *Providence Island*, pp. 1–16. For the colonizing and privateering activities of their supporters, especially Warwick, in addition to Kupperman's book, see A. P. Newton, *The Colonising Activities of the English Puritans* (New Haven, CT: Yale University Press, 1914); B. M. Levy, 'Early Puritanism in the Southern and Island Colonies', *Proceedings of the American Antiquarian Society*, 70 (1960), pp. 69–348. For the 'Feoffees', see N. Tyacke, *Aspects of English Protestantism, c. 1530–1700* (Manchester: Manchester University Press, 2001), pp. 120–6.
13. Cressy, *Coming Over*, pp. 130–43. Laud, for instance, ordered the conformity of the clergy on Bermuda, including the making of the sign of the cross at baptism, 4 September 1639, CO 1/10, f. 92.
14. See e.g., C. Robbins, *The Eighteenth-Century Commonwealth: Studies in the Transmission, Development, and Circumstance of English Liberal Thought from the Restoration of Charles II until the War with the Thirteen Colonies* (1959; Indianapolis, IN: Liberty Fund, 2004). For a withering critique of the Whiggish ('Old Hat') and Marxist ('Old Guard') views, see J. C. D. Clark, *Revolution and Rebellion: State and Society in England in the Seventeenth and Eighteenth Centuries* (Cambridge: Cambridge University Press, 1985). These schools, however, have weathered this barrage, see e.g., G. Burgess, 'On Revisionism: An Analysis of Early Stuart Historiography in the 1970s and 1980s', *Historical Journal*, 33:3 (2007), pp. 609–27; Brenner, *Merchants and Revolution*. For the enduring importance attached to the 'Puritans' by subsequent generations of Americans, see M. Kammen, *Mystic Chords of Memory: The Transformation of Tradition in American Culture* (New York: Alfred A. Knopf, 1991), pp. 206–15, 384–92.
15. For the importance of the erroneous characterization which early Americans devised of early New England history as well as a discussion of the pronouncements of migratory motives and the providential character of the migration and the 'plantation' it supported, the reality of intermittent 'Laudian persecution' of 'Puritans' and the enduring importance of the question of the motives of the New England migrants to American historians, see Cressy, *Coming Over*, pp. 74–106. Despite Cressy's findings that we cannot know the motivation for migration in the minds of the vast majority of those who left England for New England, V. D. Anderson, *New England's Generation: The Great Migration and the Formation of Society and Culture in the Seventeenth Century* (Cambridge: Cambridge University Press, 1991), launched a rearguard action maintaining the centrality of religion as a motivation. For 'reverse' migration from New England to England, see Cressy, *Coming Over*, pp. 191–212. Of course, many other 'Puritans', such as the London turner Nehemiah Wallington, never crossed the ocean, see e.g., P. Seaver, *Wallington's World: A Puritan Artisan in the Seventeenth Century* (Stanford, CA: Stanford University Press, 1985).
16. F. J. Bremer, *John Winthrop: America's Forgotten Founding Father* (New York: Oxford University Press, 2003), pp. 229–40, provides an account.
17. G. Bancroft, *A History of the United States*, 10 vols (Boston, MA, 1834–74), vol. 1, pp. 371–94, quoted in Morgan (ed.), *The Founding of Massachusetts*, pp. 29–44 (quotations

on pp. 31 and 42–3). This view, aside from ignoring the history recounted here, also fails to note that the charter was recalled, voided and replaced in 1691.
18. This grant appears through the good offices of the Avalon Project at the Yale Law School, at http://www.yale.edu/lawweb/avalon/states/me01.htm. The pair subsequently received a grant to 'Laconia' (present-day New Hampshire) on 17 November 1629 patent, see the Avalon Project, at http://www.yale.edu/lawweb/avalon/states/charter_003.htm. Charles I commissioned Gorges on 23 July 1637, see the Avalon Project, at http://www.yale.edu/lawweb/avalon/states/charter_009.htm [all accessed 24 August 2008].
19. Morton published a scathing satire of the 'godly commonwealth', *New English Canaan or New Canaan. Containing an Abstract of New England*, in 1637. For Gorges's general interest in New England, see e.g., Smith, *A Description of New England*, pp. 162–4. For Warwick's interference with Sir Ferdinando's plans, see C. M. Andrews, *The Colonial Period of American History*, 4 vols (New Haven, CT: Yale University Press, 1934–8), vol. 1, pp. 366–9. As with other colonization-related disputes between individuals connected to the Essex rebellion of 1601 (such as the Virginia Company battle between the Earl of Southampton and Sir Thomas Smythe), it is intriguing to speculate what effect that incident might have played on these subsequent events. Gorges had been one of Essex's chief lieutenants and was imprisoned after the revolt was crushed. However, he composed an 'apology' for the government and received a pardon, having freed the hostages Essex had taken and testified for the government against his chief at Essex's trial, see Fernald, 'Members of the Essex Rebellion of 1601', pp. 248–9. Did this behaviour in any way affect the attitudes of the Earls of Southampton and Warwick (for both of whose relationship with Essex see Chapters 2 and 3) towards Sir Ferdinando?
20. For the 1630s controversy over the exaction of ship money, another of the 'novelties' devised by the government to augment its revenues, and the alarm it generated for certain contemporaries, see S. P. Salt, 'Sir Simonds D'Ewes and the Levying of Ship Money, 1635–1640', *Historical Journal*, 37:2 (1994), pp. 253–87. For Gorges's history with the 'godly', see Andrews, *Colonial Period of American History*, vol. 1, pp. 400–29. Gorges's patent for New England did cause problems for the Virginia Company in the early 1620s and he supported its dissolution, see Craven, *Dissolution of the Virginia Company*, pp. 292–4. For Saghedoc, see Smith, *The Generall Historie*, pp. 588–9. For a history of the Gorges patent, see D. Dewar, 'The Mason Patents: Conflict, Controversy, and the Quest for Authority in Colonial New Hampshire', in Roper and Van Ruymbeke (eds), *Constructing Early Modern Empires*, pp. 269–99, esp. 270–83.
21. Quinn, *England and the Discovery of America*, pp. 364–92.
22. C. M. Hibbard, *Charles I and the Popish Plot* (Chapel Hill, NC: University of North Carolina Press, 1983); M. C. Questier, *Catholicism and Community in Early Modern England: Politics, Aristocratic Patronage and Religion, c. 1550–1640* (Cambridge: Cambridge University Press, 2006).
23. J. Krugler, 'Sir George Calvert's Resignation as Secretary of State and the Founding of Maryland', *MHM*, 68:3 (1973), pp. 239–54. For Matthew's activities and his relationship with the Calverts and Sir Edmund Plowden, the proprietor of New Albion, see L. H. Roper, 'New Albion: Anatomy of an English Colonisation Failure, 1632–1659', *Itinerario*, 32:1 (2008), pp. 39–57, on pp. 43–4.
24. Since Sir George was still very much part of the government and we have no evidence that he had begun to consider conversion to Rome at this time, it is unclear that he originally conceived of 'Avalon' as a haven for English Catholics, as he did of Maryland subsequently.

25. T. M. Coakley, 'George Calvert and Newfoundland: "The Sad Face of Winter"', *MHM*, 100:1 (2005), pp. 7–28.
26. 'A Briefe Relation of the Voyage unto Maryland, by Father Andrew White, 1634', in Hall, *Narratives*, pp. 25–45. The Maryland patent appears, through the Avalon Project at the Yale Law School, at http://www.yale.edu/lawweb/avalon/states/ma01.htm [accessed 25 August 2008]. The introduction of 'popery' to the English Empire in America, while a source of pride to American Catholics after independence, dismayed a number of contemporary Virginians and provided the pretext for the difficulties they gave Lord Baltimore, for which see below and Chapter 6. For Baltimore's plans and the results they generated, see D. A. Meyers, 'Calvert's Catholic Colony', in Roper and Van Ruymbeke (eds), *Constructing Early Modern Empires*, pp. 357–88.
27. 'The Petition of Sir Edmund Plowden to King Charles I', in B. M. Plowden, *Records of the Plowden Family* (privately published, 1887).
28. J. F. Merritt, 'Power and Communication: Thomas Wentworth and Government at a Distance during the Personal Rule, 1629–1635', in J. F. Merritt (ed.), *The Political World of Thomas Wentworth, Earl of Strafford, 1621–1641* (Cambridge: Cambridge University Press, 1996), pp. 109–31, on pp.117–18.
29. A. J. Loomie, 'The Spanish Faction at the Court of Charles I, 1630–8', *Bulletin of the Institute of Historical Research*, 59 (1986), pp. 37–49; H. Taylor, 'Trade, Neutrality, and the "English Road", 1630–1648', *Economic History Review*, n.s., 25:2 (1972), pp. 236–60. Cecilius Calvert acknowledged Wentworth's 'noble patronage' and kept him apprised of Maryland developments, see Lord Baltimore to Lord Deputy Wentworth, 10 January 1633/4, in *The Earl of Strafford's Letters and Dispatches*, ed. W. Knowler, 2 vols (London, 1739), vol. 1, pp. 178–9, on p. 178. While the Elizabethan government had assisted the Dutch in their war of independence from Felipe II, the degree and implementation of that assistance never completely satisfied either side and, thus, it provided the basis for resentment, see Israel, *The Dutch Republic*, pp. 220–40. Moreover, the expansion of Dutch trade, especially the Dutch East India Company (Verenigde Oostindische Compagnie), which received its charter from the States-General in 1602, began to generate alarm in English circles; the 'Amboyna massacre' of 1623 caused particular agitation, see e.g., H. Lownes, *A True Relation of the Vnvust, Cruell, and Barbarous Proceedings against the English at Amboyna in the East-Indies* (London, 1624).
30. For example, the Lord Deputy to the Lord Treasurer, Wednesday of Easter Week, 1634, in *The Earl of Strafford's Letters*, vol. 1, pp. 229–30. For Wentworth's views and behaviour as lord deputy, see D. Shaw, 'Thomas Wentworth and Monarchical Ritual in Early Modern England', *Historical Journal*, 49:2 (2006), pp. 331–55; M. Percevel-Maxwell, 'Ireland and the Monarchy in the Early Stuart Multiple Kingdom', *Historical Journal*, 34:2 (1991), pp. 279–95, on pp. 288–90.
31. J. R. Pagan, 'Dutch Maritime and Commercial Activity in Mid-Seventeenth Century Virginia', *VMHB*, 90:4 (1982), pp. 485–501. At the same time Plowden was receiving his Irish patent, on 23 September 1633, Charles I issued a 'special commission' to Captain Thomas Young 'to discover' such parts of 'Virginia, and other Parts of America', to form alliances and start trade with Indians ('of which they were very joyfull', according to Young), and to 'repell' hostile people; Young warned off a band of Dutch fur traders he encountered. Although we have no direct evidentiary connection between New Albion and this voyage of 'discovery', Young felt the need to keep Sir Toby Matthew (now Wentworth's secretary) apprised of the character and prospects of the territory that he explored: as it happens, the area included in the Plowden patent and in dis-

pute with the Dutch. The explorer also reported on the 'dangerous' situation that had developed between Maryland's proprietor and the formidable Virginia trader-planters William Claiborne and Samuel Mathews (about which much more below), see 'A Special Commission to Thomas Young, to search, discover, and find out what Parts are not yet inhabited in Virginia and America, and other Parts thereunto adjoining', T. Rymer (ed.), *Foedera*, 20 vols (London, 1704–35), vol. 19, pp. 472–4; Captain Thomas Young to Sir Toby Matthew, 13 July 1634 and 20 October 1634, Aspinwall Papers, *Collections of the Massachusetts Historical Society*, 4th series, 9 (Boston, 1881), pp. 103–12, 115–17; 'Relation of Captain Thomas Yong, 1634', in A. C. Myers (ed.), *Narratives of Early Pennsylvania, West New Jersey and Delaware, 1630–1707* (New York: Charles Scribner's Sons, 1912), pp. 37–49, esp. pp. 41–2, 44–6. For New Netherland and Dutch activities around 'South River' (the Delaware), see J. Jacobs, *New Netherland: A Dutch Colony in Seventeenth-Century America* (Leiden and Boston, MA: Brill, 2005), especially pp. 9–13, 20, 42–61, 126–31, 365–8.

32. R. M. Smuts, 'The Puritan Followers of Henrietta Maria in the 1630s', *English Historical Review*, 93:366 (1978), pp. 26–45. For Dorset's activities, see Roper, 'New Albion', pp. 46–9.

33. S. Adams, 'Spain or the Netherlands? The Dilemmas of Early Stuart Foreign Policy', in H. Tomlinson (ed.), *Before the English Civil War: Essays on Early Stuart Politics and Government* (New York: St Martin's Press, 1984), pp. 79–101. For the foreign policy of Charles I, see K. Sharpe, *The Personal Rule of Charles I* (New Haven, CT: Yale University Press, 1992), pp. 67–104.

34. 'A True Copy of the Grant of King Charles the First to Sir Edmund Plowden, Earl Palatine of Albion in America', 21 June 1634, in Plowden, *Records*, pp. 81–90. For Carolana, see P. E. Kopperman, 'Profile of a Failure: The Carolana Project, 1629–1640', *North Carolina Historical Review*, 59 (1982), pp. 1–23. The unwieldiness of the corporate form for colonization and governmental suspicion that corporate meetings served as fronts for sedition meant that the joint-stock corporation fell out of favour as a colonizing vehicle after the Providence Island Company received its charter in 1630. See e.g., 'Considerations against the Renewing of a Corporation for Virginia', [November 1631?], CO 1/6, ff. 84–5, on 84v.

35. The involvement of James Hay, first Earl of Carlisle, as proprietor of Barbados served only to inflame further the political convulsions in that colony during the first two decades of its existence, see Andrews, *Colonial Period of American History*, vol. 2, pp. 243–50.

36. 'Motives & Reasons for the Petition of the Governor & Company of New Albion', [1635], MS Bankes, 8/15, Bodleian; 'The Humble Petition of Sir John Lawrence, Knight and Baronet, Sir Edmund Plowden, Knight, Sir Boyer Worsley, Knight, John Tensler, Roger Pack, William Inwood, Thomas Ryebread, Charles Barret, & George Noble, Adventurers', [1632], CO 1/6, ff. 165–7.

37. Roper, 'New Albion', pp. 40–2, 50. New Sweden also repelled an incursion into the Delaware by an expedition from the New Haven colony in 1643, see C. A. Weslager, *The English on the Delaware, 1610–1682* (New Brunswick, NJ: Rutgers University Press, 1967), pp. 107–22, 123–40; *Winthrop's Journal*, vol. 2, pp. 70–1, 141–2, 160–1. The Swedish colony fell victim to the Dutch in 1655.

38. For Virginia's interest in present-day North Carolina, see [E. Williams], *The Discovery of New Brittaine* (1650), and Francis Yeardley to John Ferrar, 8 May 1654, both in A. S. Salley (ed.), *Narratives of Early Carolina, 1650–1708* (1911; New York: Barnes & Noble, 1967), pp. 5–21, 25–9. The Williams tract was dedicated, as were the contempo-

rary publications of the Wodenoths cited in Chapter 4, to Sir John Danvers, the former lieutenant of the Earl of Southampton in the days of the Virginia Company and 'Great Favourer of the Westerne Plantations' who had been a signatory to the death warrant of Charles I. Neither Danvers nor Ferrar had lost interest in Virginia despite the dissolution of the company with which they had so closely involved themselves 25 years previously. The continuing hazards may have become apparent, if they had not been already, to the band of Bermudans led by William Sayle, following a religious dispute, in 1649 to the island of Eleuthera in the Bahamas. So far from achieving the eponymous 'freedom', the loss of their ship and supplies to a reef forced the wretched colonists to live in the open air until they were able to fetch provisions from Virginia. The settlement managed to limp along, its population helped by continuing turmoil related to the civil wars and by the exile of 'free Negroes' to the island by the Bermuda government, see W. H. Miller, 'The Colonization of the Bahamas', *WMQ*, 3rd series, 2:1 (1945), pp. 33–46.

39. See e.g., Request to Privy Council, July 1624[?], in *RVC*, vol. 4, pp. 488–9.
40. For Cranfield's career, see Prestwich, *Cranfield*. A leading London merchant, Cranfield joined the Treasury Commission (created after the dismissal of the lord treasurer, Thomas Howard, Earl of Suffolk, in the wake of the Overbury embarrassment, for which see Chapter 4) in 1619. He became lord treasurer himself in 1621.
41. 'Declaration made to the Farmers of the Customes for the Subsidy of Commodytyes brought from Virginia and the Somer Ilands caryed thither in the severall areas underwritten', [1621?], U269/1 Ov50; 'An Abstract of what Spanish Virginia & Bermudos Tobacco hath bin imported into the porte of London and the Out-Ports from Michaelmas 1614 to Michaelmas 1621, vizt.', [1622], U269/1 Ov47, both in Sackville Papers (Virginia), Centre for Kentish Studies, Maidstone, Kent.
42. Governor Yeardley and Council in Virginia 'To the Right Honorable Earle of Southampton and others of London and to ye right worthy the Knights and the Rest of the Counsell and Company for Virginia', 23 January 1620/1, U269/1 Ov34, Sackville Papers (Virginia), Centre for Kentish Studies.
43. 'Reasons why a Free Trade for Tobacco wilbee more Benifitiall unto his Majestie then the Sole Importation to bee Graunted unto any Particular Company', [1623], U269/1 Ov62; 'A Proposition for Advancement of his Majesty's Profit and the Good of the Plantations of Virginia and the Summer Islands by Settling the Trade of Tobacco which is the Comoditie by which they nowe Cheiflie Subsist', [1622], U269/1 Ov17; 'Propositions Agreed on by the High Treasurer of England and the Companie for Virginia and the Summer Islands touching the Sole Importation of Tobacco', 27 November 1622, U269/1 Ov49, all in Sackville Papers (Virginia), Centre for Kentish Studies.
44. Prestwich, *Cranfield*, pp. 423–68.
45. Proclamation by the King (Charles I), 12 April 1632, CO 1/7. My thanks to Dr Adrian Ailes of the National Archives for his assistance with the seal which accompanies this proclamation.
46. My own enquiries have borne no further fruit, but I thank Gilles Havard, Lauric Henneton, François-Joseph Ruggiu, Bertrand Van Ruymbeke and Cécile Vidal for their kind assistance.
47. Sir William Boswell to James Hay, Earl of Carlisle, 25 September 1632, Egerton MS 2597, ff. 84–5, British Library. Boswell received specific instructions in his embassy to monitor 'what plantations [the Dutch] have possessed in America or else where, specially where they are hurtful or prejudicial unto such in anie place', SP 84/144, ff. 162–9, on f. 164r.

48. Sir William Boswell to Mr Bernard, 1/11 May 1633, Egerton MS 2597, f. 122, British Library.
49. Cogswell, '"In the Power of the State"'.
50. CO 1/6, f. 28.
51. Charles tried to solve the question of tobacco revenues in a parliamentary way from 1627, see Billings, *A Little Parliament*, pp. 15–17. The Virginians had been considering the idea of a contract in their 'parliament' since 1617, practically as soon as their staple had demonstrated its profitability, see *RVC*, vol. 4, pp. 2–3, 69–70.
52. *RVC*, vol. 4, pp. 294, 476–77, 501–4; 'Order from the Council to John Harvey, Esq. to make Enquiries concerning Virginia', 24 October 1623, CO 5/1354, f. 205.
53. J. Harvey, 'A Briefe Declaration of the State of Virginia at my comminge from thence in February 16[23/]24', in *Collections of the Massachusetts Historical Society*, 4th series, vol. 9 (Boston, 1871), pp. 60–73; 'To Sir John Harvey Knt Governor of the Colonies in Virginia', SP 9/208, f. 33.
54. Billings, *A Little Parliament*, p. 91. N. C. Hale, *Virginia Venturer: A Historical Biography of William Claiborne, 1600–1677* (Richmond, VA: Dietz Press, 1951), provides a hagiographic account of Claiborne's career. For Dorset's career, see D. L. Smith, 'The Political Career of Edward Sackville, Fourth Earl of Dorset (1590–1652)' (PhD dissertation, University of Cambridge, 1990). I am most grateful to Dr Smith for providing me with a copy of parts of his thesis.
55. Billings, *A Little Parliament*, p. 92.
56. See e.g., Council in Virginia to Privy Council, 15 June 1625, in *RVC*, vol. 4, pp. 559–62. The Council at the same time came to Harvey's defence when an anonymous author 'slandered' him, see Council in Virginia to Commissioners for Virginia, 15 June 1625, in *RVC*, vol. 4, pp. 562–7, on p. 563.
57. Governor Harvey to Viscount Dorchester, 2 April 1631, CO 1/6, ff. 22–3.
58. [Governor and Council to Commissioners for Virginia], 20 December 1631, CO 1/6, ff. 92v–3.
59. The king ordered the Virginians on 12 July 1633 to help the Baltimore colony 'in its infancy' after the Privy Council upheld the validity of the Maryland patent, CO 1/6, f. 206; Secretary Windebank applauded Harvey's efforts and commended his due obedience to authority, while noting 'that the King will be very sensible of any disobedience, presuming of impunity by [Claiborne's] far distance from hence, or some other silly hopes there', [Secretary of State Windebank] to Sir John Harvey, Governor of Virginia, 18 September 1634, abstracted in *CSPC*, p. 190, no. 26.
60. Governor Harvey to Secretary Windebank, 16 December 1634, abstracted in *CSPC*, p. 193, no. 37.
61. Brenner, *Merchants and Revolution*, pp. 140–5; Billings, *A Little Parliament*, pp. 20–2. For the early formation of the association that came to oppose Harvey, see Council in Virginia to Henry, Viscount Mandeville, 30 March 1623, in *RVC*, vol. 4, pp. 69–70. Wolstenholme supported Claiborne's enterprise on Kent Island discussed above, 'Petition from Sir John Wolstenholme and William Claiborne, November 1633, to the Privy Council', CO 1/6, f. 220.
62. Samuel Mathews to Sir John Wolstenholme, 25 May 1635, in W. M. Billings (ed.), *The Old Dominion in the Seventeenth Century: A Documentary History of Virginia, 1606–1689* (Chapel Hill, NC: University of North Carolina Press, 1975), pp. 251–4. As it happens, the king had directed that the Kent Island planters 'should in no sort be interrupted in their trade' by Baltimore or his agents, 'From the King to Lord Baltimore from

Greenwich', 14 July 1638, CO 1/9/287. The correspondence from Harvey and Mathews cited here, along with Zouch's presence in the colony at the time of the coup and his immediate departure afterwards, indicate *ex post facto* cooperation between the rebels and their friends rather than a transatlantic conspiracy against Harvey.

63. 'Summary of Pleadings, *The Virginia Company* v *Sir John Harvey*', [1635], MS Bankes 8/3; 'Petition to the Commissioners for the Plantations', [1635], MS Bankes 8/4; 'A breviat of the Declaration of the Planters of Virginia', 1 July 1635, MS Bankes 8/19, all Bodleian.

64. 'At the Star Chamber, 3rd of July 1633, the Lords of the Council Order upon the Petition from the Planters in Virginia', CO 1/6, f. 201.

65. 'Petition from John West, Samuel Mathews, John Utie, and William Peirce [to the Privy Council]', 25 May 1637, CO 1/9, ff. 132–3; 'Petition from Sergeant Major Donne on behalf of Sir John Harvey, Knt., your Majesty's Governor of Virginia', [March 1639/40], CO 1/10, f. 190.

66. Richard Kemp to Secretary of State Windebank, 20 March 1639/40, CO 1/10, f. 160; Sir John Harvey to Windebank, 6 May 1640, abstracted in *CSPC*, p. 311, no. 67; Harvey to Windebank, 20 February 1637/8, CO 1/9, f. 202, and CO 1/9, f. 204. Harvey had sequestered Mathews's estates when he sent the planter and his associates to England. The failure to make that case forced the governor to a humiliating retreat, see Governor Harvey and Council of Virginia to the Privy Council, [18 January 1638/9], abstracted in *CSPC*, p. 288, no. 6. For his 'great grief' at the 'scandals and imputations' brought before the Privy Council against his government, see Governor Harvey and Council of Virginia to Windebank, 18 January 1638/9, abstracted in *CSPC*, p. 289, no. 8. Harvey's inability to reduce Virginia's factions compelled his friend George Donne to offer a(nother) prescription to the government for solving the colony's problems, see T. H. Breen (ed.), 'George Donne's "Virginia Reviewed": A 1638 Plan to Reform Colonial Society', *WMQ*, 3rd series, 30:3 (1973), pp. 449–66.

67. Captain W. Smith from Weymouth to Windebank, 4 October 1636, CO 1/9, ff. 54–5; Smith to the Council, 23 October 1636, aboard *The Black George*, CO 1/9, ff. 60–1; documents related to Admiralty case, CO 1/9, ff. 74–5, 76–7, 78, 80. Harvey's fellow royal officials, Jerome Hawley and Richard Kemp, also complained to the government about the financial losses they routinely incurred in the course of performing their offices, 'Richard Kemp's Petition', [1638], CO 1/9, f. 206, Jerome Hawley to Windebank, 8 May 1638, CO 1/9, ff. 255–6.

68. Harvey's situation paralleled that of the Lord Deputy in Dublin the time, Sir Thomas Wentworth, in terms of distance from the centre of government, but, of course, Wentworth had far better connections and more of a governmental apparatus at his disposal than the Virginia governor had, see Merritt (ed.), *The Political World of Thomas Wentworth*.

69. Even the ability of the most notorious devotees of 'Thorough' in Charles I's government, Thomas Wentworth, Earl of Strafford and lord-lieutenant of Ireland, and William Laud, archbishop of Canterbury, ran into obstacles at both the political centre and in the localities, see Sharpe, *The Personal Rule of Charles I*, pp. 537–600, 731–65. For the character of government service in Caroline England, see G. E. Aylmer, *The King's Servants: The Civil Service of Charles I, 1625–1642* (New York: Columbia University Press, 1961).

70. Cf. the classic analysis of Bernard Bailyn, 'Politics and Social Structure in Virginia', in Smith (ed.), *Seventeenth-Century America*, pp. 90–115, on pp. 90, 115. For the enduring historiographical significance of this essay, see M. Kammen and S. N. Katz, 'Bernard

Bailyn, Historian and Teacher: An Appreciation', and J. N. Rakove, '"How Else Could It End"?', both in Henretta et al. (eds), *The Transformation of Early American History*, pp. 3–15, on p. 4; pp. 51–69, on pp. 54–7. J. P. Greene, *Pursuits of Happiness*, which offers a similar view of early Virginia society and politics, has also been influential.

71. J. Kukla, 'Order and Chaos in Early America: Political and Social Stability in Pre-Restoration Virginia', *American Historical Review*, 90:2 (1985), pp. 275–98; J. Kukla, *Political Institutions in Virginia, 1619–1660* (New York: Garland Publishing, 1989).
72. W. Hunt, *The Puritan Moment: The Coming of Revolution in an English County* (Cambridge, MA: Harvard University Press, 1983), esp. pp. 159–82, provides an illustration of this situation in East Anglia, the bailiwick of Robert Rich, second Earl of Warwick, and prominent colonizing figure of Caroline England.
73. Charles I to [Governor and Council of Virginia], 22 April 1637, CO 1/9, ff. 121–3, on ff. 121v–2. Sir John Harvey to Secretary of State Windebank, 26 June 1636, CO 1/9, ff. 40–1, recommended the issuance of farthing tokens to alleviate 'the many more incommodities the want of money brings to that country' (f. 41). Another memorandum went from Jerome Hawley, a minor official in the household of Queen Henrietta Maria now set to become treasurer in the colony, to Windebank, 'concerning the regulation of the tobacco trade in Virginia', 27 June 1636, CO 1/9, ff. 44–5 (he set out the other four recommendations on f. 44). A similar memorandum went to the governors of the Caribbean colonies, see Charles I to [Earl of Carlisle and governors of the West Indies], 22 April 1637, CO 1/9, ff. 124–5.
74. Charles I to [Earl of Carlisle and governors of the West Indies], 22 April 1637, CO 1/9, ff. 124–5, on f. 122; 'Copy of Mr. Secretary's letter to Sir John Harvey Governor of Virginia concerning Mr. Hawley passed at Hampton Court, 10 Jan. 1636/37', CO 1/9, ff. 89–90.
75. For the date of the session, see Jerome Hawley to Sir Francis Windebank, 20 March 1637/8, CO 1/9, f. 215.
76. Charles I to [Governor and Council of Virginia], 22 April 1637, CO 1/9, ff. 121–3, on f. 121. Sir Francis Windebank to the Governor and Council of Virginia, 4 August 1636, also considers tobacco issues from an imperial perspective, CO 1/9, ff. 478.
77. See e.g., 'The Lord Baltimore's Answer to the Representation delivered to His Majesty in Council the 16th October 1667 from the Governor and Council of the Colony of Virginia', CO 1/21, ff. 269–70; '[Instructions to Governor Berkeley]', 12 September 1662, CO 1/6, ff. 270–9; 'To his Highness the Lord Protector of England, Scotland & Ireland and all the Dominions thereunto belonging: The Humble Petition of Samuel Mathews, Esq. in the behalf of the Inhabitants of the Colony of Virginia' [March 1654/5], CO 1/12, f. 95; 'Certain Reasons Humbly Offered showing why the English Plantations Abroad should be Encouraged and the Planting of Tobacco in England (Contrary to Several Acts and Ordinances) Prohibited', CO 1/12, ff. 102v–3.
78. 'The Reply of the Governor and Council to the Answer of the Burgesses', [March 1638], CO 1/9, ff. 234–5. This episode and the exchange it sparked between burgesses and governor receives fuller consideration in Roper, 'Charles I'.
79. Sir John Harvey to Sir Francis Windebank, 22 March 1637/8, CO 1/9, ff. 217–18.
80. For Goring's involvement in Virginia, see e.g., 'Members of the Subcommittee for Virginia [concerning Captain Morrison's position as commander of the fort at Point Comfort]', 2 April 1639, CO 1/10, f. 37.
81. 'The Humble Remonstrance of Diverse of the Principal Planters in Virginia and others that have long continued in that Plantation touching the Contract Proposed by the Lord

Goring & others his Majesty's agents for the Regulation of Tobacco', [May 1638], CO 1/9, f. 248v. Goring apparently discussed the idea of the contract with Hawley before the latter departed for Virginia, Hawley to Windebank, 27 June 1636, CO 1/9, ff. 42–3, on f. 42.
82. Sir Francis Wyatt to [Windebank], 25 March 1640, CO 1/10, f. 162.
83. A. Thrush, 'The Personal Rule of James I, 1611–1620', in Cogswell et al. (eds), *Politics, Religion, and Popularity in Early Stuart Britain*, pp. 84–102; T. Cogswell, *The Blessed Revolution*; Russell, *Parliaments and English Politics*.
84. Sharpe, *The Personal Rule of Charles I*, pp. 783–802.
85. D. Hirst, 'Locating the 1650s in England's Seventeenth Century', *History*, 81:263 (1996), pp. 359–84.
86. For the Ranters, see e.g., A. Coppe, *A Fiery Flying Roll* (London, 1649); for the fears Coppe and others generated, see e.g., Anon., *The Ranters Creed being a True Copie of the Examinations of a Blasphemous sort of People, commonly called Ranters, whose Names are herein Particularised, together with the Name of their pretended God Almighty, and their False Profit* (London, 1651).
87. A. Woolrych, *Commonwealth to Protectorate* (Oxford: Oxford University Press, 1982), provides a careful and detailed account of the demise of the English Republic (1649–53) and should be read in conjunction with David Underdown's classic treatment of the events leading up to execution of Charles I, *Pride's Purge: Politics in the Puritan Revolution* (Oxford: Clarendon Press, 1971). For the Restoration, see R. Hutton, *The Restoration: A Political and Religious History of England and Wales, 1658–1667* (Oxford: Clarendon Press, 1985). While the restored monarch was relatively tolerant both in terms of policy and in particular, he did order the exhumation of Cromwell's body, its posthumous drawing-and-quartering, and the display of its parts on the gates of the Tower as befits traitors.
88. D. Armitage, 'The Cromwellian Protectorate and the Languages of Empire', *Historical Journal*, 35:3 (1992), pp. 531–55. For Virginia royalism, which incorporated annoyance at the Navigation Acts, see e.g., *The Speech of the Honourable Sir William Berkeley Governour and Capt. Generall of Virginea, to the Burgesses in the Grand Assembly at James Towne on the 17 of March 1651* (The Hague, 1651). For the persistence of 'secret trade with the Dutch' in Virginia, see [Report to Secretary of State Thurloe], [June 1656?], MS Rawlinson A 38, ff. 703–6, on 704, Bodleian; W. G. Duvall, 'Smuggling Sotweed: Augustine Herrman and the Dutch Connection', *MHM*, 98:4 (2003), pp. 388–407.
89. For the 'Great Western Design' and the Barbadian response to it, see L. Gragg, *Englishmen Transplanted: The English Colonization of Barbados, 1627–1660* (New York: Oxford University Press, 2003), pp. 53–5, 156–7. For the significance of its failure as the graveyard of anti-Spanish imperial ideology in England, see K. O. Kupperman, 'Errand to the Indies: Puritan Colonization from Providence Island through the Western Design', *WMQ*, 3rd series, 45:1 (1988), pp. 70–99. The eighteenth-century pre-eminence of Jamaica, generated, as in the rest of the English West Indies, by sugar cultivation, did not become immediately apparent, see T. Burnard, 'European Migration to Jamaica, 1655–1780', *WMQ*, 3rd series, 53:4 (1996), pp. 769–96.
90. 'To his Highness the Lord Protector of England, Scotland & Ireland and all the Dominions thereunto belonging: The Humble Petition of Samuel Mathews, Esq. in the behalf of the Inhabitants of the Colony of Virginia' [6 March 1654/5], CO 1/12, f. 95; 'Certain Reasons Humbly Offered showing why the English Plantations Abroad should be

Encouraged and the Planting of Tobacco in England (Contrary to Several Acts and Ordinances) Prohibited', CO 1/12, ff. 102–3.
91. W. Prynne, *A Fresh Discovery of some Prodigious new Wandring-Blasing-Stars, & Firebrands, styling themselves New-Lights* (London, 1645).
92. For Modyford's career, see C. G. Pestana, *The English Atlantic in an Age of Revolution, 1640–1661* (Cambridge, MA: Harvard University Press, 2004), pp. 116–17, 167–8, 214–15. Pestana provides a fine narrative of colonial behaviour during the civil wars, but it can be difficult to share her characterization of the period as 'an age of revolution'. For Lord Willoughby's activities, see S. Barber, 'Power in the English Caribbean', in Roper and Van Ruymbeke (eds), *Constructing Early Modern Empires*, pp. 189–212.

6 Some Measure of Success

1. Samuel Mathews and Richard Bennett to Secretary of State Thurloe, 10 October 1656, MS Rawlinson A, f. 87, Bodleian.
2. L. Gatford, *Publick Good without Private Interest: or, A Compendious Remonstrance of the Present Sad State and Condition of the English Colonie in Virginia* (London, 1657), p. 9.
3. 'The Humble Petition of Coll: Wm: Claiborne a Poor Old Servant of your Majesty's Father & Grandfather', 13 March 1676/7, *Archives of Maryland Online*, at http://www.aomol.net/html/index.html, 4:157–239.
4. We have no satisfactory treatment of the life of the extraordinary Claiborne, although his descendants have been active in perpetuating his memory, see Hale, *Virginia Venturer*. The conception of Claiborne as 'Virginia founder' tends to emphasize his 'courage' and 'recognized ability', see C. Torrence, 'The English Ancestry of William Claiborne', *VMHB*, 56:4 (1948), pp. 431–60, on p. 433. For early Maryland's political difficulties, see e.g., R. R. Menard, 'Maryland's "Time of Troubles": Sources of Political Disorder in Early St. Mary's', *MHM*, 76:2 (1981), pp. 124–40; L. G. Carr, 'Sources of Political Stability and Upheaval in Seventeenth-Century Maryland', *MHM*, 79:1 (1984), pp. 44–70.
5. The Revd Gatford, for instance, lamented the many 'miscarriages of the Planters' committed against the Indians and condemned 'their licentiousness and wickedness' as a horrible example for the 'Heathen', see *Publick Good Without Private Interest*, pp. 5–8; for Barbados, see J. P. Greene, 'Changing Identity in the British Caribbean: Barbados as a Case Study', in N. P. Canny and A. Pagden (eds), *Colonial Identity in the Atlantic World, 1500–1800* (Princeton, NJ: Princeton University Press, 1987), pp. 213–66. At least one modern historian has identified a 'half-civilized, half-savage' sensibility formed on the 'periphery' of empire as the foundation of a developing American character, see B. Bailyn, *The Peopling of British North America*, pp. 20, 36–8.
6. 'Instructions to the Colonists by Lord Baltimore, 1633', in Hall, *Narratives*, pp. 16–23, on pp. 18–20.
7. 'A Briefe Relation of the Voyage unto Maryland, by Father Andrew White, 1634', in Hall, *Narratives*, pp. 39, 41; 'Extract from a Letter of Captain Thomas Yong to Sir Toby Matthew, 1634', in Hall, *Narratives*, pp. 53–61, on pp. 54–61.
8. According to Fr White, Harvey rendered his good office to Maryland in the hopes of securing Baltimore's assistance in recovering 'a great summe of money due to him out of the exchequer', Hall, *Narratives*, p. 39.
9. Petition from Lord Baltimore to Charles I, [March 1637/8], CO 1/9, f. 211; Meeting of the Commissioners for Plantations, 4 April 1638, CO 1/9, ff. 224–5. One of Claiborne's

partners at the time, the London merchant William Clobery, wrote to the secretary of state complaining of the 'many wrongs and oppressions which we suffer from the Lord Baltimore's people' and suggested that the Earl of Stirling, with whom Clobery was working on advancing the Canadian fur trade and Stirling's Nova Scotia proprietorship, be appointed mediator of the dispute, William Clobery to Sir John Coke, 28 June 1638, CO 1/9, f. 281. For the relationship between Claiborne, Clobery and Stirling, see Brenner, *Merchants and Revolution*, pp. 122–4.

10. *Virginia and Maryland, or the Lord Baltimore's Printed Case Uncased and Answered* (1655), in Hall, *Narratives*, pp. 183–230, on pp. 199–200. For general attitudes towards Catholics at the time, especially Irish, see E. H. Shagan, 'Constructing the Discord: Ideology, Propaganda, and English Responses to the Irish Rebellion of 1641', *Journal of British Studies*, 36:1 (1997), pp. 4–34.

11. Torrence, 'The English Ancestry of William Claiborne', p. 441.

12. Pestana, *The English Atlantic in an Age of Revolution*, pp. 34–7.

13. Dorset, like many contemporaries appalled by what had happened and by the behaviour of Charles I, nevertheless refused to abandon the king (moreover, he died in 1652), see D. L. Smith, 'The Fourth Earl of Dorset and the Personal Rule of Charles I', *Journal of British Studies*, 30:3 (1991), pp. 257–87.

14. Danvers, for whom the town of Danvers, Massachusetts, is named, remains a slippery figure, perhaps because, if we are to believe Aubrey, he was a notorious 'trimmer' himself; for instance, he allegedly signed the king's death warrant solely in the hopes of having the will of his brother, the Earl of Danby, overturned, see *Aubrey's Brief Lives*, ed. O. L. Dick (Boston, MA: David R. Godine, 1999), pp. 80–1. We have no direct evidence connecting Claiborne, Mathews and Danvers, but, curiously, several pamphlets related to Virginia and Bermuda, and including defences of the Virginia Company, were produced in 1651 and 1652 (while Claiborne and Mathews were in England) by connections of John Ferrar (who would have known Danvers, the old and close friend of the Ferrars; for which connection see, e.g., Sir John Danvers to [John Ferrar], 8 April 1653, in Ransome (ed.), *The Ferrar Papers*, reel 5, #1218; at least one of these efforts was dedicated to Danvers, see W[odenoth], *A Short Collection*). A restoration of the company might have meant a restoration of its lands as it held them in 1624, including Maryland, and a voiding of subsequent grants, such as Baltimore's. This tactic, if it was ever pursued, may have been sidetracked by the dissolution of the Council of State in 1653 by Cromwell and petered out with the death of Danvers in 1655.

15. A. J. Loomie, 'Oliver Cromwell's Policy toward the English Catholics: The Appraisal by Diplomats, 1654–1658', *Catholic Historical Review*, 90:1 (2004), pp. 29–44.

16. Billings, *Berkeley and the Forging of Colonial Virginia*, pp. 105–12. Claiborne, Mathews and Bennett seem to have suffered no ill effects from the exiled Charles II having named them as Virginia councillors, under Berkeley's governorship, on 3 June 1650, CO 5/1354, ff. 243–52.

17. For an account of the Maryland civil war, see Pestana, *The English Atlantic in an Age of Revolution*, pp. 149–54. For the pamphlet war between Baltimore and the Kent Islanders, see e.g., *The Lord Baltimore's Case* (1653), in Hall, *Narratives*, pp. 163–80; *Virginia and Maryland, or the Lord Baltimore's Printed Case Uncased and Answered* (1655), in Hall, *Narratives*; R. Heamans, *An Additional brief Narrative of a late Bloody Design against the Protestants in Ann Arundel County, and Severn in Maryland* (London, 1655); J. Hammond, *Hammond versus Heamans or an Answer to an Audacious Pamphlet, Published by an Impudent and Ridiculous Fellow, named Roger Heamans* (London, [1656]).

18. Cromwell confirmed Baltimore's 'pious and noble purpose' to settle his colony from Delaware Bay to the Potomac River, CO 1/10, ff. 159–60; [Agreement between the Proprietary and Commissioners], 30 November 1657, *Archives of Maryland Online*, at http://www.aomol.net/html/index.html, 3:332–4. Cromwell was by no means a friend to Catholicism, but he did not share the fervent fear of papists held by some of his contemporaries (although he regarded them as staunch royalists and, consequently, an inevitable threat to his position) and he maintained friendships with individual papists, see Loomie, 'Oliver Cromwell's Policy toward the English Catholics'.
19. Brenner, *Merchants and Revolution*, pp. 143–4; Kupperman, *Providence Island*, pp. 213, 280.
20. This partnership also provided the form by which the Kent Island colony was maintained before it collapsed into another of Claiborne's lengthy legal disputes in the early 1640s, see 'Claiborne v Clobery', *MHM*, 27 (1932), pp. 17–28, 99–114, 337–53; 28 (1933), pp. 26–43, 172–95, 257–65.
21. 'Deposition of Thomas Brooks of Wapping, Middlesex, boatswain's mate on the *Patience*, for George Lamberton', 4 May 1636, HCA 13/51, ff. 381v–4r.
22. Cf. D. Hancock, *Citizens of the World: London Merchants and the Integration of the British Atlantic Community, 1735–1785* (Cambridge: Cambridge University Press, 1995).
23. Brenner, *Merchants and Revolution*, pp. 125–35, 161–93.
24. According to Lamberton, his voyage yielded over 80 tusks of ivory worth 1s. 7d. per pound, along with some gold (worth £5 sterling) which he had acquired in exchange for 'some knives & all his aqua vita he sold to the Negroes upon the gold coast'. The rest of the trade goods he had brought were exchanged with other Europeans, see 'Deposition of Thomas Brooks'.
25. See *Winthrop's Journal*, entry of August 1643, vol. 2, pp. 141–2, entry of 20 September 1646, 286–7, for Lamberton's demise; Weslager, *The English on the Delaware*, pp. 93–100, 107–32, 260–2, 264–5. The New England expedition against the Hudson River colony during the first Anglo-Dutch War was thwarted by the announcement of the peace, see Mr John Leverett to the Protector, 5 September 1654, in T. Birch (ed.), 'State Papers, 1654: September (1 of 5)', *A Collection of the State Papers of John Thurloe, Volume 2: 1654* (London, 1742), pp. 580–90, at http://www.british-history.ac.uk/report.aspx?compid=55341&strquery="Sedgwick" [accessed 31 August 2008]. The English captured New Netherland in 1664 during the second Anglo–Dutch War; the Dutch exchanged the province for Surinam at the conclusion of that conflict.
26. Brenner, *Merchants and Revolution*, pp. 135–7, 150–3, 181–90. For Vassall's political stance and its personal ramifications, see pp. 227, 308. For his involvement in the Massachusetts Bay Company and Rhode Island, see The Charter of Massachusetts Bay, 18 March 1628/9, at the Avalon Project at the Yale Law School, at http://www.yale.edu/lawweb/avalon/states/mass03.htm, and Patent for Providence Plantations, 14 March 1643, at the Avalon Project, at http://www.yale.edu/lawweb/avalon/states/ri03.htm [both accessed 30 August 2008]. For the African activities of Vassall and others, see R. Porter, 'The Crispe Family and the African Trade in the Seventeenth Century', *Journal of African History*, 9:1 (1968), pp. 57–77, on pp. 69, 71; Gragg, *Englishmen Transplanted*, pp. 122–4.
27. Depositions and interrogatories from *Kingswell v Vassall*, HCA 13/51, ff. 195–6, 207–8, 237, 241, 270, 436–7, 475, 523. For Vassall's incarceration, see *CSPC*, p. 197. For his second Carolina venture, see W. L. Saunders (ed.), *The Colonial Records of North Carolina*, 10 vols (Raleigh, NC, 1886–90), vol. 1, pp. 14–16, 42–3, 102–14; Andrews, *Colonial*

Period of American History, vol. 3, pp. 182–91. Despite his massive analysis, it is hard to accept the fundamental conclusion of Brenner's characterization of the beliefs and behaviour of these 'new men', although there can be no questioning of the extent of their ambition and of their determination to preserve their interests: those of his 'revolutionary' subjects who lived to 1660, such as Thompson and Vassall, not only survived the Restoration, but seem to have suffered no ill consequences of their Interregnum status. Indeed, Charles II appointed Thompson a governor of the East India Company.

28. P. F. Campbell, 'Editor's Note', in *Chapters in Barbados History*, 1st series (Bridgetown: Barbados Museum and Historical Society, 1986), pp. 56–8. While Sir John certainly benefited from marrying his partner's widow and he certainly assisted in her assault on Berringer's English will, it remains unclear how, in the first instance, such a will would have survived the dower claims of the widow and, second, why seeking to preserve those rights, along with those of Berringer's children on Barbados, constitutes a necessarily dubious act; cf. Campbell (ed.), 'Editor's Note', in *Chapters in Barbados History*, pp. 58–9.

29. For Sir John's early years, see D. H. Sacks, *The Widening Gate: Bristol and the Atlantic Economy, 1450–1700* (Berkeley and Los Angeles, CA: University of California Press, 1991), pp. 264–5. For his career on Barbados, see E. M. Shilstone, 'Nicholas Plantation and some of its Associations', in Campbell (ed.), *Chapters in Barbados History*, pp. 49–60. For his involvement in Carolina, see Roper, *Conceiving Carolina*, pp. 42–5.

30. Aside from the playwrights cited in Chapter 2, the Revd Joseph Hall, later bishop of Norwich, was an acerbic critic of colonization. His *The Discovery of a New World or A Description of the South Indies Hetherto Unknowne* (London, 1609), with its satirical 'descriptions of 'Tenter-belly', 'Shee-lands' and 'Fooliana', lampoons the efforts of promoters. It is unclear how its dedicatee, William Herbert, third Earl of Pembroke, who, as we saw in Chapter 4, joined the Virginia Company, regarded this effort. The closing of the playhouses by parliament in 1642 may have helped the cause.

31. Sir John Elliott has noted that the performance of the English Navy in the first Anglo-Dutch War signalled the arrival of England as a stiff competitor for the Dutch Republic, Spain and France (as well as, presumably, Sweden). Even though it disappointed, the 'Western Design' also demonstrated that the English state had now the will and the way to pursue overseas policy directly even though it took rather longer to create the sort of bureaucracy the Spanish had created and established to run their empire, see J. H. Elliott, *Empires of the Atlantic World: Britain and Spain in America, 1492–1830* (New Haven, CT: Yale University Press, 2006), p. 114. It is interesting to speculate what course the Castilian Empire might have taken had the revolt of the *comuneros* of Castile in 1520 not disrupted the metropolis to the same degree that the civil wars did in England, especially given that the geographical scope of the respective empires was about the same, albeit 150 years apart, at the time rebellion began, see P. Zagorin, *Rebels and Rulers, 1500–1660*, 2 vols (Cambridge: Cambridge University Press, 1982), vol. 1, pp. 253–74. In any event, Elliott's observations do not note that the 1652–4 war contributed to the demise of the English Republic, despite its military success, see Woolrych, *Commonwealth to Protectorate*, pp. 277–88, 323–5. In the succeeding two conflicts between the nations, the Dutch held sway despite early English victories (including the capture of New Netherland) and the predicted end of the Republic at the hands of a Franco-English alliance in 1672 (which proved nearly true): de Ruyter's humiliating raid on the English fleet at anchor in the Medway (since the government could not pay its crews) punctuated the second war (1664–7), while the third (1672–4) confirmed Dutch control of Suri-

nam (with the English again having to settle for a consolation, New York), see J. Israel, *The Dutch Republic: Its Rise, Greatness, and Fall* (Oxford: Clarendon Press, 1995), pp. 756–825.

32. Thus, the battery of promotional pamphlets extolling the qualities of the various Anglo-American colonies which emanated from early modern printing presses continued, invariably, to stress the ready and relative availability of land as the primary attraction for relocating across the Atlantic, see e.g., [B. Clark], *A Brief Account of the Province of East-Jersey in America* (London, 1682), R. Frane, *A Short Description of Pennsylvania or a Relation what things are Known* (Philadelphia, 1692), R. Montgomery, *A Discourse concerning the Design'd Establishment of a New Colony to the South of Carolina* (London, 1717).

33. For Maryland, see D. A. Meyers, 'Lord Calvert's Catholic Colony', for Carolina, L. H. Roper, 'Conceiving an Anglo-American Proprietorship: Early South Carolina History in Perspective', both in Roper and Van Ruymbeke (eds), *Constructing Early Modern Empires*, pp. 356–88, 389–409.

34. D. Hirst, 'The Privy Council and the Problem of Enforcement in the 1620s', *Journal of British Studies*, 18:1 (1978), pp. 46–66.

35. For Dorset, see Smith, 'The Political Career of Edward Sackville'; for Warwick as patron, see Hunt, *The Puritan Moment*, pp. 240–50; as political figure, pp. 194–6, 210–6, 267–72. Warwick, like other colonizers, spread across the Atlantic as well, possessing colonial estates, see *The Rich Papers: Letters from Bermuda, 1615–1646*, ed. V. A. Ives (Toronto and Buffalo, NY: University of Toronto Press, 1984).

36. Although they did not immediately or necessarily resort to warfare, see e.g., J. H. Merrell, 'The Indians' New World: The Catawba Experience', *WMQ*, 3rd series, 41:4 (1984), pp. 538–65.

37. Billings, *Berkeley and the Forging of Colonial Virginia*, pp. 96–9. For continuing concerns about the colonial disinclination to settle in towns, see e.g., 'An Answere to a Declaracon of the Present State of Virginia', May, 1623, in *RVC*, vol. 4, pp. 130–51, on p. 133; Governor and Council of Virginia to Lords Commissioners for Virginia, 18 January 1638/9, CO 1/10, ff. 8–13, on f. 10v; Joseph West to Lords Proprietors of Carolina, 30 December 1674, MS Locke c. 30, ff. 6–7, Bodleian.

38. M. Rowlandson, *The Sovereignty and Goodness of God* (London, 1682); J. Lepore, *In the Name of War: King Philip's War and the Origins of American Identity* (New York: Alfred A. Knopf, 1998).

39. Roper, *Conceiving Carolina*, pp. 140–2.

40. Servitude numbers from England declined as the population levelled off in the latter half of the seventeenth century and as more colonial options, notably Pennsylvania (founded 1682), became available to prospective migrants, but overall numbers were maintained by servants from Scotland, Ireland and the Continent, especially Germany, see D. W. Galenson, 'The Rise and Fall of Indentured Servitude in the Americas: An Economic Analysis', *Journal of Economic History*, 44:1 (1984), pp. 1–26.

41. 'Instructions for Capt. Thomas Newman', 23 June 1636, CO 1/9, ff. 31–8, on f. 36.

42. 'From the Council', 11 November 1637, CO 1/9, f. 169. The Council was concerned with allegations that John Crisp had encroached on the Guinea Company's monopoly under false pretences 'to take Negroes, and to carry them to other foreign parts, whereby to defeat his Majesty of his customs, and to the great prejudice of the said company'. On the character of servitude in early Anglo-America, see Hatfield, *Atlantic Virginia*, pp. 136–9.

43. The fate of those, for instance, captured by the English in the 'Pequot War', see M. L. Fickes, '"They Could Not Endure That Yoke": The Captivity of Women and Children after the War of 1637', *New England Quarterly*, 73:1 (2000), pp. 58–81. The trade in Indian slaves (customarily to the West Indies) assumed particular importance after the founding of South Carolina in 1669, although it was officially illegal, see A. Gallay, *The Indian Slave Trade: The Rise of the English Empire in the American South, 1670–1717* (New Haven, CT: Yale University Press, 2002).
44. According to Betty Wood's synthesis of the subject, by the 1630s 'the English in Barbados had already devised a slave status for those West Africans already on the island'. This entailed 'the right to do as they pleased with their African workers', see Wood, *The Origins of American Slavery: Freedom and Bondage in the English Colonies* (New York: Hill & Wang, 1997), pp. 40, 60, 89.
45. In 1648, according to the Dutch visitor to the colony David Pietersz de Vries, Virginia had some 300 slaves, of whom Samuel Mathews, the running partner of William Claiborne, owned 40, or 13 per cent, the second highest total, see Hatfield, *Atlantic Virginia*, p. 168. By comparison, his Barbadian contemporary Major William Hilliard had houses on his plantation for 96 'Negroes', three Indian women slaves and 28 servants (Ligon used the term 'Christians'), see R. Ligon, *A True and Exact History of the Island of Barbados* (1657; London: Frank Cass, 1970), p. 22
46. Ligon, *A True and Exact History*, pp. 51, 53–4.
47. Ibid., p. 46.
48. A number of Virginia planters also had connections with the Dutch, who had become the leading slave-trading nation by this time, including Mathews, see Hatfield, *Atlantic Virginia*, pp. 140, 164–8. The degree to which fear of disorder led to extraordinary punishments in the 'New World' (and the early formation and spread of intercolonial networks) is demonstrated in a 1643 incident on Barbados reported by John Winthrop: the governor, Philip Bell 'Esq.' (a client of the Earl of Warwick's and former governor of Bermuda), 'complaining of the distracted condition of that island in regard of divers sects of familists [the Family of Love had been notorious since Elizabethan times for their alleged anarchical practices, including free love] sprung up there, and their turbulent practices, which had forced him to proceed against some of them by banishment, and others of mean quality by whipping'. Bell asked Winthrop to send ministers to reform the morals of his colonists, but to no avail, see *Winthrop's Journal*, entry of August 1643, vol. 2, pp. 142–3. For the Family of Love and its reputation, see C. W. Marsh, *The Family of Love in English Society, 1550–1630* (Cambridge: Cambridge University Press, 1994).
49. On his plantation of 500 acres, Thomas Modyford had devoted 200 acres to sugar by 1647 and 70 to provisions, see Ligon, *A True and Exact History*, p. 22; for this general tendency, see Hatfield, *Atlantic Virginia*, pp. 154–68; Gragg, *Englishmen Transplanted*, pp. 98–112.
50. For Barbados, see R. S. Dunn, 'The Barbados Census of 1680: Profile of the Richest Colony in America', *WMQ*, 3rd series, 26:1 (1969), pp. 4–30; R. S. Dunn, *Sugar and Slaves: The Rise of the Planter Class in the West Indies, 1624–1713* (Chapel Hill, NC: University of North Carolina Press, 1972). The purportedly rabid pursuit of colonial wealth and power via staple agriculture and the enslavement of Africans spread all too readily to the Carolina Lowcountry on the mainland, where the population developed a 'black majority' as early as 1708. For the characterization of Yeamans, which accepts without question the belief that Sir John 'murdered' Bellinger, and of the West Indies in the seventeenth century, see A. Taylor *American Colonies: The Settling of North America* (New

York: Penguin, 2001), p. 223. J. P. Greene, *Imperatives, Behaviors and Identities: Essays in Early American Cultural History* (Charlottesville, VA: University of Virginia Press, 1992), characterizes Barbados as an Anglo-American 'cultural hearth' at p. 69. These West Indian effects, both in terms of their general distinctiveness and their particular impact on Carolina, have been overstated, see Roper, *Conceiving Carolina*, pp. 6–13; L. H. Roper, 'Big Fish in a Bigger Transatlantic Pond: The Social and Political Leadership of Early Modern Anglo-American Colonies', in C. Laux, F.-J. Ruggiu and P. Singaravelou (eds), *Les élites européennes dans les colonies du début du XVI siècle au milieu du XXe siècle* (Bern: Peter Lang, forthcoming).

51. Berlin, *Generations of Captivity*, pp. 9–10, 67–8; R. R. Menard, 'Financing the Lowcountry Export Boom: Capital and Growth in Early South Carolina', *WMQ*, 3rd series, 51:4 (1994), pp. 659–76; R. R. Menard, 'The Africanization of the Lowcountry Labor Force, 1670–1730', in W. D. Jordan and S. L. Skemp (eds), *Race and Family in the Colonial South* (Jackson, MS, and London: University Press of Mississippi, 1987), pp. 81–105.
52. Ligon, *A True and Exact History*, p. 1. Involuntary migrants, especially, of course, enslaved Africans and Indians, had no 'motive for migration'.
53. For the Spanish Empire under the later Habsburgs, see H. Kamen, *Empire: How Spain Became a World Power, 1492–1763* (New York: HarperCollins, 2003), pp. 381–437.
54. Cf. E. Mancke, 'Negotiating an Empire: Britain and its Overseas Peripheries, c. 1550–1780', in C. Daniels and M. V. Kennedy (eds), *Negotiated Empires: Centers and Peripheries in the Americas, 1500–1820* (New York and London: Routledge, 2002), pp. 235–65, which gives the metropolitan government too great a role, at least for the seventeenth century, in imperial development.
55. While a 'Glorious Revolution' was effected in terms of the official character and ideology of the monarchy, this rethink about the nature of state and local relations which ultimately prompted reorientation of state and empire in fact largely stemmed from the activities and attitudes of James II from his days as Duke of York, see J. Miller, 'The Crown and the Borough Charters in the Reign of Charles II', *English Historical Review*, 100:394 (1985), pp. 53–84; S. C. A. Pincus, 'From Butterboxes to Wooden Shoes: The Shift in English Popular Sentiment from Anti-Dutch to Anti-French in the 1670s', *Historical Journal*, 38:2 (1995), pp. 333–61. For the continuation of certain behaviour and even personnel between the governments of James II and William III, notwithstanding the 'Glorious Revolution' of 1688–9, see S. S. Webb, 'Imperial Fixer: From Popish Plot to Glorious Revolution', *WMQ*, 3rd series, 25:1 (1968), pp. 4–21; S. S. Webb, 'Imperial Fixer: Muddling through to Empire, 1689–1717', *WMQ*, 3rd series, 26:3 (1969), pp. 373–415; cf. J. P. Greene et al., 'Roundtable', *WMQ*, 3rd series, 64:2 (2007), pp. 235–86. Despite increasing 'centralization' and 'state-building' after the Restoration, 'private' entities continued to take the lead in founding colonies, such as the Georgia Trustees in 1732, see J. O. Spady, 'Bubbles and Beggars and the Bodies of Laborers: the Georgia Trusteeship's Colonialism Reconsidered', in Roper and Van Ruymbeke (eds), *Constructing Early Modern Empires*, pp. 213–68.
56. Although the need to resort to the terminology of the social sciences to comprehend this history remains unclear, cf. J. P. Greene, 'Social and Cultural Capital in Colonial British America: A Case Study', *Journal of Interdisciplinary History*, 29:3 (1999), pp. 491–509.
57. In addition to those careers discussed here, such non-English families as the Delanceys (Huguenots), Livingstons (Scots), Phillipses and van Cortlandts (both Dutch) became preeminent in New York and spent the eighteenth century battling each other for pre-

eminence in that colony; the Draxes, Modyfords and Codringtons did the same in seventeenth-century Barbados; the Lee, Harrison, and Carter families joined William Byrd at the top of Virginia society by the end of the seventeenth century; the descendants of John Winthrop formed a similar endogamy with the Dudley, Sewall and Bradstreet families in Massachusetts Bay, see P. U. Bonomi, *A Factious People: Politics and Society in Colonial New York* (New York: Columbia University Press, 1971); Dunn, *Sugar and Slaves*; R. Isaac, *The Transformation of Virginia, 1740–1790* (Chapel Hill, NC: University of North Carolina Press, 1982); R. L. Bushman, *King and People in Provincial Massachusetts* (Chapel Hill, NC: University of North Carolina Press, 1985).

58. See e.g., I. Altman and J. P. P. Horn (eds), *'To Make America': European Emigration in the Early Modern Period* (Berkeley and Los Angeles, CA: University of California Press, 1991); N. P. Canny (ed.), *Europeans on the Move: Studies on European Migration, 1500–1800* (Oxford: Clarendon Press, 1994); P. Clark and D. Souden (eds), *Migration and Society in Early Modern England* (Totowa, NJ: Barnes & Noble, 1988).

59. Cf. e.g., B. Bailyn, *Atlantic History*; Games, 'Atlantic History', pp. 741–57; Games, 'Beyond the Atlantic', pp. 675–92. Washington, of course, used a most advantageous marriage to the wealthy widow Martha Dandridge Custis, his surveying skills and his association with Thomas Fairfax, sixth Lord Fairfax of Cameron, to move from the minor gentry to the upper strata of Virginia society, while his military and political lieutenant Alexander Hamilton, born the illegitimate son of a Scottish merchant on St Croix in the Danish Virgin Islands, rose to prominence in a similar way in New York, see M. Cunliffe, *George Washington: Man and Monument* (Boston: Little Brown, 1958); J. E. Cooke, *Alexander Hamilton: A Biography* (New York: Hill and Wang, 1967).

60. Even today, despite decades of clamour for reform, the primary means of raising revenue for local governments in New York State remains the tax on real property.

61. W. D. Smith, 'Complications of the Commonplace: Tea, Sugar, and Imperialism', *Journal of Interdisciplinary History*, 23:2 (1992), pp. 259–78; E. Chalus, 'Elite Women, Social Politics, and the Political World of Late Eighteenth-Century England', *Historical Journal*, 43:3 (2000), pp. 666–97; R. Mukherjee, 'Trade and Empire in Awadh, 1765–1804', *Past and Present*, 94 (1982), pp. 85–102; F. Anderson, *Crucible of War: the Seven Years War and the Fate of Empire in British North America, 1754–1766* (New York: Alfred A. Knopf, 2000).

WORKS CITED

Manuscripts

Beinecke Rare Book and Manuscript Library, Yale University, James Marshall and Marie-Louise Osborn Collection.

Bodleian Library, University of Oxford
  MS Bankes, Papers of Sir John Bankes.
  MS Rawlinson, Papers of Dr Richard Rawlinson.

British Library, Egerton MS.

Centre for Kentish Studies, Maidstone, Kent, Sackville Papers (Virginia).

National Archives of Great Britain, Kew, Richmond, Surrey
  High Court of Admiralty Papers.
  State Papers, Colonial Office Series.

Primary Sources

Alexander, W., *An Encouragement to Colonies* (London, 1624).

Anon., *The Ranters Creed being a True Copie of the Examinations of a Blasphemous sort of People, commonly called Ranters, whose Names are herein Particularised, together with the Name of their pretended God Almighty, and their False Profit* (London, 1651).

—, *Some Reasons Humbly Offered to the Consideration of the Parliament for the Continuance of the Writs of Capias, and Process of Arrest, in Actions of Debt, &c.* (London, 1671).

Archives of Maryland, at http://www.aomol.net/html/index.html.

Aspinwall Papers, *Collections of the Massachusetts Historical Society*, 4th series, vol. 9 (Boston, MA, 1881).

Aubrey, J., *Aubrey's Brief Lives*, ed. O. L. Dick (Boston, MA: David R. Godine, 1999).

Barret, W., *A True Declaration of the Estate of the Colonie in Virginia* (1610), in Force (ed.), *Tracts and Other Papers*, vol. 3.

Berkeley, W., *The Speech of the Honourable Sir William Berkeley Governour and Capt. Generall of Virginea, to the Burgesses in the Grand Assembly at James Towne on the 17 of March 1651* (The Hague, 1651).

[Berkeley, W.], *A Discourse and View of Virginia* (London, 1663).

Beverly, R., *The History and Present State of Virginia* (London, 1705).

Billings, W. M. (ed.), *The Old Dominion in the Seventeenth Century: A Documentary History of Virginia, 1606–1689* (Chapel Hill, NC: University of North Carolina Press, 1975).

— (ed.), *The Papers of Sir William Berkeley* (Richmond, VA: Library of Virginia, 2007).

Birch, T. (ed.), 'State Papers, 1654: September (1 of 5)', *A Collection of the State Papers of John Thurloe, Volume 2: 1654* (London, 1742).

[Bradford, W.], *Bradford's History 'Of Plimoth Plantation'* (Boston, MA: Wright and Potter, 1928).

Breen, T. H. (ed.), 'George Donne's "Virginia Reviewed": A 1638 Plan to Reform Colonial Society', *William and Mary Quarterly*, 3rd series, 30:3 (1973), pp. 449–66.

Brereton, J., *A Briefe and True Relation of the Discouerie of the North Part of Virginia* (London, 1602).

Brown, A. M., (ed.), *The Genesis of the United States*, 2 vols (Boston, MA, and New York: Houghton Mifflin and Company, 1897).

Chamberlain, J., *The Letters of John Chamberlain*, ed. N. E. McClure, 2 vols (Philadelphia, PA: Memoirs of the American Philosophical Society, 1939).

'Claiborne v Clobery in the High Court of Admiralty', *Maryland Historical Magazine*, 27 (1932), pp. 17–28, 99–114, 337–53; 28 (1933), pp. 26–43, 172–95, 257–65.

[Clark, B.], *A Brief Account of the Province of East-Jersey in America* (London, 1682).

Coppe, A., *A Fiery Flying Roll* (London, 1649).

Crashaw, W., *A New-Yeeres Gift to Virginiea, a Sermon Preached in London before the Right Honourable the Lord Lawarre, Lord Gouernour and Captaine Generall of Virginea, and others of his Maiesties Counsell for that Kingdome, and the Rest of the Aduenturers in that Plantation* (London, 1610).

Edwards, E., *The Life of Sir Walter Ralegh ... together with his Letters* (London: Macmillan, 1868).

Ferrar, N., *Sir Thomas Smith's Misgovernment of the Virginia Company* (1625), ed. D. R. Ransome (Cambridge: Roxburghe Club, 1990).

Force, P. (ed), *Tracts and Other Papers Related to the Settlement of the United States*, 4 vols (Washington, DC, 1838–46).

Frane, R., *A Short Description of Pennsylvania or a Relation what things are Known* (Philadelphia, 1692).

Gatford, L., *Publick Good without Private Interest: or, A Compendious Remonstrance of the Present Sad State and Condition of the English Colonie in Virginia* (London, 1657).

Hakluyt, R., and R. Hakluyt, *The Original Writings and Correspondence of the Two Richard Hakluyts*, ed. E. G. R. Taylor (London: Hakluyt Society, 1935).

Hall, C. C. (ed.), *Narratives of Early Maryland 1633–1683* (New York: Charles Scribner's Sons, 1910).

H[all], J., *The Discovery of a New World or A Description of the South Indies Hetherto Unknowne* (London, 1609).

Hammond, J., *Hammond versus Heamans or an Answer to an Audacious Pamphlet, Published by an Impudent and Ridiculous Fellow, named Roger Heamans* (London, [1656]).

Hamor, R., *A True Discourse of the Present Estate of Virginia, and the Successe of the Affaires there till the 18 of June 1614* (1615), in Smith, *Writings*, pp. 1115–68.

Harrison, W., *The Description of England: The Classic Contemporary Account of Tudor Social Life*, ed. G. Edelen (1587; New York: Dover Publications, Inc., 1994).

Harvey, J., 'A Briefe Declaration of the State of Virginia at my comminge from thence in February 16[23/]24', *Collections of the Massachusetts Historical Society*, 4th series, vol. 9 (Boston, MA, 1871).

Heamans, R., *An Additional brief Narrative of a late Bloody Design against the Protestants in Ann Arundel County, and Severn in Maryland* (London, 1655).

Herford, C. H., and P. Simpson (eds), *Works of Ben Jonson*, 10 vols (Oxford: Clarendon Press, 1932).

James I, *His Maiesties Gracious Letter to the Earle of Southampton, Treasurer, and to the Councell and Company of Virginia here: Commending the present setting up of Silke Works, and Planting of Vines in Virginia* (London, 1622).

Johnson, R., *Nova Britannia Offering Most Excellent Fruits by Planting in Virginia* (1609), in *American Colonial Tracts Monthly*, 1:6 (1897–8).

—, *The New Life of Virginia Declaring the Former Success and Present Estate of the Plantation, being the Second Part of Nova Britannia* (1612), in *American Colonial Tracts Monthly*, 1:7 (April–May 1897).

Kingsbury, S. M. (ed.), *The Records of the Virginia Company of London*, 4 vols (Washington, DC: Library of Congress, 1906–35).

Lawne, C., *Brownisme Turned the In-Side Out-Ward* (London, 1613).

Ligon, R., *A True and Exact History of the Island of Barbados* (1657; London: Frank Cass, 1970).

Lownes, H., *A True Relation of the Vnvust, Cruell, and Barbarous Proceedings against the English at Amboyna in the East-Indies* (London, 1624).

Montgomery, R., *A Discourse concerning the Design'd Establishment of a New Colony to the South of Carolina* (London, 1717).

More, T., *Utopia* (1516), ed. G. M. Logan and R. M. Adams (Cambridge: Cambridge University Press, 1989).

Morgan, E. S. (ed.), *The Founding of Massachusetts: Historians and the Sources* (Indianapolis, IN: Bobbs-Merrill Co., 1964).

Morton, T., *New English Canaan or New Canaan. Containing an Abstract of New England* (Amsterdam, 1637).

Myers, A. C. (ed.), *Narratives of Early Pennsylvania, West New Jersey and Delaware, 1630–1707* (New York: Charles Scribner's Sons, 1912).

Percy, G., 'Observations Gathered out of a Discourse of the Plantation of the Southerne Colonie in Virginia' (London, 1606/7), in Smith, *Writings*, pp. 920–34.

—, 'A Trewe Relaycion of the Proceedings and Ocurrentes of Momente which have Hapned in Virginia', in Smith, *Writings*, pp. 1093–114.

Plowden, B. M., *Records of the Plowden Family* (privately published, 1887).

Prynne, W., *A Fresh Discovery of some Prodigious new Wandring-Blasing-Stars, & Firebrands, styling themselves New-Lights* (London, 1645).

Purchas, S., *Hakluytus Posthumus or Purchas His Pilgrimes: Contayning a History of the World in Sea Voyages and Lande Travells by Englishmen and others*, 20 vols (New York: AMS Press, 1965).

Ransome, D. R. (ed.), *The Ferrar Papers, 1590–1790 in Magdalene College, Cambridge* (East Ardsley, Yorkshire: Microform Academic Publishers, 1992).

Rich, N., *The Rich Papers: Letters from Bermuda, 1615–1646*, ed. V. A. Ives (Toronto and Buffalo, NY: University of Toronto Press, 1984).

Robinson, J., *A Iustification of Separation from the Church of England* ([Amsterdam], 1610).

Rolfe, J., *A True Relation of the State of Virginia lefte by Sir Thomas Dale Knight in May last 1616* (1617), in Smith, *Writings*, pp. 1174–85.

Rowlandson, M., *The Sovereignty and Goodness of God* (London, 1682).

Sainsbury, W. N. (ed.), *Calendar of State Papers, Colonial Series, 1574–1660, preserved in the State Paper Department of Her Majesty's Public Record Office* (London, 1860).

Salley, A. S. (ed.), *Narratives of Early Carolina, 1650–1708* (1911; New York: Barnes & Noble, 1967).

Saunders, W. L. (ed.), *The Colonial Records of North Carolina*, 10 vols (Raleigh, NC, 1886–90).

Shakespeare, W., *The Tempest*, ed. V. M. Vaughan and A. T. Vaughan (London, Arden Shakespeare Edition, 1999).

Sidney, P., *The Countesse of Pembrokes Arcadia* (London, 1590).

Smith, J., *The Complete Works of Captain John Smith (1580–1631)*, ed. P. L. Barbour, 3 vols (Chapel Hill, NC: University of North Carolina Press, 1986).

—, *A True Relation of such Occurrences and Accidents of Noate as hath Hapned in Virginia since the First Planting of that Collony, which is now Resident in the South part thereof, till the Last Returne* (1608), in Smith, *Writings*, pp. 5–40.

—, *The Proceedings of the English Colonie in Virginia* (1612), in Smith, *Writings*, pp. 35–118.

—, *A Description of New England* (1616), in Smith, *Writings*, pp. 119–71.

—, *New England's Trials* (1622), in Smith, *Writings*, pp. 175–97.

—, *The Generall Historie of Virginia, New-England, and the Summer Isles* (1624), in Smith, *Writings*, pp. 199–670.

—, *The True Travels, Adventures, and Obsevations of Captaine John Smith* (1630), in Smith, *Writings*, pp. 671–770.

—, *Advertisements for the Unexperienced Planters of New-England or any where* (1631), in Smith, *Writings*, pp. 771–816.

—, *Writings with Other Narratives of Roanoke, Jamestown, and the First English Settlement of America*, ed. J. Horn (New York: The Library of America, 2007).

Strachey, W., *A True Reportory of the Wracke, and Redemption of Sir Thomas Gates Knight* (1612), in Smith, *Writings*, pp. 979–1037.

[Strachey, W.], *For the Colony in Virginea Britannia. Laws Divine, Morall and Martiall* (London, 1612).

Strafford, T. W., *The Earl of Strafford's Letters and Dispatches*, ed. W. Knowler, 2 vols (London, 1739).

Tyler, L. G. (ed.), *Narratives of Early Virginia 1606–1625* (New York: Charles Scribner's Sons, 1907).

[Virginia Company], *A True and Sincere Declaration of the Purpose and Ends of the Plantation begun in Virginia* (London, 1610).

West, T., Baron de la Ware, *Relation of the Lord De-La-Warre* (1611), in Tyler (ed.), *Narratives*, pp. 209–14.

Wingfield, E. M., 'A Discourse of Virginia' (1608), in Smith, *Writings*, pp. 950–66.

Winthrop, J., 'A Modell of Christian Charity' (1630), in Morgan (ed.), *The Founding of Massachusetts*, pp. 190–204.

—, *Winthrop's Journal: 'History of New England'*, ed. J. K. Hosmer, 2 vols (New York: Charles Scribner's Sons, 1908).

W[odenoth], A., *A Short Collection of the Most Remarkable Passages from the Original to the Dissolution of the Virginia Company* (London, 1651).

Wodenoth, R., *A New Description of Virginia* (London, 1649).

—, *A Rare and New Discovery* (London, 1652).

Wroth, M., *The Countesse of Mountgomeries Urania* (London, 1621).

Secondary Sources

Abrams, A. U., *The Pilgrims and Pocahontas: Rival Myths of American Origin* (Boulder, CO: Westview Press, 1999).

Adams, S., 'Spain or the Netherlands? The Dilemmas of Early Stuart Foreign Policy', in H. Tomlinson (ed.), *Before the English Civil War: Essays on Early Stuart Politics and Government* (New York: St Martin's Press, 1984), pp. 79–101.

Alsop, J. D., 'William Welwood, Anne of Denmark and the Sovereignty of the Sea', *Scottish Historical Review*, 59 (1980), pp. 171–4.

Altman, I., and J. P. P. Horn (eds), *'To Make America': European Emigration in the Early Modern Period* (Berkeley and Los Angeles, CA: University of California Press, 1991).

Anderson, F., *Crucible of War: the Seven Years War and the Fate of Empire in British North America, 1754–1766* (New York: Alfred A. Knopf, 2000).

Anderson, V. D., *New England's Generation: The Great Migration and the Formation of Society and Culture in the Seventeenth Century* (Cambridge: Cambridge University Press, 1991).

Andrews, C. M., *The Colonial Period of American History*, 4 vols (New Haven, CT: Yale University Press, 1934–8).

Andrews, K. R., *Elizabethan Privateering: English Privateering during the Spanish War, 1585–1603* (Cambridge: Cambridge University Press, 1964).

Appelbaum, R., and J. Wood Sweet (eds), *Envisioning an English Empire: Jamestown and the Making of the North Atlantic World* (Philadelphia, PA: University of Pennsylvania Press, 2005).

Armitage, D., 'The Cromwellian Protectorate and the Languages of Empire', *Historical Journal*, 35:3 (1992), pp. 531–55.

—, 'Making the Empire British: Scotland in the Atlantic World, 1542–1707', *Past and Present*, 155 (May, 1997), pp. 34–63.

—, 'Literatures and Empire', in Canny (ed.), *The Origins of Empire*, pp. 99–123.

—, 'Greater Britain: A Useful Category of Analysis?', *American Historical Review*, 104:2 (1999), pp. 427–45.

—, *The Ideological Origins of the British Empire* (Cambridge: Cambridge University Press, 2001).

Armitage, D., and M. Braddick (eds), *The British Atlantic World, 1500–1800* (New York and Houndmills, Hampshire: Palgrave Macmillan, 2002).

Aston, M., 'English Ruins and English History: The Dissolution and the Sense of the Past', *Journal of the Warburg and Courtauld Institutes*, 36 (1973), pp. 231–55.

Aylmer, G. E., *The King's Servants: The Civil Service of Charles I, 1625–1642* (New York: Columbia University Press, 1961).

—, 'Buckingham as an Administrative Reformer?', *English Historical Review*, 105:415 (1990), pp. 355–62.

Bailey, M., 'Demographic Decline in Late Medieval England: Some Thoughts on Recent Research', *Economic History Review*, n.s., 49:1 (1996), pp. 1–19.

—, 'The Commercialization of the English Economy, 1086–1500', *Journal of Medieval History*, 24:3 (1998), pp. 297–311.

Bailyn, B. 'Politics and Social Structure in Virginia', in J. M. Smith (ed.), *Seventeenth-Century America: Essays in Colonial History* (Chapel Hill, NC: University of North Carolina Press, 1959), pp. 90–115.

—, *The Peopling of British North America: an Introduction* (New York: Alfred A. Knopf, 1986).

—, *Atlantic History: Concepts and Contours* (Cambridge, MA: Harvard University Press, 2005).

Barker, F., and P. Hulme, 'Nymphs and Reapers Heavily Vanish: The Discursive Contexts of *The Tempest*', in Graff and Phelan (eds), *The Tempest*, pp. 229–46.

Banerjee, P., 'The White Othello: Turkey and Virginia in John Smith's *True Travels*', in Appelbaum and Wood Sweet (eds), *Envisioning an English Empire*, pp. 135–51

Barbour, P. L., 'Captain John Smith's Route through Turkey and Russia', *William and Mary Quarterly*, 3rd series, 14:3 (1957), pp. 358–69.

—, 'Captain George Kendall: Mutineer or Intelligencer?', *Virginia Magazine of History and Biography*, 70:3 (1962), pp. 297–313.

Barroll, J. L., 'The Court of the First Stuart Queen', in Peck (ed.), *The Mental World of the Jacobean Court*, pp. 191–208.

—, 'The Arts at the English Court of Anna of Denmark', in S. P. Cerasano and M. Wynne-Davies (eds), *Readings in Renaissance Women's Drama: Criticism, History, and Performance, 1594–1998* (London and New York: Routledge, 1998), pp. 47–59.

—, *Anna of Denmark, Queen of England: A Cultural Biography* (Philadelphia, PA: University of Pennsylvania Press, 2001).

Bellany, A., *The Politics of Court Scandal in Early Modern England: News Culture and the Overbury Affair, 1603–1660* (Cambridge: Cambridge University Press, 2002).

Berlin, I., *Generations of Captivity: A History of African-American Slaves* (Cambridge, MA: Harvard University Press, 2003).

Bernhard, V., 'Beyond the Chesapeake: The Contrasting Status of Blacks in Bermuda, 1616–1663', *Journal of Southern History*, 54:4 (1988), pp. 545–64.

Billings, W. M., *A Little Parliament: The Virginia General Assembly in the Seventeenth Century* (Richmond, VA: Library of Virginia, 2007).

—, *Sir William Berkeley and the Forging of Colonial Virginia* (Baton Rouge, LA: Louisiana State University Press, 2004).

Bonomi, P. U., *A Factious People: Politics and Society in Colonial New York* (New York: Columbia University Press, 1971).

Braddick, M. J., *State Formation in Early Modern England, c. 1550–1700* (Cambridge: Cambridge University Press, 2000).

Bremer, F. J., *John Winthrop: America's Forgotten Founding Father* (New York: Oxford University Press, 2003).

Brennan, M., *Literary Patronage in the English Renaissance: The Pembroke Family* (London and New York: Routledge, Chapman & Hall, Inc., 1988).

Brenner, R., 'The Civil War Politics of London's Merchant Community', *Past and Present*, 58 (1973), pp. 53–107.

—, *Merchants and Revolution: Commercial Change, Political Conflict, and London's Overseas Traders, 1550–1653* (1993; London: Verso, 2003).

Brigden, S., 'Religion and Social Obligation in Early Sixteenth-Century London', *Past and Present*, 103 (May 1984), pp. 67–112.

Britnell, R., 'Town Life', in Horrox and Ormrod (eds), *A Social History of England*, pp. 134–78.

Brown, K. M., *Good Wives, Nasty Wenches, and Anxious Patriarchs: Gender, Race, and Power in Colonial Virginia* (Chapel Hill, NC: University of North Carolina Press, 1996).

Brown, P., '"This Thing of Darkness I Acknowledge Mine": *The Tempest* and the Discourse of Colonialism', in Graff and Phelan (eds), *The Tempest*, pp. 205–29.

Burgess, G., 'On Revisionism: An Analysis of Early Stuart Historiography in the 1970s and 1980s', *Historical Journal*, 33:3 (2007), pp. 609–27.

Burnard, T., 'European Migration to Jamaica, 1655–1780', *William and Mary Quarterly*, 3rd series, 53:4 (1996), pp. 769–96.

Bushman, R. L., *King and People in Provincial Massachusetts* (Chapel Hill, NC: University of North Carolina Press, 1985).

Campbell, P. F. (ed.), *Chapters in Barbados History*, 1st series (Bridgetown: Barbados Museum and Historical Society, 1986), pp. 49–60.

Cañizeras-Esguerra, J., *Puritan Conquistadors: Iberianizing the Atlantic* (Stanford, CA: Stanford University Press, 2006).

Canny, N. P., 'The Ideology of English Colonization from Ireland to America', *William and Mary Quarterly*, 3rd series, 30:4 (1973), pp. 573–98.

— (ed.), *The Origins of Empire*, vol. 1 in W. R. Louis (ed.), *The Oxford History of the British Empire*, 5 vols (Oxford: Oxford University Press, 1998–2000).

Carr, L. G., 'Sources of Political Stability and Upheaval in Seventeenth-Century Maryland', *Maryland Historical Magazine*, 79:1 (1984), pp. 44–70.

Carr, L. G., and L. S. Walsh, 'The Planter's Wife: The Experience of White Women in Seventeenth-Century Maryland', *William and Mary Quarterly*, 3rd series, 34:4 (1977), pp. 542–71.

—, 'The Standard of Living in the Colonial Chesapeake', *William and Mary Quarterly*, 3rd series, 45:1 (1988), pp. 135–59.

Carr, L. G., P. D. Morgan and J. B. Russo (eds), *Colonial Chesapeake Society* (Chapel Hill, NC: University of North Carolina Press, 1988).

Cell, G. T., *Newfoundland Discovered: English Attempts at Colonisation, 1610–1630* (London: Hakluyt Society, 1982).

Chalus, E., 'Elite Women, Social Politics, and the Political World of Late Eighteenth-Century England', *Historical Journal*, 43:3 (2000), pp. 666–97.

Clark, G., and A. Clark, 'Common Rights to Land in England, 1475–1839', *Journal of Economic History*, 61:4 (2001), pp. 1009–36.

Clark, J. C. D., *Revolution and Rebellion: State and Society in England in the Seventeenth and Eighteenth Centuries* (Cambridge: Cambridge University Press, 1985).

—, *The Language of Liberty, 1660–1832: Political Discourse and Social Dynamics in the Anglo-American World* (Cambridge: Cambridge University Press, 1994).

—, 'The Strange Death of British History? Reflections on Anglo-American Scholarship', *Historical Journal*, 40:3 (1997), pp. 787–809.

—, *English Society, 1688–1832: Ideology, Social Structure, and Political Practice during the Ancien Regime*, 2nd edn (Cambridge: Cambridge University Press, 2000).

Clark, P., and P. Slack (eds), *Crisis and Order in English Towns 1500–1700: Essays in Urban History* (Toronto and Buffalo, NY: University of Toronto Press, 1972).

Clark, P., and D. Souden (eds), *Migration and Society in Early Modern England* (Totowa, NJ: Barnes & Noble, 1988).

Coakley, T. M., 'George Calvert and Newfoundland: "The Sad Face of Winter"', *Maryland Historical Magazine*, 100:1 (2005), pp. 7–28.

Cogswell, T., *The Blessed Revolution: English Politics and the Coming of War, 1621–1624* (Cambridge: Cambridge University Press, 1989).

—, '"In the Power of the State": Mr Anys's Project and the Tobacco Colonies, 1616–1628', *English Historical Review*, 123:500 (2008), pp. 35–64.

Cogswell, T., R. Cust and P. Lake (eds), *Politics, Religion, and Popularity in Early Stuart Britain: Essays in Honour of Conrad Russell* (Cambridge: Cambridge University Press, 2002).

Collinson, P. (ed.), *Elizabethan Essays* (London: Hambledon Press, 1994).

Cooke, J. E., *Alexander Hamilton: A Biography* (New York: Hill and Wang, 1967).

Craig, J., 'Reformers, Conflict, and Revisionism', *Historical Journal*, 42:1 (1999), pp. 1–23.

Craven, W. F., *Dissolution of the Virginia Company: The Failure of a Colonial Experiment* (1932; Gloucester, MA: Peter Smith, 1964).

—, 'The Earl of Warwick, a Speculator in Piracy', *Hispanic American Historical Review*, 10:4 (1930), pp. 457–79.

Cressy, D., *Coming Over: Migration and Communication between England and New England in the Seventeenth Century* (Cambridge: Cambridge University Press, 1987).

—, *Bonfires and Bells: National Memory and the Protestant Calendar in Elizabethan and Stuart England* (London: Weidenfeld and Nicolson, 1989).

Cuddy, N., 'The Conflicting Loyalties of a "Vulgar Counselor": The Third Earl of Southampton, 1597–1624', in A. Fletcher and P. Roberts (eds), *Religion, Culture, and Society in Early Modern Britain: Essays in Honour of Patrick Collinson* (Cambridge: Cambridge University Press, 1994), pp. 121–50.

Cunliffe, M., *George Washington: Man and Monument* (Boston: Little Brown, 1958).

Cust, R., and A. Hughes (eds), *Conflict in Stuart England: Studies in Religion and Politics, 1603–1642* (London: Longman, 1989).

D'Alton, C. W., 'Cuthbert Tunstall and Heresy in Essex and London, 1528', *Albion*, 35:2 (2003), pp. 210–28.

Dewar, D., 'The Mason Patents: Conflict, Controversy, and the Quest for Authority in Colonial New Hampshire', in Roper and Van Ruymbeke (eds), *Constructing Early Modern Empires*, pp. 269–99.

Dodd, A. H., 'North Wales in the Essex Revolt of 1601', *English Historical Review*, 59:235 (1944), pp. 348–70.

Dunn, R. S., *Sugar and Slaves: The Rise of the Planter Class in the West Indies, 1624–1713* (Chapel Hill, NC: University of North Carolina Press, 1972).

—, 'The Barbados Census of 1680: Profile of the Richest Colony in America', *William and Mary Quarterly*, 3rd series, 26:1 (1969), pp. 4–30.

—, 'John Winthrop, Jr., Connecticut Expansionist: The Failure of His Designs on Long Island, 1663–1675', *William and Mary Quarterly*, 3rd series, 29:1 (1956), pp. 3–26.

Duvall, W. G., 'Smuggling Sotweed: Augustine Herrman and the Dutch Connection', *Maryland Historical Magazine*, 98:4 (2003), pp. 388–407.

Dyer, C., *An Age of Transition? Economy and Society in England in the Late Middle Ages* (Oxford: Clarendon Press, 2001).

—, 'Small Places with Large Consequences: The Importance of Small Towns in England, 1000–1540', *Historical Research*, 75:187 (2002), pp. 1–24.

Elliott, J. H., *Empires of the Atlantic World: Britain and Spain in America, 1492–1830* (New Haven, CT: Yale University Press, 2006).

Fausz, J. F., 'The Invasion of Virginia: Indians, Colonialism, and the Conquest of Cant: A Review Essay on Anglo-Indian Relations in the Chesapeake', *Virginia Magazine of History and Biography*, 95:2 (1987), pp. 133–56.

—, 'An Abundance of Blood Shed on Both Sides: England's First Indian War, 1609–1614', *Virginia Magazine of History and Biography*, 98:1 (1990), pp. 3–56.

Eales, J., 'The Rise of Ideological Politics in Kent, 1558–1640', in Zell (ed.), *Early Modern Kent*, pp. 279–313.

Fernald, M. H., 'Members of the Essex Rebellion of 1601' (PhD dissertation, Brown University, 1976).

Fickes, M. L., '"They Could Not Endure That Yoke": The Captivity of Women and Children after the War of 1637', *New England Quarterly*, 73:1 (2000), pp. 58–81.

Fitzmaurice, A., *Humanism and America: An Intellectual History of English Colonisation, 1500–1625* (Cambridge: Cambridge University Press, 2003).

—, 'The Commercial Ideology of Colonization in Jacobean England: Robert Johnson, Giovanni Botero, and the Pursuit of Greatness', *William and Mary Quarterly*, 3rd series, 64:4 (2007), pp. 791–820.

Foster, W., 'An English Settlement in Madagascar in 1645–6', *English Historical Review*, 27:106 (1912), pp. 239–50.

Friis, A., *Alderman Cockayne's Project and the Cloth Trade: The Commercial Policy of England in its Main Aspects, 1603–1625* (London: Humphrey Milford, 1927).

Fuchs, B., 'Conquering Islands: Contextualizing *The Tempest*', *Shakespeare Quarterly*, 48:1 (1997), pp. 45–62.

Galenson, D. W., 'The Rise and Fall of Indentured Servitude in the Americas: An Economic Analysis', *Journal of Economic History*, 44:1 (1984), pp. 1–26.

Gallay, A., *The Indian Slave Trade: The Rise of the English Empire in the American South, 1670–1717* (New Haven, CT: Yale University Press, 2002).

Games, A., *Migration and the Origins of the English Atlantic World* (Cambridge, MA: Harvard University Press, 1999).

—, 'Atlantic History: Definitions, Challenges, and Opportunities', *American Historical Review*, 111:3 (2006), pp. 741–57.

—, 'Beyond the Atlantic: English Globetrotters and Transoceanic Connections', *William and Mary Quarterly*, 3rd series, 63:4 (2006), pp. 675–92.

—, 'England's Global Transition and the Cosmopolitans Who Made it Possible', *Shakespeare Studies*, 35 (2007), pp. 24–31.

Gardiner, S. R., *History of England from the Accession of James I to the Outbreak of the Civil War*, 10 vols (London: Longman, Green, and Co., 1883–4).

Gillingham, J., 'Images of Ireland 1170–1600: The Origins of English Imperialism', *History Today*, 37:2 (1987), pp. 16–22.

—, 'The Beginnings of English Imperialism', *Journal of Historical Sociology*, 5:4 (1992), pp. 392–409.

—, *The English in the Twelfth Century: Imperialism, National Identity, and Political Values* (Woodbridge, Suffolk, and Rochester, NY: Boydell Press, 2000).

Gookin, W. F., 'Who was Bartholomew Gosnold?', *William and Mary Quarterly*, 3rd series, 6:3 (1949), pp. 398–415.

Graff, G., and J. Phelan (eds), *The Tempest: A Case Study in Critical Controversy* (Boston, MA: Bedford/St Martin's, 2000).

Gragg, L., *Englishmen Transplanted: The English Colonization of Barbados, 1627–1660* (New York: Oxford University Press, 2003).

Green, D., 'Lordship and Principality: Colonial Policy in Ireland and Aquitaine in the 1360s', *Journal of British Studies*, 47:1 (2008), pp. 3–29.

Greenblatt, S. 'The Best Way to Kill Our Literary Inheritance is to Turn it into a Decorous Celebration of the New World Order', in Graff and Phelan (eds), *The Tempest*, pp. 113–15.

Greene, J. P., 'Changing Identity in the British Caribbean: Barbados as a Case Study', in N. P. Canny and A. Pagden (eds), *Colonial Identity in the Atlantic World, 1500–1800* (Princeton, NJ: Princeton University Press, 1987), pp. 213–66.

—, *Pursuits of Happiness: The Social Development of Early Modern British Colonies and the Formation of American Culture* (Chapel Hill, NC: University of North Carolina Press, 1988).

—, *Imperatives, Behaviors & Identities: Essays in Early American Cultural History* (Charlottesville, VA: University of Virginia Press, 1992).

—, 'Social and Cultural Capital in Colonial British America: A Case Study', *Journal of Interdisciplinary History*, 29:3 (1999), pp. 491–509.

Greene, J. P., et al., 'Roundtable', *William and Mary Quarterly*, 3rd series, 64:2 (2007), pp. 235–86.

Gurr, A., 'Industrious Ariel and Idle Caliban', in J.-P. Maquerlot and M. Willems (eds), *Travel and Drama in Shakespeare's Time* (Cambridge: Cambridge University Press, 1996), pp. 193–208.

Guy, J., 'The 1590s: The Second Reign of Elizabeth I?', in Guy (ed.), *The Reign of Elizabeth I*, pp. 1–19.

— (ed.), *The Reign of Elizabeth I: Court and Culture in the Last Decade* (Cambridge: Cambridge University Press, 1995).

Hadden, S., *Slave Patrols: Law and Violence in Virginia and the Carolinas* (Cambridge, MA: Harvard University Press, 2001).

Hale, N. C., *Virginia Venturer: A Historical Biography of William Claiborne, 1600–1677* (Richmond, VA: Dietz Press, 1951).

Hammer, J., *Plague, Population, and the English Economy, 1348–1550* (London: Macmillan, 1977).

Hammer, P. E. J., 'Patronage at Court, Faction and the Earl of Essex', in Guy (ed.), *The Reign of Elizabeth I*, pp. 65–86.

—, 'A Welshman Abroad: Captain Peter Wynn of Jamestown', *Parergon*, n.s., 16 (1998), pp. 59–92.

—, *The Polarization of English Politics: the Political Career of Robert Devereux, 2nd Earl of Essex, 1585–1597* (Cambridge: Cambridge University Press, 1999).

Hancock, D., *Citizens of the World: London Merchants and the Integration of the British Atlantic Community, 1735–1785* (Cambridge: Cambridge University Press, 1995).

Handlin, O., and M. F. Handlin, 'The Origins of the Southern Labor System', *William and Mary Quarterly*, 3rd series, 7:2 (1950), pp. 199–222.

Harris, T., *London Crowds in the Reign of Charles II: Propaganda and Politics from the Restoration until the Exclusion Crisis* (Cambridge: Cambridge University Press, 1987).

—, *Politics under the Later Stuarts: Party Conflict in a Divided Society, 1660–1715* (London, Longman, 1993).

Haskell, A. B., 'The Affections of the People: Ideology and the Politics of State Building in Colonial Virginia' (PhD dissertation, Johns Hopkins University, 2004).

Hatfield, A. L., *Atlantic Virginia: Intercolonial Relations in the Seventeenth Century* (Philadelphia, PA: University of Pennsylvania Press, 2004).

Hecht, I. W. D., 'The Virginia Muster of 1624/5 as a Source for Demographic History', *William and Mary Quarterly*, 3rd series, 30:1 (1973), pp. 65–92.

Henretta, J. A., M. Kammen and S. N. Katz (eds), *The Transformation of Early American History: Society, Authority, and Ideology: How the Writings and Influence of Bernard Bailyn have Changed our Understanding of the American Past* (New York: Alfred A. Knopf, 1991).

Hibbard, C. M., *Charles I and the Popish Plot* (Chapel Hill, NC: University of North Carolina Press, 1983).

Hindle, S., *The State and Social Change in Early Modern England, c. 1550–1640* (New York: St Martin's Press, 2000).

Hirst, D., 'The Privy Council and the Problem of Enforcement in the 1620s', *Journal of British Studies*, 18:1 (1978), pp. 46–66.

—, 'Locating the 1650s in England's Seventeenth Century', *History*, 81:263 (1996), pp. 359–84.

Howard, J. E., *Theater of a City: The Places of London Comedy, 1598–1642* (Philadelphia, PA: University of Pennsylvania Press, 2007).

Horn, J., *A Land As God Made It* (New York: Basic Books, 2005).

Horn, J. P. P., *Adapting to a New World: English Society in the Seventeenth-Century Chesapeake* (Chapel Hill, NC: University of North Carolina Press, 1994).

Horrox, R., and W. M. Ormrod (eds), *A Social History of England, 1200–1500* (Cambridge: Cambridge University Press, 2006).

Hunt, W., *The Puritan Moment: The Coming of Revolution in an English County* (Cambridge, MA: Harvard University Press, 1983).

Hutton, R., *The Restoration: A Political and Religious History of England and Wales, 1658–1667* (Oxford: Clarendon Press, 1985).

Hyde, P., and M. Zell, 'Governing the County', in Zell (ed.), *Early Modern Kent*, pp. 7–38.

Isaac, R., *The Transformation of Virginia, 1740–1790* (Chapel Hill, NC: University of North Carolina Press, 1982).

Israel, J., *The Dutch Republic: Its Rise, Greatness, and Fall* (Oxford: Clarendon Press, 1995).

Iwanisziw, S., 'England, Morocco, and Global Geopolitical Upheaval', in Appelbaum and Sweet (eds), *Envisioning an English Empire*, pp. 152–71.

Jacobs, J., *New Netherland: A Dutch Colony in Seventeenth-Century America* (Leiden and Boston, MA: Brill, 2005).

James, M., 'At a Crossroads of the Political Culture: The Essex Revolt, 1601', in M. James (ed.), *Society, Politics and Culture: Studies in Early Modern England* (Cambridge: Cambridge University Press, 1988), pp. 416–65.

Johnson, R. C., 'The Lotteries of the Virginia Company, 1612–1621', *Virginia Magazine of History and Biography*, 74:3 (1966), pp. 259–92.

Jones, H. M., 'The Colonial Impulse: An Analysis of the "Promotion" Literature of Colonization', *Proceedings of the American Philosophical Society*, 90 (1946), pp. 131–61.

Jordan, W. D., *White over Black: American Attitudes toward the Negro, 1550–1812* (Chapel Hill, NC: University of North Carolina Press, 1968).

Kamen, H., *Empire: How Spain Became a World Power, 1492–1763* (New York: HarperCollins, 2003).

Kammen, M., *Mystic Chords of Memory: The Transformation of Tradition in American Culture* (New York: Alfred A. Knopf, 1991).

Kiracofe, D. J., 'The Jamestown Jubilees: "State Patriotism" and Virginia Identity in the Early Nineteenth Century', in *Virginia Magazine of History and Biography*, 110:1 (2002), pp. 35–68.

Kishlansky, M., *A Monarchy Transformed: Britain, 1603–1714* (London: Penguin, 1996).

Kopperman, P. E., 'Profile of a Failure: The Carolina Project, 1629–1640', *North Carolina Historical Review*, 59 (1982), pp. 1–23.

Krugler, J., 'Sir George Calvert's Resignation as Secretary of State and the Founding of Maryland', *Maryland Historical Magazine*, 68:3 (1973), pp. 239–54.

Kukla, J., *Political Institutions in Virginia, 1619–1660* (New York: Garland Publishing, 1989).

—, 'Order and Chaos in Early America: Political and Social Stability in Pre-Restoration Virginia', *American Historical Review*, 90:2 (1985), pp. 275–98.

Kupperman, K. O., 'The Puzzle of the American Climate in the Early Colonial Period', *American Historical Review*, 87:5 (1982), pp. 1262–89.

—, 'Errand to the Indies: Puritan Colonization from Providence Island through the Western Design', *William and Mary Quarterly*, 3rd series, 45:1 (1988), pp. 70–99.

—, *Indians and English: Facing Off in Early America* (Ithaca, NY: Cornell University Press, 2000).

—, *The Jamestown Project* (Cambridge, MA: Harvard University Press, 2007).

—, *Providence Island, 1630–1641: The Other Puritan Colony* (Cambridge: Cambridge University Press, 1993).

Kussmaul, A., *Servants in Husbandry in Early Modern England* (Cambridge: Cambridge University Press, 1981).

LeMaster, M., 'Pocahontas: (De)Constructing an American Myth', *William and Mary Quarterly*, 3rd series, 62:4 (2005), pp. 774–81.

Lepore, J., *In the Name of War: King Philip's War and the Origins of American Identity* (New York: Alfred A. Knopf, 1998).

Levy, B. M., 'Early Puritanism in the Southern and Island Colonies', *Proceedings of the American Antiquarian Society*, 70 (1960), pp. 69–348.

Levin, C., J. E. Carney and D. Barrett-Graves (eds), *High and Mighty Queens of Early Modern England* (New York: Palgrave Macmillan, 2003).

Lewalski, B. K., 'Lucy, Countess of Bedford: Images of a Jacobean Courtier and Patroness', in K. Sharpe and S. N. Zwicker (eds), *Politics of Discourse: The Literature and History of Seventeenth-Century England* (Berkeley and Los Angeles, CA: University of California Press, 1987), pp. 52–77.

—, *Writing Women in Jacobean England* (Cambridge, MA: Harvard University Press, 1993).

Limerick, P. N., 'Turnerians All: The Dream of a Helpful History in an Intelligible World', *American Historical Review*, 100:3 (1995), pp. 697–716.

Lindgren, J. M., '"Whatever is Un-Virginian is Wrong": The APVA's Sense of the Old Dominion', *Virginia Cavalcade*, 38 (1989), pp. 112–23.

Lockyer, R., *Buckingham: The Life and Political Career of George Villiers, first Duke of Buckingham, 1592–1628* (London: Longman, 1981).

Loomie, A. J., 'Gondomar's Selection of English Officers in 1622', *English Historical Review*, 88:348 (1973), pp. 574–81.

—, 'The Spanish Faction at the Court of Charles I, 1630–8', *Bulletin of the Institute of Historical Research*, 59 (1986), pp. 37–49.

—, 'Oliver Cromwell's Policy toward the English Catholics: The Appraisal by Diplomats, 1654–1658', *Catholic Historical Review*, 90:1 (2004), pp. 29–44.

Lorimer, J., (ed.), *English and Irish Settlement on the River Amazon, 1550–1646* (London: Hakluyt Society, 1989).

—, 'The Failure of the English Guiana Ventures 1595–1667 and James I's Foreign Policy', *Journal of Imperial and Commonwealth History*, 21 (1993), pp. 1–30.

McClure, P., 'Patterns of Migration in the late Middle Ages: The Evidence of English Place-Name Surnames', *Economic History Review*, 2nd series, 32:2 (1979), pp. 167–82.

McConville, B., *The King's Three Faces: The Rise and Fall of Royal America, 1688–1776* (Chapel Hill, NC: University of North Carolina Press, 2006).

McDougall, E. A., 'The Caravel and the Caravan: Reconsidering Received Wisdom in the Sixteenth-Century Sahara', in Mancall (ed.), *The Atlantic World and Virginia*, pp. 143–69.

Macfarlane, A., *The Origins of English Individualism: The Family, Property, and Social Transition* (Cambridge: Cambridge University Press, 1978).

Macinnes, A., and A. H. Williamson, 'Introduction: Connecting and Disconnecting with America', in A. Macinnes and A. H. Williamson (eds), *Shaping the Stuart World, 1603–1714: The Atlantic Connection* (Leiden and Boston, MA: Brill Academic Publishers, 2006), pp. 1–30.

McMullan, G., and J. Hope (eds), *The Politics of Tragicomedy: Shakespeare and After* (London and New York: Routledge, 1992).

Madden, P. C., 'Social Mobility', in Horrox and Ormrod (eds), *A Social History of England*, pp. 113–33.

Mancall, P. C., *Hakluyt's Promise: An Elizabethan's Obsession for an English America* (New Haven, CT: Yale University Press, 2007).

— (ed.), *The Atlantic World and Virginia, 1550–1624* (Chapel Hill, NC: University of North Carolina Press, 2007).

—, 'Review Essay: Savagery in Jamestown', *Huntington Library Quarterly*, 70 (2007), pp. 661–70.

—, 'Native Americans and Europeans in English America, 1500–1700', in Canny (ed.), *The Origins of Empire*, pp. 328–50.

Mancke, E., 'Empire and State', in Armitage and Braddick (eds), *The British Atlantic World*, pp. 175–95.

—, 'Negotiating an Empire: Britain and its Overseas Peripheries, c. 1550–1780', in C. Daniels and M. V. Kennedy (eds), *Negotiated Empires: Centers and Peripheries in the Americas, 1500–1820* (New York and London: Routledge, 2002), pp. 235–65.

Marsh, C. W., *The Family of Love in English Society, 1550–1630* (Cambridge: Cambridge University Press, 1994).

Marshall, T., '*The Tempest* and the British Imperium in 1611', *Historical Journal*, 41:2 (1998), pp. 375–400.

Martin, J. W., 'Elizabethan Familists and English Separatism', *Journal of British Studies*, 20:1 (1980), pp. 53–73.

Maycock, A., *Chronicles of Little Gidding* (London: Society for the Propagation of Christian Knowledge, 1954).

Meinig, D. W., *The Shaping of America: A Geographical Perspective on 500 Years of History, Volume 1, Atlantic America, 1492–1800* (New Haven, CT: Yale University Press, 1986).

Menard, R. R., 'Maryland's "Time of Troubles": Sources of Political Disorder in Early St. Mary's', *Maryland Historical Magazine*, 76:2 (1981), pp. 124–40.

—, 'Financing the Lowcountry Export Boom: Capital and Growth in Early South Carolina', *William and Mary Quarterly*, 3rd series, 51:4 (1994), pp. 659–76.

—, 'The Africanization of the Lowcountry Labor Force, 1670–1730', in W. D. Jordan and S. L. Skemp (eds), *Race and Family in the Colonial South* (Jackson, MS, and London: University Press of Mississippi, 1987), pp. 81–105.

Merrell, J. H., 'The Indians' New World: the Catawba Experience', *William and Mary Quarterly*, 3rd series, 41:4 (1984), pp. 538–65.

—, 'Some Thoughts on Colonial Historians and American Indians', *William and Mary Quarterly*, 3rd series, 46:1 (1989), pp. 94–119.

Merritt, J. F. (ed.), *The Political World of Thomas Wentworth, Earl of Strafford, 1621–1641* (Cambridge: Cambridge University Press, 1996).

Miller, J., 'The Crown and the Borough Charters in the Reign of Charles II', *English Historical Review*, 100:394 (1985), pp. 53–84.

Miller, W. H., 'The Colonization of the Bahamas', *William and Mary Quarterly*, 3rd series, 2:1 (1945), pp. 33–46.

Morgan, E. S., *American Slavery, American Freedom: the Ordeal of Colonial Virginia* (New York: W. W. Norton, 1975).

—, 'The First American Boom: Virginia, 1618 to 1630', *William and Mary Quarterly*, 3rd series, 28:2 (1971), pp. 169–98.

Morgan, P. D., *Slave Counterpoint: Black Culture in the Eighteenth-Century Chesapeake and Lowcountry* (Chapel Hill, NC: University of North Carolina Press, 1998).

Mukherjee, R., 'Trade and Empire in Awadh, 1765–1804', *Past and Present*, 94 (1982), pp. 85–102.

Newton, A. P., *The Colonising Activities of the English Puritans* (New Haven, CT: Yale University Press, 1914).

Nicholl, C., *The Reckoning: The Murder of Christopher Marlowe* (Chicago, IL: University of Chicago Press, 1992).

Nicholls, M., 'The "Wizard Earl" in Star Chamber: The Trial of the Earl of Northumberland, June 1606', *Historical Journal*, 30:1 (1987), pp. 173–89.

—, '"As Happy a Fortune as I Desire": The Pursuit of Financial Security by the Younger Brothers of Henry Percy, 9th Earl of Northumberland', *Historical Research*, 65 (1992), pp. 296–314.

— (ed.), 'George Percy's "Trewe Relaycion" [1625]: A Primary Source for the Jamestown Settlement', *Virginia Magazine of History and Biography*, 113:3 (2005), pp. 212–75.

Pagan, J. R., 'Dutch Maritime and Commercial Activity in Mid-Seventeenth Century Virginia', *Virginia Magazine of History and Biography*, 90:4 (1982), pp. 485–501.

Peck, L. L., *Northampton: Patronage and Policy at the Court of James I* (London and Boston, MA: Allen & Unwin, 1982).

—, *Court Patronage and Corruption in Early Stuart England* (London: Allen & Unwin, 1990).

— (ed.), *The Mental World of the Jacobean Court* (Cambridge: Cambridge University Press, 1992).

Percevel-Maxwell, M., 'Ireland and the Monarchy in the Early Stuart Multiple Kingdom', *Historical Journal*, 34:2 (1991), pp. 279–95.

Pestana, C. G., *The English Atlantic in an Age of Revolution, 1640–1661* (Cambridge, MA: Harvard University Press, 2004).

Pincus, S. C. A., 'From Butterboxes to Wooden Shoes: The Shift in English Popular Sentiment from Anti-Dutch to Anti-French in the 1670s', *Historical Journal*, 38:2 (1995), pp. 333–61.

Porter, H. C., *Reform and Reaction at Tudor Cambridge* (Cambridge: Cambridge University Press, 1958).

Porter, R., 'The Crispe Family and the African Trade in the Seventeenth Century', *Journal of African History*, 9:1 (1968), pp. 57–77.

Prestwich, M., *Cranfield: Politics and Profits under the Early Stuarts* (Oxford: Clarendon Press, 1966).

Price, D. A., *Love and Hate in Jamestown: John Smith, Pocahontas, and the Heart of a New Nation* (New York: Alfred A. Knopf, 2003).

Pursell, B. C., 'James I, Gondomar and the Dissolution of the Parliament of 1621', *History*, 85:3 (2000), pp. 428–45.

Questier, M. C., *Catholicism and Community in Early Modern England: Politics, Aristocratic Patronage and Religion, c. 1550–1640* (Cambridge: Cambridge University Press, 2006).

Quinn, D. B., *Raleigh and the British Empire* (London: English Universities Press, 1962).

—, 'Sir Thomas Smith (1513–1577) and the Beginnings of English Colonial Theory', *Proceedings of the American Philosophical Society*, 89 (1945), pp. 543–60.

—, 'Thomas Hariot and the Virginia Voyages of 1602', *William and Mary Quarterly*, 3rd series, 27:2 (1970), pp. 268–81.

—, *England and the Discovery of America, 1481–1620* (New York: Alfred A. Knopf, 1974).

—, 'James I and the Beginnings of Empire in America', *Journal of Imperial and Commonwealth History*, 2 (1974), pp. 135–52.

Rabb, T. K., *Jacobean Gentleman: Sir Edwin Sandys, 1561–1629* (Princeton, NJ: Princeton University Press, 1998).

Rakove, J. N., '"How Else Could It End"?', in Henretta et al. (eds), *The Transformation of Early American History*, pp. 51–69.

Ransome, D. R., 'Village Tensions in Early Virginia: Sex, Land, and Status at the Neck of Land in the 1620s', *Historical Journal*, 43:2 (2000), pp. 365–81.

Ravi, Z., 'The Myth of the Immutable English Family', *Past and Present*, 140 (1993), pp. 3–44.

Richter, D. K., 'Whose Indian History?', *William and Mary Quarterly*, 3rd series, 50:2 (1993), pp. 379–93.

Rives, R. H., 'The Jamestown Celebration of 1857', *Virginia Magazine of History and Biography*, 66:3 (1958), pp. 259–71.

Robbins, C., *The Eighteenth-Century Commonwealth: Studies in the Transmission, Development, and Circumstance of English Liberal Thought from the Restoration of Charles II until the War with the Thirteen Colonies* (1959; Indianapolis, IN: Liberty Fund, 2004).

Roper, L. H., 'Unmasquing the Connections between Jacobean Politics and Colonization: The Circle of Anna of Denmark and the Beginning of the English Empire, 1614–1618', in Levin et al. (eds), *High and Mighty Queens of Early Modern England*, pp. 45–59.

—, *Conceiving Carolina: Proprietors, Planters, and Plots, 1662–1729* (New York and Houndmills, Hampshire: Palgrave Macmillan, 2004).

—, 'Charles I, Virginia, and the Idea of Atlantic History', *Itinerario*, 30:2 (2006), pp. 33–53.

—, 'New Albion: Anatomy of an English Colonisation Failure, 1632–1659', *Itinerario*, 32:1 (2008), pp. 39–57.

—, 'Big Fish in a Bigger Transatlantic Pond: the Social and Political Leadership of Early Modern Anglo-American Colonies' in C. Laux, F-J. Ruggiu, and P. Singaravelou (eds), *Les élites européennes dans les colonies du début du XVI siècle au milieu du XXe siècle* (Bern: Peter Lang, forthcoming).

Roper, L. H., and B. Van Ruymbeke, (eds), *Constructing Early Modern Empires: Proprietary Ventures in the Atlantic World, 1500–1750* (Leiden and Boston, MA: Brill Academic Publishers, 2007).

Rorke, M., 'English and Scottish Overseas Trade, 1300–1600', *Economic History Review*, 59:2 (2006), pp. 265–88.

Rose, E., 'The Politics of Pathos: Richard Frethorne's Letters Home', in Appelbaum and Sweet (eds), *Envisioning an English Empire*, pp. 92–108.

Rowse, A. L., *Shakespeare's Southampton, Patron of Virginia* (New York: Harper & Row, 1965).

Russell, C., *Parliaments and English Politics, 1621–1629* (Oxford: Clarendon Press, 1979).

Russell, J., 'Medieval Midland and Northern Migration to London, 1100–1365', *Speculum*, 34:4 (1959), pp. 641–5.

Sacks, D. H., *The Widening Gate: Bristol and the Atlantic Economy, 1450–1700* (Berkeley and Los Angeles, CA: University of California Press, 1991).

—, 'Discourses of Western Planting: Richard Hakluyt and the Making of the Atlantic World', in Mancall (ed.), *The Atlantic World and Virginia*, pp. 410–53.

St George, R. B. (ed.), *Possible Pasts: Becoming Colonial in Early America* (Ithaca, NY: Cornell University Press, 2000).

Salt, S. P., 'Sir Simonds D'Ewes and the Levying of Ship Money, 1635–1640', *Historical Journal*, 37:2 (1994), pp. 253–87.

Scott, J., *England's Troubles: Seventeenth-Century English Political Instability in European Context* (Cambridge: Cambridge University Press, 2000).

Schwarz, P. J., *Slave Laws in Virginia* (Athens, GA: University of Georgia Press, 1996).

Seaver, P., *Wallington's World: A Puritan Artisan in the Seventeenth Century* (Stanford, CA: Stanford University Press, 1985).

Seeley, J. R., *The Expansion of England: Two Courses of Lectures* (1895; Chicago, IL: University of Chicago Press, 1971).

Shagan, E. H., 'Constructing the Discord: Ideology, Propaganda, and English Responses to the Irish Rebellion of 1641', *Journal of British Studies*, 36:1 (1997), pp. 4–34.

Sharpe, K., *The Personal Rule of Charles I* (New Haven, CT: Yale University Press, 1992).

Shaw, D., 'Thomas Wentworth and Monarchical Ritual in Early Modern England', *Historical Journal*, 49:2 (2006), pp. 331–55.

Sluiter, E., 'New Light on the "20. and Odd Negroes" Arriving in Virginia, August 1619', *William and Mary Quarterly*, 3rd series, 54:2 (1997), pp. 395–8.

Smith, D. L., 'The Political Career of Edward Sackville, Fourth Earl of Dorset (1590–1652)', (PhD dissertation, University of Cambridge, 1990).

—, 'The Fourth Earl of Dorset and the Personal Rule of Charles I', *Journal of British Studies*, 30:3 (1991), pp. 257–87.

Smith, J. M. (ed.), *Seventeenth-Century America: Essays in Colonial History* (Chapel Hill, NC: University of North Carolina Press, 1959).

Smith, W. D., 'Complications of the Commonplace: Tea, Sugar, and Imperialism', *Journal of Interdisciplinary History*, 23:2 (1992), pp. 259–78.

Smuts, R. M., 'The Puritan Followers of Henrietta Maria in the 1630s', *English Historical Review*, 93:366 (1978), pp. 26–45.

Sokol, B. J., 'Text-in-History: *The Tempest* and New World Cultural Encounter', in E. D. Hill and W. Kerrigan (eds), *The Wit to Know: Essays on English Renaissance Literature for Edward Taylor* (Fairfield, CO: George Herbert Journal Special Studies and Monographs, 2000), pp. 21–40.

Spady, J. O., 'Bubbles and Beggars and the Bodies of Laborers: the Georgia Trusteeship's Colonialism Reconsidered', in Roper and Van Ruymbeke (eds), *Constructing Early Modern Empires*, pp. 213–68.

Sprunger, K. L., *Dutch Puritanism: a History of English and Scottish Churches of the Netherlands in the Sixteenth and Seventeenth Centuries* (Leiden: Brill, 1982).

Statt, D., 'The City of London and the Controversy over Immigration, 1660–1722', *Historical Journal*, 33:1 (1990), pp. 45–61.

Striker, L. P., and B. Smith, 'The Rehabilitation of Captain John Smith', *Journal of Southern History*, 28:4 (1962), pp. 474–81.

Sweet, J. H., 'African Identity and Slave Resistance in the Portuguese Atlantic', in Mancall (ed.), *The Atlantic World and Virginia*, pp. 225–49.

Takaki, R. 'The "Tempest" in the Wilderness', in Graff and Phelan (eds), *The Tempest*, pp. 140–72.

Taylor, A., *American Colonies: The Settling of North America* (New York: Penguin, 2001).

Taylor, H., 'Trade, Neutrality, and the "English Road", 1630–1648', *Economic History Review*, n.s., 25:2 (1972), pp. 236–60.

Thirsk, J., 'Agriculture in Kent, 1540–1640', in Zell (ed.), *Early Modern Kent*, pp. 75–103.

Thompson, P., 'William Bullock's "Strange Adventure": A Plan to Transform Seventeenth-Century Virginia', *William and Mary Quarterly*, 3rd series, 61:1 (2004), pp. 107–28, and supplemental material accessible at http://oieahc.wm.edu/wmq/Jan04/Thompson-Web.pdf.

Thorndale, W., 'The Virginia Census of 1619', *Magazine of Virginia Genealogy*, 33:3 (1996), pp. 155–70.

Thornton, J., 'The African Experience of the "20. and Odd Negroes" Arriving in Virginia in 1619', *William and Mary Quarterly*, 3rd series, 55:3 (1998), pp. 421–34.

Thrush, A., 'The Personal Rule of James I, 1611–1620', in Cogswell et al. (eds), *Politics, Religion, and Popularity in Early Stuart Britain*, pp. 84–102.

Tittler, R., *Townspeople and Nation: English Urban Experiences, 1540–1640* (Stanford, CA: Stanford University Press, 2001).

Torrence, C., 'The English Ancestry of William Claiborne', *Virginia Magazine of History and Biography*, 56:4 (1948), pp. 431–60.

Turner, F. J., *The Frontier in American History* (New York: Henry Holt, 1920).

Tyacke, N., *Aspects of English Protestantism, c. 1530–1700* (Manchester: Manchester University Press, 2001).

Underdown, D., *Pride's Purge: Politics in the Puritan Revolution* (Oxford: Clarendon Press, 1971).

Van Ruymbeke, B., 'Refuge or Diaspora? Historiographical Reflections on the Huguenot Dispersion in the Atlantic World', in C. Schnurmann and S. Lachenicht (eds), *Religious Refugees in Europe, Asia, and the Americas (6th–20th Centuries)* (Münster: Lit Verlag, 2007), pp. 167–82.

Vaughan, A. T., '"Expulsion of the Savages": English Policy and the Virginia Massacre of 1622', *William and Mary Quarterly*, 3rd series, 35:1 (1978), pp. 57–84.

Wall, A., 'Faction in Local Politics, 1580–1620: Struggles for Supremacy in Wiltshire', *Wiltshire Archaeological Magazine*, 72/73 (1980), pp. 119–33.

Webb, S. S., 'Imperial Fixer: From Popish Plot to Glorious Revolution', *William and Mary Quarterly*, 3rd series, 25:1 (1968), pp. 4–21.

—, 'Imperial Fixer: Muddling through to Empire, 1689–1717', *William and Mary Quarterly*, 3rd series, 26:3 (1969), pp. 373–415.

Wertenbaker, T. J., *Virginia under the Stuarts, 1607–1688* (Princeton, NJ: Princeton University Press, 1914).

Weslager, C. A., *The English on the Delaware, 1610–1682* (New Brunswick, NJ: Rutgers University Press, 1967).

Will, G., 'Literary Politics', in Graff and Phelan (eds), *The Tempest*, pp. 110–13.

Wilson, R., 'Voyage to Tunis: New History and the Old World of *The Tempest*', *ELH*, 64:2 (1997), pp. 333–57.

Wood, B., *The Origins of American Slavery: Freedom and Bondage in the English Colonies* (New York: Hill & Wang, 1997).

Wood, G. S., 'The Creative Imagination of Bernard Bailyn', in Henretta et al. (eds), *The Transformation of Early American History*, pp. 16–50.

Wood, P. H., '"I Did the Best I Could for My Day": The Study of Early Black History during the Second Reconstruction, 1960 to 1976', *William and Mary Quarterly*, 3rd series, 35:2 (1978), pp. 185–225.

Woolrych, A., *Commonwealth to Protectorate* (Oxford: Oxford University Press, 1982).

Wright, I. A., 'Spanish Policy toward Virginia, 1606–1612: Jamestown, Ecija, and John Clark of the Mayflower', *American Historical Review*, 25:3 (1920), pp. 448–79.

Wright, J., 'The World's Worst Worm: Conscience and Conformity during the English Reformation', *Sixteenth Century Journal*, 30:1 (1999), pp. 113–33.

Wrightson, K., *English Society, 1580–1680* (New Brunswick, NJ: Rutgers University Press, 1982).

Wrigley, E. A., and R. S. Schofield, *The Population of England, 1541–1871* (Cambridge, MA: Harvard University Press, 1981).

Young, M. B., 'Illusions of Grandeur and Reform at the Jacobean Court: Cranfield and the Ordnance', *Historical Journal*, 22:1 (1979), pp. 53–73.

Zagorin, P., *Rebels and Rulers, 1500–1660*, 2 vols (Cambridge: Cambridge University Press, 1982).

Zell, M. (ed.), *Early Modern Kent, 1540–1640* (Woodbridge, Suffolk: Boydell Press, 2000).

—, 'Landholding and the Land Market in Early Modern Kent', in Zell (ed.), *Early Modern Kent*, pp. 39–74.

—, 'Walter Morrell and the New Draperies Project, c. 1603–1631', *Historical Journal*, 44:3 (2001), pp. 651–75.

INDEX

Abbott, George, archbishop of Canterbury
    opponent of Howard family, 76–7
    Virginia investor, 78
    see also Anna of Denmark
Africans, 33
    in Barbados, 134–5
    in Bermuda, 82
    in Virginia, 1, 80–2, 158, 178
    trade with English, 126–8
    see also William Claiborne; Richard Ligon; slavery; John Yeamans
Alcazarquivir, Morocco, Battle of the Three Kings (1578), 22
Amazon, English colonizing activities in, 35–7, 92
    see also Walter Ralegh
Amboina (Indonesia) see Dutch Republic
Andrews, Charles McLean, 100
Anglicization, 3, 8
Angola, 22
    see also Ndongo
Anna of Denmark, queen-consort of James I, 15
    council, 77
    promoter of colonization, 74–8
    see also Eastward Hoe!; William Herbert; James I; Pocahontas; Walter Ralegh; John Rolfe; John Smith; Henry Wriothesley
Antigua, 36
    see also English West Indies
Antwerp, 24, 26
Anys, William, 107
Archer, Gabriel, 52, 57–8, 60, 62
Argall, Sir Samuel, 13, 53, 85–6, 89
    see also Robert Rich

Armitage, David, 4, 7, 37
Atlantic history, as historiographical concept, 3–5, 22
Atlantic World, as historiographical concept, 7, 137–8
Avalon see Sir George Calvert; Newfoundland

Bacon's Rebellion, 3, 121
Bailyn, Bernard, x, 48
Barbados, 36, 48, 114, 119
    population, 135
    social formation, 133–6
    see also English West Indies; James Hay; Richard Ligon; slavery; sugar; John Yeamans
Bargrave, Captain John, 87–8
Barret, William, 42–3
Barroll, J. Leeds, 74
Battle of Dunbar, 124
Battle of Preston, 124
Battle of the Severn (Maryland), 125–6
Battle of Worcester, 124
Bell, Philip, governor of Barbados, 178
Bennett, Richard, 125
    see also William Claiborne
Berkeley, Sir Maurice
    as parliamentary figure, 31, 78
    member of Queen Anna's council, 75
Berkeley, Sir William, governor of Virginia, 19
    and English Civil Wars, 124–5
    promoter of diversifying Virginia economy, 31–2, 91
Berlin, Ira, 135–6

Bermuda, 64, 65, 81–2, 94–6
  dispute between Independents and Presbyterians on, 119
  Independents settling in Bahamas, 19, 168
  tobacco production on, 106, 114–15
  see also Thomas Gates; William Prynne; slavery; George Somers
Berringer, Benjamin, 129
  see also John Yeamans
Berringer, Margaret, 129
  see also John Yeamans
Black Death, 9, 24
Boswell, Sir William, 19
  receiver-general of tobacco customs, 107
Bouchier, Sir Henry, 88
  see also Jones Commission; Virginia Company
Braddick, Michael, 5–6, 8
Brenner, Robert, 127
Bristol, Gloucestershire, 129, 163
  see also John Yeamans
Brownism, 100, 163
  see also Plymouth
Butler, Nathaniel, governor of Bermuda and Africans, 81–2
  supporter of Robert Rich, 85–6, 89
  see also Robert Rich

Calais, 54
Calvert, Cecilius, second Lord Baltimore, 101, 121, 123–4
  see also William Claiborne; Maryland; Thomas Wentworth
Calvert, George, first Lord Baltimore, 18–19, 28, 101–2, 165
  see also England, situation of Roman Catholics; Maryland
Calvert, Leonard, governor of Maryland, 124
Cape Fear, North Carolina (settlement) see Samuel Vassall; John Yeamans
Carleton, Sir Dudley, Viscount Dorchester, 72, 108, 109
Carolana see Robert Heath; Samuel Vassall
Carolina, 129–31
  see also Samuel Vassall; Yamassee War; John Yeamans

Carr, Robert, Earl of Somerset, 16, 31, 76
Cavendish, William, Lord, 89
  see also John Ferrar; Nicholas Ferrar; Edwin Sandys; Virginia Company; Henry Wriothesley
Cecil, Sir Robert, Earl of Salisbury, 38, 75
  attitude towards Spain, 36–7
  death, 76
  supports Virginia Company (1618), 47
  see also Scotland; Spain
Cecil, William, Lord Burghley, 12–13, 15
Chaloner, Sir Thomas, 55
Chamberlain, John, 72
Chapman, George see Eastward Hoe!
Charles I, King of England (1625–49), 11
  character of English state under, 93–4, 97–9, 102–3, 112–15
  as Prince of Wales, 77, 92, 95
  trial and execution, 124
  see also England; imperialism; Ireland; liberty; Scotland; Spain
Charles II, King of England (1660–85), 117, 121–2, 138
chartered companies, 6
  see also Massachusetts Bay Company; Providence Island Company; Virginia Company
Chesapeake school of historians, 3
Christian IV, King of Denmark, 74
Claiborne, William, 17, 19–20, 32, 89, 109–11, 131–2, 136–7
  dispute with Maryland, 121–6, 166–7
  significance of career, 126–8
  see also Cecilius Calvert; England; factionalism; John Harvey; Maryland; Samuel Mathews; Edward Sackville; Virginia
Clobery, William, 18, 126–7, 133, 173–4
  see also William Claiborne
Cockayne, William, plan for English cloth industry, 32
Cogswell, Thomas, 108–9
Company of Grocers, 78
comuneros (Castile), revolt, 176
Connecticut, 96, 128
Cranfield, Lionel, Earl of Middlesex, 17, 28
  attempts to regulate tobacco customs, 105–7

Index

Cressy, David, 98
Cromwell, Oliver, Lord Protector, 19
   character of English Empire under, 118–19
   death, 33, 94
   'Great Western Design' (1655), 20, 95–6, 118
   and Roman Catholics, 125–6
   see also Dutch Republic; England; imperialism; Ireland; Jamaica; Scotland; Spain
Cromwell, Sir Oliver, 78

Dale, Sir Thomas, governor of Virginia
   effects of arrival at Jamestown, 65–7, 78–9
   enacts laws, 70
   see also tobacco
Danvers, Sir John, 13, 29, 108, 125, 167–8, 174
   advocate for Virginia Company, 90
   connections with Essex circle, 55
   leader of Virginia Company, 74
   supporter of Southampton and Sandys, 85
   Wiltshire political activity, 29
   see also John Ferrar; Nicholas Ferrar; Edward Sackville; Edwin Sandys; Henry Wriothesley
Dee, John, 7, 96
Delaware River valley, 19, 128, 166–7
   Dutch presence in, 18, 101, 103, 166–7
   Swedish settlement, 18, 101, 105
   see also George Lamberton; New Albion; New Haven colony; New Sweden
de Licques, Pierre, 19
   receiver-general of tobacco customs, 107
Deventer, handover to Spanish (1587) *see* William Stanley
de Vere, Elizabeth, Countess of Derby, 77
de Vere, Susan, Countess of Montgomery, 77
Devereux, Robert, second Earl of Essex
   as champion of international Protestantism, 12
   circle of and Virginia, 55–6, 73–8, 85
   enmity between him and Ralegh, 148–9
   political patronage, 12–15, 30–1, 55–6
   revolt (1601), 13–14, 31, 38, 159
   as socio-political example, 28–31
   see also John Danvers; Thomas Gates; Ferdinando Gorges; Edward Maria Wingfield; Henry Wriothesley; Peter Wynn
Dorset Commission (Virginia), 110–13
   see also Edward Sackville; Maurice Thompson; Samuel Vassall; Virginia; John Wolstenholme; John Zouch
Drake, Sir Francis, 22
Dudley, Robert, Earl of Leicester, 12, 28, 76
Dutch Republic, 158
   relations with England, 19–20, 32–3, 103–4, 118, 166, 176
   see also Brownism; Oliver Cromwell; Low Countries; Navigation Acts; New Albion; Johan van Oldenbarneveldt; Spain; Maurice Thompson
Dutch Revolt *see* Low Countries, wars in

East India Company *see* Robert Rich; Thomas Smythe
Eastward Hoe!, as spoof of colonization, 38–41, 46–8, 75
Egerton, Thomas, Baron Ellesmere, 77
Eleuthera Island (Bahamas), 19
Elfrith, Daniel, 85
Elizabeth I, Queen of England (1558–1603), 12–15, 21, 47
   see also Robert Cecil; William Cecil; Robert Devereux; Richard Hakluyt; Ireland; Walter Ralegh
Endecott, John, governor of Massachusetts Bay, 99
England
   civil wars, 117–18, 129
      effects on colonies, 19, 118–19, 123–6
      see also William Claiborne; Richard Ingle; Maryland
   fears of social disorder, and colonization, 10, 25–8, 31, 36–41, 44–7, 82–3, 96–9, 122–4, 130–1, 139, 178
      see also Eastward Hoe!; factionalism; *The Tempest*; Virginia Company; John Winthrop
   importance of locality, 29

medieval
  character, 23–4
  colonization in Ireland and France, 53–4
  historiography, 23–5
  trade, 24–5
  overseas trade, 32
    see also Thomas Smythe; Maurice Thompson; Samuel Vassall
  plague, 25
  population, 23–6
  republican government, 124
  servitude, 82
  situation of Roman Catholics, 19, 26–7, 55–6, 100–1, 105, 123–6, 153
    see also Cecilius Calvert; George Calvert; Oliver Cromwell; Guy Fawkes; Maryland; Toby Matthew; New Albion
  social character and pursuit of advancement, 22–33, 130–9
  in American colonies, 130–9
    see also William Claiborne; factionalism; imperialism; George Lamberton; John Rolfe; slavery; Maurice Thompson; Samuel Vassall; John Yeamans
  theatre see Eastward Hoe!; The Tempest
  see also Charles I; Oliver Cromwell; imperialism; James I; Reformation
English West Indies, 36
  and Virginia social model, 47–8, 133
  see also Antigua; Barbados; St Christopher; Providence Island; slavery
estates, pursuit of by Anglo-American colonists, 28, 132–3, 136

factionalism, 32, 41–3, 54–6, 130–1
  and foreign policy of Charles I, 103–4
  in Kent, 30
  in Virginia and Virginia Company, 56–64, 84–89, 109–14
  and historiography, 67–8
  in Wiltshire, 29–30
  see also Anna of Denmark; William Claiborne; John Danvers; Robert Devereux; Henry Howard; Henry Wriothesley

Fawkes, Guy, conspiracy, 27, 55, 69
Felipe II, King of Spain (1556–98), 21
Felipe III, King of Spain (1598–1621), 36
  see also Diego Sarmiento de Acuña
Feoffees for Impropriations, 97
Ferrar, John, 16–17, 19, 74, 85, 91, 108, 162
  see also Edwin Sandys; Henry Wriothesley
Ferrar, Nicholas, 16–17, 74, 91, 108, 162
  see also Edwin Sandys; Henry Wriothesley
Ferrar, Virginia, 162
Fiennes, William, Viscount Saye and Sele, 97
  see also New England; Providence Island
Fortescue, Sir Nicholas, 88
  see also Jones Commission; Virginia Company
France
  activities in North America, 52, 102
  relations with England, 103–4, 116
  see also Low Countries; Nova Scotia; Henry Rich; Robert Rich; Edward Sackville; Spain
Frethorne, Richard, 87

Gates, Sir Thomas, governor of Virginia, 14, 42, 51, 85
  client of Essex, 55
  effects of arrival at Jamestown, 61, 65–7
  fleet shipwrecked on Bermuda, 64, 69
  see also Robert Devereux; George Somers
Gatford, Revd Lionel, 121–2
Gilbert, Sir Humphrey, 35, 47, 54
'Glorious Revolution' (1688–9), 3, 179
Gofton, Sir Francis, 88
  see also Jones Commission; Virginia Company
Gorges, Sir Ferdinando, 96, 99–100, 112, 136, 165
Goring, Sir George, 115
Gorton, Samuel, 96
Gosnold, Bartholomew, 14, 37, 41, 52
  death, 57
'Great Contract', failure, 116
'Great Puritan Migration' see New England

Guinea Company, 133
  see also William Clobery
'Gunpowder Plot' (1605) see Guy Fawkes

Habsburg monarchy, alleged universal pretensions, 55–6, 58
  see also Robert Devereux; Low Countries; Spain
Hakluyt, Richard ('the younger'), 7, 10, 14–15, 21–6, 35, 37–8, 42, 52, 96
  death, 62
  Virginia investor, 51, 64
  see also Walter Ralegh; Virginia Company
Hall, Revd Joseph, 176
Hammer, Paul, 56
Hamor, Ralph, 66–7, 70, 77, 89
Hampden, John, 97
  see also New England; Providence Island
Harington, Sir John, 78
Hariot, Thomas, 22
Harrison, Revd William, 26
Harvey, Sir John, governor of Virginia, 18, 20, 108–15, 136
  see also William Claiborne; factionalism; tobacco; Virginia
Harvey, William, 22
Hatfield, April Lee, 134
Hawley, Jerome, 170, 171
  see also William Claiborne; John Harvey
Hay, James, Earl of Carlisle, 95, 104, 107, 167
Heath, Sir Robert, 19, 104, 128
Henry, Prince of Wales, 74
Herbert, William, third Earl of Pembroke, 38
  leads revitalization of Virginia Company, 73–4
  opponent of Howard family, 74–6
  patron of Rolfe, 69–70, 77–8
  see also Pocahontas; John Rolfe; Henry Wriothesley
Howard, Frances, 31, 76
Howard, Henry, Earl of Northampton, 15
  death, 77
  political views, 31, 76
  see also factionalism

Howard, Thomas, Earl of Suffolk, 76, 77, 168
  Virginia investor, 47, 78
Howard of Effingham, Charles, Lord, 15, 77
Hudson, Henry, explorer, 158
Huguenots, migration to Virginia, 158
Hungary, as background for Virginia colonists see John Smith; Peter Wynn
Hutchinson, Anne, 96

imperialism
  character of English pre-1660, 11–20, 42–3, 53–5, 94–9, 101–5, 112–16, 117–19, 131–2, 136–7
  historiography of British, 5–9
  see also Amazon; Charles I; Oliver Cromwell; Dutch Republic; England; factionalism; John Harvey; Ireland; James I; Maryland; modernization; New Albion; John Smith; Spain; tobacco; Virginia; Thomas Wentworth
indentured servitude see Virginia, labour systems in
Ingle, Richard, 19, 124
  see also William Claiborne; Maryland
Ireland
  English colonization, model for Virginia, 53–5
  as locus of grant for New Albion colony, 102
  rebellion, 105, 123
  subjugation by English, 117
  see also Thomas Wentworth

Jacob, Abraham, 106
Jamaica, English capture from Spain, 117–18
James I, King of England (1603–25), 11, 13, 15–16
  attempts to proscribe tobacco cultivation, 106
  intervenes in Virginia Company dispute, 88–9
  as James VI of Scotland, 36
  policy towards Spain, 35–7, 39, 92
  complaints about, 15–16
  see also Diego Sarmiento de Acuña

promotion of Scots at court, 15, 38, 75–6
visit to Scotland (1617), 77
see also 'Great Contract', Guy Fawkes; imperialism; Scotland
Johnson, Robert, 37–8, 151
supporter of Smythe, 85–6
see also factionalism; Virginia Company
Jones, Inigo, 72
Jones, Sir William see Jones Commission
Jones Commission, 88–9, 161
see also Virginia Company
Jonson, Ben, 14, 22, 72
see also Eastward Hoe!

Kemp, Richard, 170
see also William Claiborne; John Harvey
Kendall, George, 52, 64
arrest and execution as Spanish spy, 57–8
Kendall, Captain, deputy governor of Bermuda, 81–2
Kent (county), 30
Kent Island see William Claiborne; Maryland; Samuel Mathews
Killigrew, Sir Robert, 108

Lamberton, George, 127–8, 131
see also Africans; Delaware River valley; New Haven colony
Lane, Sir Ralph, governor of Roanoke, 54
Laud, William, archbishop of Canterbury, 96, 164, 170
and Committee for Foreign Plantations, 97, 99–100
execution, 117
see also liberty
Leeward Islands see English West Indies
liberty, as historiographical concept, 2, 5, 98–9
see also modernization; Whig interpretation of history
Ligon, Richard, 133–4, 136
London, population, 24
Long Island, New York see New England; New Netherland
Louis XIV, King of France (1648–1714), 137
Low Countries
trade with England, 24–5, 32

wars in, 25–6, 83, 152
as background for Virginia careers, 13–14, 54–9
see also Robert Devereux; imperialism; Spain; Virginia

Madagascar, failed attempt to colonize by English, 163
Madoc, Prince of Wales, 42
Mancall, Peter, 68
Marlowe, Christopher, 13
Marston, John see Eastward Hoe!
Martin, John, 52, 57–8, 64, 67, 89
Mary, Queen of Scots, 12, 153
Maryland, 131
founding, 101–2
social development, 6
target of Virginia interests, 110–11
see also Cecilius Calvert; George Calvert; William Claiborne; England
Mason, Captain John, 99–100
Massachusetts Bay colony, 99, 105, 128
see also John Endecott; New England; John Winthrop
Massachusetts Bay Company, 96, 98, 100
see also Samuel Vassall
Mathews, Samuel, 17, 89, 109–10, 119
servants, 83
as slaveholder, 178
see also William Claiborne; factionalism; John Harvey; Maryland; Edward Sackville
Matthew, Sir Toby, 102–3, 166
Menefie, George, 90
Metacom ('King Philip'), Wampanoag sachem, 132
modernization
and empire, 9–11
as historiographical concept, 2–5, 7–8, 10–11, 23–4, 48, 137–9
see also imperialism
Modyford, Sir Thomas, 119
Montagu, Henry, first Earl of Manchester, 89
More, Sir Thomas, 25
Utopia (1516), 40, 45
Morton, Thomas, 100

Navigation Acts (1651), 19, 93, 105, 118
Ndongo (Angola), kingdom, 82
  see also Africans
New Albion, failed English colony, 19, 101–5
  see also Sir Edmund Plowden
New Amsterdam, Dutch colony at, 18
  see also Virginia
New England, 122
  expansion, 105, 163–4
  migration to, 96–9
  see also Connecticut; Massachusetts Bay colony; Massachusetts Bay Company; New Haven colony; Plymouth; Rhode Island and Providence plantations; John Winthrop
Newfoundland, 162–3
  see also George Calvert
New Haven colony, 19, 96, 128
Newman, Captain Thomas, 133
New Netherland, 19, 103, 128, 163–4
Newport, Captain Christopher, 41, 52, 60–1
New Sweden, 128, 167
North, Roger see Amazon
Northwest Passage, search for, 1, 14, 15, 37, 52, 63
Nova Scotia
  French settlement at, 53
  Scottish attempt to colonize, 163

Oldenbarneveldt, Johan van, 159
Opechancanough, Powhatan sachem, 84
  attack on Virginia (1644), 132
  see also Powhatan Indians
Ottoman Empire see John Smith; Peter Wynn
Overbury, Sir Thomas, 31
  murder, 76

Palatinate, 92, 104
  see also Spain
Parliament, 31, 54, 75, 86, 90, 103, 108, 116
  of 1604, 76
  of 1621, 87–8
  of 1624, 17, 106
  of 1629, dissolution, 97
  'Cavalier' (1661), 118

Long, 18, 94, 97, 105, 117, 123, 124
Rump, 19, 118
Short, 117
  see also Charles I; Lionel Cranfield; Oliver Cromwell; England; Guy Fawkes; 'Great Contract'; Ireland; James I; Maryland; Navigation Acts; Edwin Sandys; Scotland; Virginia
Parsons, Robert, 101
patronage see factionalism
Peace of Prague (1635) see Spain
Peckham, Sir George, 13, 100
Peircey, Abraham, 81, 89, 109
  servants, 83
  see also William Claiborne
Percy, George, 7, 52
  connections with Essex circle, 55
  dispute with Smith, 62
  historiographical view, 69
  possible motives for migration, 69
  temporary governor of Virginia, 64–5
  see also factionalism; John Smith
Peter, Revd Hugh, 97
pilgrim colonists see Brownism; Plymouth
piracy see Robert Rich
Pitt, Sir William, 88
  see also Jones Commission; Virginia Company
Plowden, Sir Edmund, 19, 102
  see also England, situation of Roman Catholics; New Albion
Plymouth, Massachusetts, settlement, 94–6, 160, 162–3
Pocahontas, 1, 10, 16–17
  kidnap by English, 53
  marriage to Rolfe, 47, 71
  and Smith, 67, 76–7
  visit to England, 72–3, 76–8
  see also Powhatan Indians; John Rolfe; John Smith
Poor Law of 1597, 25
Pory, John, 7, 89
Powhatan Indians, 10
  attack on Virginia (1622), 1, 17, 47, 80, 84, 88, 132
  peace with Virginia, 70

relations with English, 51–3, 59–61, 64–5, 83–4, 155
  see also Opechancanough; Pocahontas; Virginia; Wahunsonacock
'Pride's Purge', 124
Printz, Johan, governor of New Sweden, 128
Providence Island, 36, 42, 95, 133
  see also slavery
Providence Island Company, 97, 98, 126
Prynne, William, 119
Purchas, Revd Samuel, 80, 96
Pym, John, 97, 128
  see also New England; Providence Island

Ralegh, Sir Walter, 11, 47
  career in Ireland, 54
  colonizing and political failures, 11–15, 35, 38–9
  friendship with Queen Anna, 76–7
  patronage of Hakluyt, 21–2
  see also Amazon; Robert Devereux
Ratcliffe (a.k.a. Sicklemore), John, 52, 64
  as president at Jamestown, 57–60
  sent home by Smith, 61
Read, James, 58
Reformation
  effects upon historiography, 23–4
  social and religious effects in England, 26–7
Rhode Island and Providence plantations, 96, 128
Rich, Henry, first Earl of Holland, 126
  pro-French views, 103–4
  see also Providence Island
Rich, Sir Nathaniel, and Virginia Company dispute, 85–8
  see also John Bargrave; Richard Frethorne; Robert Rich; Virginia Company
Rich, Penelope
  member of Queen Anna's circle, 74–6
  supporter of Essex rebellion, 155
Rich, Robert, second Earl of Warwick, 17, 126
  and English East India Company, 85
  and 'godly' circles, 97
  involvement in civil wars, 117
  and New England, 97, 99–100, 128
  and piracy, 85–6
  and Virginia Company, 81–2, 84–6, 88–9
  see also factionalism; Massachusetts Bay Company; New England; Providence Island; Nathaniel Rich; Edwin Sandys; Somers Island Company; Virginia Company; Henry Wriothesley
Ridgeway, Sir Thomas, 75
Roanoke, 'Lost Colony' see Walter Ralegh
Roe, Sir Thomas, 108
  and farm of tobacco customs, 106
Rolfe, John, 1, 10, 16–17
  importance of career, 69–71, 127, 131–2
  report of arrival of Africans, 81
  visit to England, 72–3, 77
  see also William Herbert; Pocahontas; Henry Wriothesley
Roman Catholics see England, situation of Roman Catholics
Ruatan Island (Honduras), 126
  see also William Claiborne
Rudyerd, Sir Benjamin, 75–6
  see also Anna of Denmark
Russell, Edward, third Earl of Bedford, 78
Russell, Lucy, Countess of Bedford
  friend of Queen Anna, 74–6
  supporter of Essex, 14–15, 149
  see also Anna of Denmark; Eastward Hoe!

Sackville, Edward, fourth Earl of Dorset, 17, 108
  advocate for Virginia Company, 90
  colonial connections, 109, 112, 124
  pro-French views, 103–4
  supports Sandys in Virginia Company, 86–7
  see also William Claiborne; factionalism; Samuel Mathews; Edwin Sandys
Saghedoc (Maine) see Virginia Company of Plymouth
St Christopher, 36, 48, 95, 114, 130
  see also English West Indies
Sandys, Sir Edwin, 9
  leader of Virginia Company, 16–17, 74, 77–81, 106, 127
  opponent of Rich faction, 84–9
  member of Queen Anna's circle, 15, 75–6

parliamentary opponent of royal plans, 31, 75, 86–8, 160–1
  see also Anna of Denmark; John Bargrave; factionalism; Robert Rich; Thomas Smythe; Virginia Company; Henry Wriothesley
Sandys, George, 18, 89–90
  servants, 83
  proposes restoration of Virginia Company, 90
Sarmiento de Acuña, Diego, Count Gondomar
  contemporary view, 92
  and Spanish ambassador to England, 13, 36
Scotland
  proposed union with England, 31, 116–17
  rebellion (1637), 100, 116–17, 162
  subjugation by English, 117
  visit of Charles I (1633), 107
  see also Anna of Denmark; Charles I; James I
Scrivener, Matthew, 60
Seeley, Sir J. R., 5
Shakespeare, William, 14, 22
  and colonialism, 150–1
  see also The Tempest
Sidney, Sir Philip, 12, 76
Sidney, Robert, Viscount L'isle, 78
silk *see* Virginia; Virginia Company
slavery, 81–3, 133–6, 138
  and Indians, 133, 178
  see also Africans; Bermuda; English West Indies; Virginia, labour systems in
Smith, Captain John, 1, 2, 7, 13, 52, 78
  colonial career, 56–62
  colonial promotion, 11–12, 62
    as model for others, 91
  contempt for fellow colonists, 60–2
  Habsburg service, 22
  Hungarian service, 154
  impact of writings on historical record, 11–12, 58–69
  injury and departure from Jamestown, 61–2
  opponent of Wingfield, 57–9
  possible motives for migration, 68–9

pursuit of patronage, 68, 76–7
  see also factionalism; George Percy; Pocahontas; Powhatan Indians; Edward Maria Wingfield
Smythe, Sir Thomas, 9, 14, 16
  involvement in overseas trade, 32, 85, 127
  leadership of Virginia Company, 56, 63–4, 77–8, 80
    place in dispute within, 85, 89
  see also Robert Rich; Edwin Sandys; Henry Wriothesley
Society of Jesus *see* England, situation of Roman Catholics
Somers, Sir George, arrives at Jamestown, 65
  see also Thomas Gates
Somerset, Edward, Earl of Worcester, 77
Somers Islands *see* Bermuda
Somers Island Company, 81
  see also Bermuda; Robert Rich; Edwin Sandys; Thomas Smythe; Virginia Company; Henry Wriothesley
South Carolina *see* Carolina
South Sea (Pacific Ocean), search for passage to, 53, 78
Spain
  colonizing experience as model for English, 12, 51–2
  English relations with, 35–7, 39, 55–9, 95, 97, 103–4, 152
  see also Anna of Denmark; Robert Cecil; Charles I; Robert Devereux; Henry Howard; James I; George Kendall; Low Countries; Walter Ralegh; Diego Sarmiento de Acuña
Spiller, Sir Henry, 88
  see also Jones Commission; Virginia Company
Squanto, 95
Stanley, Sir William, 56, 58
state formation
  as historiographical concept, 2, 5–7, 21–2, 136–7, 179
  see also factionalism; imperialism
Stegge, Thomas, 125
  see also William Claiborne
Strachey, William, 44
Strode, Sir William, 75

sugar, 135
Surinam, 119, 175, 176
Susquehannock Indians, 53
  see also Powhatan Indians
Sutton, Sir Henry, 88
  see also Jones Commission; Virginia Company

Tempest, The
  scholarship on, 43–4
  as spoof of colonization, 43–8
Thirty Years War, 92, 104
Thompson, Maurice, 18, 32, 110, 126–7, 131–2
  see also William Claiborne
Thorpe, George, 84
  supporter of Southampton and Sandys, 85
Thurloe, John, 125
tobacco
  attempts to regulate customs, 17, 105–8, 114–16, 119, 160
    see also William Anys; William Boswell; Lionel Cranfield; Pierre de Licques; George Goring; John Harvey; imperialism; Abraham Jacob; Thomas Roe; Virginia
  importance to English Empire, 103, 119
  overdependence upon in Virginia, 2, 70
  reaction to, 32–3, 86, 90–2, 114–16
  preference for Spanish by English smokers, 106
Treaty of London (1604) *see* Spain
Tucker, Captain William, servants, 83
Turner, Frederick Jackson, 2–3

United Provinces *see* Dutch Republic

Vassall, Samuel, 32, 110, 127, 128–30, 131–2
Villiers, George, Earl and Duke of Buckingham, 16, 28, 80, 92, 95, 97, 105
  as socio-political example, 28–9
  promotion to favour, 43, 77
Virginia
  degree of socio-political novelty, 7–10
  desperate condition of early settlers, 59–60, 64–5
  Dutch and, 81, 83, 111, 114–15, 125, 127, 178
  encouragement of silk production, 67, 78, 86, 91, 161–2
  expansion, 19, 105, 167
  history of historiography, 1–5, 7–8, 59, 62–3
  House of Burgesses, 2, 9, 79
    and tobacco regulation, 108, 114–15
  labour systems in, 47–8, 79, 81–4, 133, 135–6
  migration to, 80–1
  as military endeavour, 51–7
  as model for subsequent colonies, 47–8, 136–7
  political culture, 8, 20, 112–14
  population, 80, 83–4
    see also Africans
  promotion by Virginia Company, 41–3, 47
  revitalization, 43, 66–7, 78–80
  social development, 6, 132–3
  tobacco production, 67, 78–9, 105–6
  see also Africans; chartered companies; William Claiborne; Dorset Commission; factionalism; John Harvey; George Kendall; John Martin; Powhatan Indians; Christopher Newport; John Ratcliffe; Edward Sackville; Edwin Sandys; slavery; John Smith; tobacco; Virginia Company; Edward Maria Wingfield; Henry Wriothesley
Virginia Company (of London), 1, 2, 6, 9–11
  dissolution, 9, 88–90
    see also Jones Commission
  factions within, 84–8, 92
  'first fleet', 47
  formation, 51
  historiographical views, 63–4
  lotteries, 86
  promotion of colony, 37–8, 41–3, 66–7
  relationship with Virginia colony, 63–7
  see also Bermuda; John Ferrar; Nicholas Ferrar; Richard Hakluyt; William Herbert; Plymouth; Robert Rich; Edwin Sandys; George Sandys; Tho-

mas Smythe; Virginia; Thomas West; Henry Wriothesley
Virginia Company of Plymouth, 152

Wahunsonacock, Powhatan sachem, 1, 16, 52, 63, 64, 66, 67
  'coronation' by Virginians, 61
  see also Powhatan Indians
Waldo, Richard, 61
Washington, George, 137
Welwood, William, *De Domino Maris*, 76
Wentworth, Thomas, Earl of Strafford, 19, 170
  interest in colonization, 102–3, 166
West, Thomas, Lord de la Ware, governor of Virginia, 1, 42, 72
  effects of arrival at Jamestown, 65–7
  Virginia investor, 78
Weymouth, Thomas, 16
Whig interpretation of history, 2, 4, 98, 164
White, Andrew, 173
Williams, Roger, 96
Willoughby of Parham, Francis, Lord, 119
Wiltshire *see* John Danvers; factionalism
Windebank, Sir Francis, 105, 112, 169, 171
  see also Charles I
Wingfield, Edward Maria, governor of Virginia, 14, 51, 52, 56–7, 64
  as client of Essex, 55
  departure from Virginia, 60
  opponent of Smith, 57–9
  see also Robert Devereux; factionalism; John Smith
Winthrop, John, governor of Massachusetts Bay, 25, 96, 99–100, 128
Wolstenholme, Sir John, 17, 89–90, 108, 110
Wriothesley, Thomas, third Earl of Southampton, 9, 63
  concerns about Scots at court of James I, 76–7
  leadership of Virginia Company, 16–17, 73–4, 77–81, 84, 106, 127, 157
  opponent of Howard family, 38, 43, 74–6
  political patronage, 30
  supporter of Essex, 13–15, 55, 165
  see also factionalism; William Herbert; Robert Rich; Edwin Sandys; Thomas Smythe; Virginia Company
Wrote, Samuel, attacks Sandys-Ferrar administration, 86–7, 89
Wroth, John, 85
  see also Virginia Company
Wroth, Mary, 12
Wyatt, Sir Francis, governor of Virginia, 17, 89, 90, 108, 116
Wyatt, Sir Thomas, rebellion (1549), 30
Wynn, Peter, 13
  charged with negligence by Smith, 61
  client of Essex, 55
  death, 64
  Hungarian service, 154
  possible motives for migration, 68–9
  see also Robert Devereux; Low Countries, wars in
Wynne, Captain Edward, 102
  see also George Calvert

Yamassee War, 132
Yeamans, Sir John, 127, 129–30, 131–2
  see also Barbados
Yeardley, Sir George, governor of Virginia, 66, 81, 89
Young, Captain Thomas, 166–7

Zouch, Sir John, 17, 51, 110